Interactions 1

Integrated Skills Edition

Instructor's Manual

Mc Graw Hill

Interactions 1 Integrated Skills Instructor's Manual

Published by McGraw-Hill   a business unit of The McGraw-Hill Companies,
Inc., 1221 Avenue of the Americas, New York, NY 10020. Copyright © 2003
by The McGraw-Hill Companies, Inc. All rights reserved. No part of this publication may be
reproduced or distributed in any form or by any means, or stored in a database or retrieval
system, without the prior written consent of The McGraw-Hill Companies, Inc., including,
but not limited to, in any network or other electronic storage or transmission, or broadcast for
distance learning.

 This book is printed on recycled, acid-free paper containing 10% postconsumer waste.

4 5 6 7 8 9 QSR/QSR 0 9 8 7

ISBN 978-0-07-233051-9
MHID 0-07-233051-1

Editorial director: *Tina B. Carver*
Developmental editor: *Annie Sullivan*
Director of marketing: *Thomas P. Dare*
Production manager: *Genevieve Kelley*
Compositor: *Tracey Harris*
Typeface: *10/13 Garamond*
Printer: *Quebecor World Dubuque*

www.mhcontemporary.com/interactionsmosaic

The **McGraw·Hill** Companies

TABLE OF CONTENTS

General Teaching Suggestions

Multi-Level Classes

Students have different needs and learning styles, so there will usually be a range of levels within a class. By varying the types of activities, you can address the needs of all students. Use whole class activities for presenting and modeling activities. Allow students to work individually, in pairs, or small groups to practice and prepare responses. During this time, give individual attention as needed. Have students work together in cooperative groups, not competitive groups. In this way, all students will participate, contribute, help, and learn from each other rather than compete against each other. You may want to provide additional activities for more advanced learners if they finish earlier than others. If possible, allow students to explore the Internet for readings and information related to the chapter topics to share with the class.

You may want to ask students to evaluate their own progress halfway through the course. Ask them to write down if they feel they are making progress and what they feel they have learned so far in the course. Also ask them to write down what they hope to achieve in the second half of the course and how you can best help them achieve their goals. As you read through their self-evaluations, make notes about students' common goals and incorporate them into your course planning.

Groupwork

Small groups allow students more of a chance to participate in the discussion activities. It is often easier to speak in a small group than in front of the whole class, so the small group situation is more secure for those who are less proficient in their speaking skills. In addition, it allows time for students to help each other with vocabulary. Students can practice saying something in a small group before addressing a larger audience. Groupwork promotes discussions and the sharing of ideas and cultural understanding. Students can learn from each other. Groupwork also allows you to address individual needs of students.

When students are working in groups, be sure that:

- Students understand the directions of the activity
- Everyone in the group is involved or has a role
- Students show respect for each other
- There is a time limit for the activity
- Groups have a chance to share what they discussed or prepared.

Form groups of 4—6 students for discussion and group writing activities. Prepare for groupwork. Have the following roles clearly defined for each member of the group:

- *reader*, or *facilitator*, who reads instructions, guides the group, is the leader
- *recorder*, who takes notes on discussions and answers for the activity
- *checker*, who makes sure everyone in the group understands points, watches the time, etc.
- *reporter*, who will share the group's information with the rest of the class

As groups are working, walk around the room listening. You may need to assist with vocabulary or give other guidance. Your job is to facilitate the group activity, not to lead it. Make a note of types of problems that arise and address them later.

Dealing with Unknown Vocabulary

Look the activity over beforehand to identify problem words. Teach these before you start the activity. If students encounter an unknown word, supply the definition (or translation) as quickly as possible and move on. Don't get sidetracked into a vocabulary lesson. Your class will forget what you are trying to teach.

Feedback and Error Correction

Student errors can be useful because they show you problem areas. Correct answers simply tell you what students already know. Remind students that errors provide important learning opportunities. Experimenting and receiving feedback help students learn how a language works. Students should be working slightly above their ability, so if they aren't making errors, they are not getting the right amount of challenge.

When / What to Correct

As a general rule, errors that interfere with communication are more important than those that don't. Distinguish between error correction in accuracy activities and error correction in fluency activities. Accuracy activities (such as the grammar activities) require more error correction. But when the objective is fluency and communication, it is best to correct errors only when communication is impeded. Note other errors to be worked on later.

Using the Video

At the end of each chapter there is a Video Activities page. It is placed at the end of the lessons so that students will be familiar with the topic of the video, and so they will have had a chance to learn or review the vocabulary and grammatical structures needed to comprehend and discuss the video clip.

The *Before You Watch* activity asks students to call on their own prior knowledge to answer some questions related to the video. When appropriate, bring in visual materials, such as maps and photographs, to help students build background that will help them understand what they are about to see.

Before playing the video, discuss the *Watch* section with students. Make sure they understand the meanings of all the words and that they also know what information the questions are asking them to watch for.

The *Watch Again* section asks students to look for more specific information than they did in the *Watch* section. Again, go over the questions carefully before replaying the video and answer any questions students may have. Invite individuals to put their responses on the board and have the class check their own answers.

You can have the students do the *After You Watch* activity in the whole-class setting, or divide students into small groups. If you choose to have small groups,

move among them to be sure that they are focusing on the task in the book and to provide language support. Afterwards, ask the groups to report back to the whole class.

Administering the Placement Test

The Placement Test helps teachers and administrators place students into the proper level of the **Interactions Integrated Skills** series. The test has been carefully designed to assess a student's language proficiency as it relates to the three levels of the series. The test has been divided into four sections: Listening/Speaking, Reading, Writing, and Grammar.

The Listening/Speaking section is divided into two parts. The Listening part requires the students to listen to a prompt (available on the assessment program) and choose an appropriate answer. In the Speaking part, students read a prompt and choose the correct conversational rejoinder.

The Reading section also consists of two parts. The first part tests the students' ability to derive meaning by using context. In the second part, students read selections and answer comprehension questions about them.

The Writing section consists of three parts. The first part tests students' ability to use key grammatical patterns. The second part tests the students' ability to apply organizational principles and cohesion. The third part provides a prompt and asks students to write an essay.

With the exception of the essay part of the Writing section, all of the test items are in multiple-choice format to make scoring easier. For the essay, a scoring rubric is provided on page 164.

Use the following chart as a guide to place your students in the correct level of the series. The parts of the test, excepting the essay, total 100 points. If a student scores significantly better or worse on the essay than on the other parts of the test, consider adjusting his or her placement accordingly.

Placement Guidelines

Score	Placement
Below 20	Needs a more basic text
21—50	Interactions Access Integrated Skills
51—80	Interactions 1 Integrated Skills
81—100	Interactions 2 Integrated Skills

Using the Chapter Quizzes

Description

Each chapter of **Interactions Integrated Skills** is accompanied by a quiz. There are also two cumulative quizzes: a Midterm Quiz, which covers Chapters 1—5, and a Final Quiz covering Chapters 6—10. You will notice that:

- These exercises measure how well students have mastered the listening/speaking, reading, writing, and grammar skills presented in the chapter.

- The first exercise in each quiz requires students to listen to a recorded speech or conversation. You may wish to play this segment more than once. The first time, you can ask students to just listen. The second time, they can mark their answers as they listen.

Suggestions

- Explain that the purpose of the quizzes is to give students an idea of how they are doing and what areas they may need to work on.

- Emphasize that the quizzes are a learning device.

- Go over the instructions for all exercises. Make sure students understand what they are supposed to do before they begin writing their answers.

- Allow students time to complete the quiz. They are meant to be brief and should take from ten to fifteen minutes to complete.

- For some quizzes, you may wish to have students work in pairs and small groups. This activity helps emphasize that the quizzes are primarily a learning activity, not a way of discovering errors.

- Always correct quizzes as soon as possible so that students find out about their errors while the questions and answers are still fresh in their minds. One way to give immediate feedback is to have students correct each other's papers in class. This provides the additional advantage of allowing for a classroom discussion of the questions most people missed.

Scoring

Each quiz contains six or seven exercises. The number of points for each exercise is indicated at its beginning. If an exercise with five items is worth 10 points, then the items are worth 2 points each.

All quizzes are worth 50 points. If you are using a system based on 100, simply multiply the results by 2.

School Life Around the World

Part 1 Listening to Conversations

Before You Listen

1 Prelistening Questions. Page 2.

Explain that the young people in the picture are continuing characters who will appear throughout the book. Point out the three people in the picture and ask students who they think they are and where they think the conversation is taking place. Then read the questions aloud and call on volunteers to answer. This discussion acquaints students with the characters as well as two of the chapter goals: introducing yourself and others and understanding body language.

2 Vocabulary Preview. Page 2.

Explain that the words at the top will appear in the recording and that this activity will make it easier for them to understand what they are going to hear. Read aloud the words at the top and have students circle any of them that they don't know. Discuss these words with the whole class, giving sample sentences to illustrate the meaning of each. Another approach is to have pairs of students work together to write definitions and sample sentences clarifying the meaning of each term. When they finish, ask them to present their explanations to the class.

Answers: 1. sounds 2. stop by 3. No kidding 4. (just) call me 5. comes over 6. take (Chinese) 7. you guys

Listen

3 Listening for Main Ideas. Page 3. [on tape/CD]

Read the introduction to the activity aloud and review the names of the three students in the picture on page 2. (Jack is on the left and Peter is

in the middle.) Then ask a confident student to read aloud the instructions and the questions. To be sure they understand what is being asked, ask different students to paraphrase each question item. Remind them that they won't understand every word and that that isn't the goal of the activity: they should be listening for main ideas. Then play the tape or CD and have students go over the answers in pairs. During the first chapter or two, you may wish to play the recording again and go over the answers together to provide confirmation and allow students to ask questions about anything they don't understand.

Answers:

1. Jack introduces Ming to Peter.
2. No, they aren't.
3. No, she wasn't.
4. He might study Chinese.
5. They want to get something to eat.
6. Jack, Peter, and Ming live in the same building.

Tapescript

Jack: Hi. How're you doing?

Peter: Hi. You're...Jack, right?

Jack: Yeah. And, sorry, you're...?

Peter: Peter. Peter Riley.

Jack: Oh, yeah, we met on campus last week. Peter, this is my friend, Ming Lee. She's just moved into the building.

Peter: Hi, Ming Lee.

Ming: Nice to meet you. You can just call me Ming. Lee's my last name.

Peter: Oh. "Ming"...That sounds...?

Ming: Chinese. My parents came over from Hong Kong before I was born.

Peter: Really? I was thinking of taking Chinese this term. Maybe you could help me.

Ming: Well, my Chinese really isn't very good...

Jack: Listen, Peter. We're really hungry. Do you want to get something to eat with us?

Peter: Sorry, I can't. I have to go meet my new roommate.

Jack: Oh, okay. Well, stop by sometime. I'm up in 212.

Peter: Hey, I'm on the same floor. I'm in 220.

Jack: No kidding...

Peter: Well, nice meeting you, Ming. I'm sure I'll see you guys soon.

Ming and Jack: See you later.

Stress

Explain that not all words are equally stressed in English. This is important to know because the stressed words usually give the most important information in a given sentence. Focusing on the stressed words can often give the listener enough information to understand an utterance. For example, in the sentence *Please put your homework on the desk at the end of class*, most people would stress the words *homework—desk—end—class*. The message is unmistakable.

Review the information at the top with students. Ask them to give examples of the parts of speech listed as words that are usually stressed. Then point out the bold words with stress marks in the sample sentences and explain that these words are stressed; they are said louder than the other words in the sentences. Demonstrate by reading the sentences aloud, emphasizing the stressed words. Have students take turns repeating the sentences, being careful to stress the words indicated. During this introduction, you may wish to allow somewhat exaggerated stress patterns to help clarify which words are stressed.

4 Listening for Stressed Words. Page 4. [on tape/CD]

One activity in each chapter asks students to listen for stressed words. It is important for them to begin to hear the difference between stressed and unstressed syllables and words. Read the instructions and point out the blanks below where students will fill in the missing stressed words. Then point out the words they will use to fill in the blanks and go over the list together. You might have a different student read aloud each of the four columns. Answer any questions they may have about meaning or pronunciation.

Explain that after each pause in the recording students must do two things: repeat after the speaker and write in the missing words. There is enough time for both, so make sure students repeat audibly before writing. This will help them practice normal word stress. Then play the tape or CD again and ask students to fill in the missing words using the list at the top. After that, have students correct their own work using the tapescript at the back of the student book. Another approach is to have students exchange books and correct each other's work.

Reductions

This section focuses on the reductions native speakers often produce when they run two words together. For example, *Do you...* becomes *D'ya...* Review the introductory information and read the examples aloud. Then give some additional examples, such as *hafta* and *why're* and ask students to guess the long forms. Invite students to think of other examples of reduced forms in English. Emphasize that although these are not standard English forms, they are commonly used in informal spoken English, and that the corresponding long forms may sound too formal and even be considered unfriendly in some situations. Finally, remind students that reduced forms are never written.

5 Comparing Long and Reduced Forms. Page 5. [on tape/CD]

Play the tape or CD and have students follow along in their books. Then have students repeat the sentences after the recording. Students might enjoy practicing some of the reductions in the form of a short chant:

Meetcha, meetcha
Wanna, wanna
Hafta, hafta
Seeya, seeya

6 Listening for Reductions. Page 5. [on tape/CD]

Read the directions for item 1. Remind students that the recording leaves enough time for students to repeat each sentence. Make sure students repeat audibly before writing. Remind them that they will have to write the full forms because the reduced forms are never written. Play the tape or CD. Then write the correct answers on the board and have them correct their own activities. For item 2, have students read the sentences to a partner for pronunciation practice. Move around the room checking their progress and modeling pronunciation as needed.

Answers:
1. How are you feeling?
2. See you in an hour.
3. Jack, do you want to eat at the cafeteria?
4. When do you have to meet your roommate?

Tapescript
1. How're ya feeling?
2. See ya in an hour.
3. Jack, d'ya wanna eat at the cafeteria?
4. When d'ya hafta meet your roommate?

After You Listen

7 Vocabulary Review. Page 6.
This activity reinforces the vocabulary introduced in Activity 2. Point out the pair icon in the student book. Explain that activities marked in this way are always done by partners. Review the instructions with the class and do the first item as an example. The answer might be: *In my community, no one ever stops by a friend's house without calling first.* When students finish, ask volunteers to share some of their responses.

Pronunciation

The -s Ending [on tape/CD]
Read through the information on pronouncing the *-s* ending with the class. Then go back and work on each of the different pronunciations individually. First play the tape or CD or read the examples and have students listen to the lists of sample words. Focus on an ending, for example /iz/, and have students repeat it in several times

in isolation. Then ask them to try to think of other words that feature that particular pronunciation of the *-s* ending.

8 Distinguishing between -s Endings. Page 6. [on tape/CD]
Read and discuss the instructions. Explain to students that they will have to listen very carefully to hear the differences among the three *-s* endings. Play the tape or CD and have students mark their answers. If you feel it is appropriate, you can play the recording a second time so that students can check their answers. Then put the correct answers on the board and have students correct their work.

Answers: 1. plays /z/   2. misses /iz/
3. hopes /s/   4. stops /s/   5. drives /z/
6. phones /z/   7. washes /iz/
8. summarizes /iz/   9. mothers /z/
10. puts /s/

Tapescript
1. plays
2. misses
3. hopes
4. stops
5. drives
6. phones
7. washes
8. summarizes
9. mothers
10. puts

Using Language

Introducing Yourself and Others
Explain that students are going to practice making introducing themselves introducing one person to another. Have three students read the dialogue. Then review the chart showing the other expressions they might use. Invite other sets of students to read the other sample dialogues given there. Discuss the meaning of any words or phrases that are confusing to students.

Explain that each *Using Language* activity is unique and that there is no set pattern followed throughout the book. Here are a few suggestions for introducing students to the various types of activities:

- After reading the directions for an activity, ask students to repeat back to you in their own words what they are going to do first, second, etc.

- Appoint one student in each group to be the "captain" or "chair" whose job it is to keep the activity moving and to ensure that every person in the group has a chance to speak.

- Set a reasonable time limit for the activity.

- Circulate from group to group while students talk.

- Plan a way to bring the whole class back together at the conclusion of the activity in order to consolidate what they have done. For example, the captain can report on a decision the group has made, students from each group can share what they learned from the activity, or students might role-play a conversation that they had.

- Always go over common errors that you heard students make as they talked.

- Sometimes you may wish to plan a follow-up reading or writing activity.

9 Making Introductions. Page 7.

Review the five steps of the activity and ask students to explain in their own words what is involved in each step. Rehearse the expressions in step five with the class. Then form small groups and appoint a captain for each. Set a time limit for the first four steps (perhaps ten minutes). When the time is up, have students do step five, walking around the room and seeing how many people they can identify by name. Remind them to use the expressions in the book to check that they have remembered correctly.

Part 2 Recalling Main Ideas

Before You Listen

1 Prelistening Questions. Page 8.

Every *Before You Listen* section begins with a set of prelistening questions. This activity gives students an introduction to the material they will be hearing. It also helps them bring to mind facts and language items they already know that are related to the topic. Read and discuss the instructions and questions with the whole class. Then help them form pairs and complete the activity. Set a time limit of about five minutes. Then review their responses with the whole class.

2 Vocabulary Preview. Page 8.

The second activity in each *Before You Listen* is always a vocabulary preview. Although many different formats are used, the purpose is always to provide an introduction to words that are essential to the understanding of the recorded listening segment. Have students complete the activity individually. This may be a review/reinforcement activity for some students, but for others it may be their first exposure to some of the words. As you review the answers with the class, ask students to raise their hands if they are still having difficulty with any of the terms. Invite other students to explain these terms in their own words.

Answers: 1. d 2. a 3. b 4. e 5. c

Listen

The *Listen* section of each chapter includes some or all of the following activities: Listening for Main Ideas, Listening for Specific Information, Taking Notes on Specific Information, and Reviewing Notes. Once students understand how each one works, they will have no difficulty in doing the activity on their own.

Culture Note

Most colleges and universities conduct formal orientation sessions for incoming students. Some institutions even have week-long programs in which new students get to know each other as they learn about the school. Certain colleges even take new students on a camping trip away from the school where they take part in activities designed to help them form friendships before the school year begins.

3 Listening for Main Ideas. Page 9.
[on tape/CD]

Focus first on the *Hints for Remembering* section, which appears only in this chapter. Ask students to rephrase each suggestion in their own words. Then play the tape or CD and ask students to take their own notes. Mention that the speech is quite long and that students should aim to take only five or six short notes on the whole thing. Otherwise, they may get bogged down in writing and miss important points. If students say they don't know how to take notes, ask them to do their best.

Tapescript

Gina: Hello everybody. Welcome to the American Language Center! I'm Gina Richards, your academic advisor. You can all just call me Gina. I know today is your first day at our school, so you're probably a little nervous and maybe a little shy, too. So, I want to tell you right at the beginning: if you don't understand something, please ask questions. Okay? And listen very carefully because we're going to give you a lot of important information —information that

will make your experience here enjoyable and useful. Okay, here we go.

Let me tell you about the plan for today. There are three things on your schedule. First, you will take a placement test. This test will measure your English level. You'll take a reading, grammar, and composition test. Oh, and also listening. A listening test. The whole test takes three hours.

Next, you will meet in small groups, with a teacher, for an orientation. This orientation meeting will be about important things you need to know, like where to buy your books, what type of classes you'll have, how to find a roommate, things like that. This is where you can ask a lot of questions.

Then, finally, this afternoon, you will take a campus tour. We'll show you the main buildings where your classrooms are; you'll see some of the sports facilities, you know, the tennis courts, the swimming pool, places like that; and you'll also visit the library and the computer lab. I think you'll be surprised how large and how beautiful our campus is. All right. Are there any questions before we begin?

4 Reviewing Notes. Page 9.

You might wish to have several students copy their notes onto the blackboard so that you can compare what they wrote with the notes suggested in the book. You can expect that various students' notes will be quite different in form and content.

5 Listening for Specific Information. Page 9.
[on tape/CD]

Read aloud the three questions. Give students time to read the sample notes. Then ask students to listen and add details to the outline given in the book. When they are finished, go over the answers together. Ask students to suggest some elements that make for useful notes. They may mention:

• Use only key words, not whole sentences.

• Use abbreviations, symbols, and numbers whenever possible.

• Put main ideas at the left margin and indent less important information (if any).

• Include only one piece of information per line.

After You Listen

6 Summarizing Main Ideas. Page 10.

Read the instructions and example with the class. Then help them find partners and practice summarizing the speech. As they work, listen to different pairs, helping them with any aspects of the task that are proving difficult for them. If time permits, have one or more students present their summary to the class.

7 Vocabulary Review. Page 10.

This is an open-ended oral activity that reviews key vocabulary words and provides listening and speaking practice. If possible, match up students of differing ability. You may wish to have less fluent students focus on only two or three of the questions so that they have time to receive plenty of feedback from their partners. More fluent students can try answering all the questions.

Part 3 Reading

Before You Read

1 Discussing Pictures. Page 10.

Point out the three pictures and ask students to identify the people, places, and objects. Have students tell what the people are doing in each of the pictures. Then read the questions aloud and call on volunteers to answer. Encourage students to talk about things that are the same and things that are different from the pictures and their own school. Make a list of vocabulary on the board as students describe the pictures.

Sample Answers:
1. People: students, teachers, professors, instructors. Places: snack bar (snack room), classroom, hallway,

registration/administration line. Other things: snack machines, tables, chairs, soda machine, books, signs; map, student desks, chalkboard, eraser, course listings, bookbag, program of studies, a line.

2. The first place may be in a dormitory or student lounge. It's a place for students to relax and talk. The people look like they might be from different countries. They are drinking coffee and studying.

   The second picture is in a school building, in classrooms. The students are studying or learning. They are listening and looking. The professors are teaching and explaining.

   The third picture is a registration line. The students are waiting in line to sign up (or register) for classes. They are looking at books and papers and talking.

3. In my school, there are soda machines and places to buy snacks. We have classrooms. We wait in line to sign up for classes. My school has different desks in the classrooms.

2 Thinking about the Answers. Page 11.

Read the questions aloud and call on volunteers to answer. Point out key vocabulary: *international students, institutions of higher learning, universities.* As students suggest answers, record students' responses and ideas on an overhead projector or on a large piece of paper. You may want to review these responses later after students have read the selection.

Sample Answers:
1. International students are students who study in a foreign country. Colleges, community colleges, and universities are institutions of higher learning.

2. Most international students go to school in universities.

3. Some students attend colleges or universities far from home because they want to practice a new language, they want to study a particular subject, they

have a scholarship, or the schools in their country may not offer advanced studies.

4. Colleges and universities want students from other countries because the students bring new ideas and enrich the school.

3 Vocabulary Preview. Page 11.

Read the words aloud and have student circle the ones they don't know. Students can look for the words they don't know in the reading. Have students check their understanding of the circled words after they complete the reading selection.

Read

4 International Students. Page 12. [on tape/CD]

Play the tape or CD as students follow along in their books. You may want to stop the tape or CD after every paragraph to check understanding and point out vocabulary words. Listen a second time as students read along.

Culture Note

Since there are so many different types of institutions of higher education in the United States, this level of education is available to nearly every post-secondary student. But, higher education is not free. All students pay tuition and other fees, although some do receive scholarships to help cover the costs.

After You Read

5 Recognizing Reading Structure: Readings, Chapters, and Paragraphs. Page 13.

Read the instructions. Refer to the book to show examples of chapters in books and paragraphs in reading selections. Have students look back at the reading on page 12 and indicate the number of paragraphs in this selection. Point out the letters

for the various paragraphs. Students can complete the exercise. Go over the answers together.

Answers: 1. C 2. B 3. A 4. D 5. E

6 Understanding the Main Idea. Page 13.

Explain "main idea." Read the instructions and have students complete the exercise. Then discuss the answers with the whole class.

Answers: 1. T 2. F 3. F 4. T 5. F

Ask students to point out the information that is not true in the false statements. Students can look back in the reading selection for the correct information. Ask volunteers to restate the false statements to make them true.

Sample Answers:
3. High school and college graduates go to school in foreign countries for many reasons.
5. Some students may not like to go to school abroad. Colleges and universities want learners from other countries.

7 Finding Definitions in Context. Page 14.

Read together the instructions. Have students work individually in pairs to write the definitions of the words in Exercise 7. If some students finish before the rest of the class, ask them to find the definitions of the other vocabulary items. Go over the answers with the group.

Answers:
1. the other words in the sentence or paragraph
2. the meanings of new words and phrases
3. an institution of higher learning with one or more undergraduate colleges and graduate schools
4. a college student with a bachelor's degree or higher
5. a post-secondary student from another country
6. university, college, or school
7. in a foreign place
8. nations that don't yet have a high level or industrialization or technology

9. legal members of a nation or country

Students can develop definitions based on context clues in the reading for additional words.

Sample Answers:

College: an institution of higher learning

School: an institution of (higher) learning

Undergraduate: a post-secondary student without a college degree

Foreign: of a different country or culture

Tuition: the fee charged for instruction

Structure: organization or form

Chapter: the largest division of a book

Paragraph: a division or part about one idea or one kind of information

8 Answering Paragraph Questions with Details. Page 14.

Be sure students understand the difference between main idea and details. Read together the instructions. Ask students to complete the exercise. Go over the answers together.

Answers: 1. c 2. b 3. c 4. a

Discussing the Reading

9 Small Group Discussion. Page 15.

This activity allows students to use the vocabulary from the reading to talk about their own experiences related to the content. Arrange students in groups of four. Assign each person in the group a role:

Student 1: reading the questions to the group

Student 2: restating answers

Student 3: recording information

Student 4: reporting the answers to the whole class.

Model the activity and the four roles. Give the groups about 15-20 minutes to discuss the questions. Circulate among the groups, listening, and giving assistance as needed. When all groups

are finished, ask the reporters from each group to share the most interesting information from their groups.

Answers will vary.

Part 4 Writing

Before You Write

Exploring Ideas

1 Interviewing Someone. Page 16.

Direct students' attention to the photo, and tell them that the young man is asking the other student questions. He is recording her answers on a tape machine. Tell students that this is an interview.

Have students take about five minutes to brainstorm a list of questions they would like to ask during their own interviews. They can look at the list of questions at the top of the page to help get them started.

Give students at least fifteen minutes each to conduct their interviews. They might want to record the interviews if recording equipment is available. Or, they can simply take notes as they conduct the interview. Afterwards, they should prepare a transcript of the questions and answers.

Organizing Ideas
Fact vs. Opinion

2 Page 17.

Answers:

1. F	6. O
2. F	7. O
3. F	8. O
4. O	9. F
5. F	10. O

3   Page 18.

Have students determine whether each statement in their interview is a fact or an opinion. Then have students number each of the answers in the order that they want to present it in their paragraphs. Point out that it is common to begin biographical sketches with factual information which leads into subjective statements, or opinions.

Allow students to take some time to have a conference with their interview subjects. This is an opportunity for the interview subject to add or change any information contained in the interview.

Writing Topic Sentences

4   Page 18.

Tell students to read the entire interview and to extract the main idea or general impression from it. The main idea is the basis for the topic sentence. Students can review the tips in the box for guidance in creating a topic sentence.

Write

Developing Cohesion and Style

Connecting Ideas

5   Page 18.

Have students read the article on page 19, then point out that the words *and* and *also* introduce new information; *so* introduces a result; *but* contrasts information.

Using *and* to Connect Phrases and Sentences

6   Page 19.

Answers:
2. Amelia eats breakfast and lunch in the cafeteria.
3. Reiko is 19 years old and likes music a lot.

4. Salma is married and is a student.
5. Enrique likes soccer and plays every Saturday.
6. The school offers a good program in business and its recreational facilities are excellent.

Using *but* or *so* to Connect Sentences

7   Page 20.

Answers:
1. She has to work all day, so she doesn't have time to do all her homework.
2. He likes his English class, but he doesn't think the American students are very friendly.
3. Her company is opening an office in the United States, so it needs English-speaking workers.
4. She likes school life, but she is homesick for her family.
5. Pedro wants to work in Japan, so he wants to learn Japanese.

8   Page 21.

Answers will vary. Review students' work for grammar and sense.

Writing the First Draft

9   Page 21.

Explain the idea of the *first draft* and have students read the information in the box on page 21. Then have them write a first draft of a paragraph about the person they just interviewed. They should use the organization and topic sentence that they created for Activities 3 and 4. Remind them to try to use connecting words like *and, so, but,* and *also.*

Edit and Revise

Editing Practice

10 Page 21.

In this exercise, students are to look at the writer's ideas and organization. The following is an example of how students might edit the paragraph:

Wichai Tongkhio is a new member of the English composition class at Amarin Community College. Wichai is 18 years old, and he is originally from a village in the north. In general, Wichai likes life in Bangkok and Amarin Community College, but he doesn't like his dormitory. He is studying business administration, accounting, and English. Wichai plans to visit the United States next summer, so he needs to learn English. In his free time, Wichai plays basketball and he likes going to the movies.

11 Page 22.

In this exercise, students are to edit for form. Refer to the edited paragraph above in Activity 10 for corrections to grammar and form.

Editing Your Writing

12 Editing Using a Checklist. Page 23.

Have students focus on one item in the checklist before moving on to the next one. For example, students should check their writing for interest, completeness, and accuracy of content before moving on to check for organization. In a similar way, they should make separate passes for cohesion and style, grammar, and form. Have students refer to the checklist for guidance.

13 Peer Editing. Page 23.

Use the suggestions in the Student Book to conduct peer conferences. Give pairs of students time to exchange papers and read each other's work. They can write comments in the margins of their partners' papers. Pairs can then reconvene and give each other verbal feedback, explaining the main points of their written comments. Afterwards, students can rewrite their articles, incorporating the feedback as appropriate.

As an additional step, students can exchange their work with other students besides their interview subjects. This will give them "cold" feedback that may be helpful in making final corrections.

Writing the Second Draft

14 Page 23.

Explain the importance of the *second draft* and have students rewrite their paragraph about the interview, based on the suggestions of their peers and teacher, as well as their own edits from Activity 12.

Part 5 Grammar

A. Present Tense of *Be*: Affirmative and Negative Statements, Contractions

Before reading the chart, ask students to give you sentences with the verbs *am, are,* and *is.* Write the correct sentences on the board. Ask students to say which pronouns go with which verb forms. Have students read the examples and notes in the affirmative part of the first chart. Then, ask students to make one of the sentences on the board negative. Have students read the negative part of the first chart before having students make similar sentences of their own.

Point to one of the affirmative sentences you have on the board in its full form. Say it in its contracted form. Ask students what has changed. Rewrite it in its contracted form. Have students read the affirmative part of the next chart to themselves. Then, have selected students read the contracted sentences. Have students make the contracted sentence on the board negative. Point out the two ways to make the sentence negative. Have students read the negative part of the chart silently. Have selected students read the contracted forms.

1 Page 24.

Have students look at the picture. Explain that the two women entering the classroom are Kami and Yumiko. Read the instructions. Ask students to read the conversation first without filling in the blanks. Then, have students say what Yumiko's problem is (she isn't ready for class yet). Ask students if Kami thinks the homework is easy or difficult. Have students reread the conversation to fill in the blanks individually. Put students in pairs to check their answers.

Answers: 2. She's 3. isn't 4. It's
5. It's not / isn't 6. aren't 7. bar's 8. I'm
9. homework's / is 10. are 11. isn't
12. You're 13. I'm 14. is 15. You're / are

B. *Be: Yes/No Questions and Short Answers*

Ask students some simple affirmative *yes/no* questions such as *"Are you a student?"* Write one of your questions on the board. Then write the equivalent affirmative statement beside it. Ask students to say what the difference between them is. Then ask a student a *yes/no* question that you are pretty sure you know the answer to such as *"Aren't you [Yuko]?"* Write it on the board. Ask students to say why you used the negative form. Have students read the first chart to themselves. Then ask students more affirmative or negative *yes/no* questions. Write your questions and their answers on the board. Point out that contractions can't be used in short answers to affirmative *yes/no* questions. Have students read the second chart to themselves.

2 Page 25.

Read the instructions. Go over the example. Ask students to provide other questions for the same answer such as *"Isn't Jana a good student?"* Have students write their questions individually or in pairs. Add a game element to this activity by having students read their questions out of order while the rest of the class guesses which answer it is for.

Sample Answers: 1. Is Mr. Dawson in the History department? 2. Isn't Marcy from California? 3. Are you students? 4. Are the exams easy? 5. Aren't you in my English class?

C. Simple Present Tense: Affirmative and Negative Statements

Read the information above the chart. Go over the examples for each of the four different categories in the left-hand column. To check students' comprehension of the differences in meaning between each category, have them give examples of their own. Then, go back to each category and have students read the notes. Have students supply more examples illustrating each note. Give examples of everyday activities and habits that don't include objects following the verb such as *I run every morning before school.* Give examples of opinions in the affirmative such as: *He teaches math very well.*

Have students read the spelling rules for *–s* endings and the three pronunciation notes. Have students provide additional examples for each spelling rule. Also have students practice the pronunciation of the third person verbs.

3 Page 26.

Read the instructions. Go over the examples. Ask students to say which person in the picture is Mr. Sommers. Have students read the list of items. Then, check their comprehension of them. Have students write their sentences while you circulate to answer individual questions. Put students in pairs to compare answers.

Answers:
1. Mr. Sommers is a teaching assistant.
2. He isn't a professor.
3. He helps Mr. Michaels.
4. He teaches three days a week.
5. He doesn't give lectures.
6. He works with students in small groups.
7. He doesn't wear a suit and a tie.
8. He likes to wear jeans every day.
9. He doesn't carry a briefcase.
10. He doesn't have a board in his classroom.

D. Simple Present Tense: *Yes/No Questions* and Short Answers

Ask students a *yes/no* question and write it on the board. Below it write the corresponding affirmative and negative sentences. Have students contrast the three forms. Ask students what the differences are, pointing out the use of *do(n't)* or *does(n't)* in the question and the negative statement. With arrows, indicate the inversion of the verb *do* with the subject. Read the information above the chart. Have individual students read each example in the affirmative questions chart while other students respond affirmatively and negatively. Put a negative simple present tense question and a question with the negative present tense of the verb *be* on the board. Ask students when it is you use the negative question with the present tense of the verb *be*. Explain that it is the same with negative questions in the simple present tense. Have individual students read each example in the negative questions chart while other students respond affirmatively and negatively.

Optional Activity: As a class, have students return to their sentences about Mr. Sommers in Exercise 3. Put them in pairs to take turns asking and answering *yes/no* questions. For more advanced classes, have one student in the pair keep his/her book open while asking the first ten questions while his/her partner closes the book and tries to respond from memory. Then have them switch roles for the next ten questions.

4   Page 27.

Read the instructions. Go over the example. Ask students to try to think of other questions they could ask based on the example. Point out how Student B provided additional information in some of his answers. Make sure that students are clear on the difference between *yes/no* questions and responses in the simple present tense and with the verb *be*. Have students read the items to check their comprehension. Put students in pairs to do the exercise. Check students' answers as a class.

Sample Answers:
1. Does this school have a cafeteria? Yes, it does. / No, it doesn't.
2. Do students study there? Yes, they do. / No, they don't.
3. Is it open late? Yes, it is. It is open until midnight. / No, it isn't. It closes at 9:00.
4. Do any students work there? Yes, they do. Many students work there. No, they don't.
5. Does it have coffee? Yes, it does but it is bad. / No, it doesn't.
6. Are the prices high? Yes, they are. / No, they aren't. They are very low.

5   Page 27.

Repeat the procedure from Exercise 4.
Sample Answers:
1. Is your English class difficult? Yes, it is. / No, it isn't. It's very easy.
2. Do you like your English class? Yes, I do. It's a lot of fun. / No, I don't. It's boring.
3. Does the instructor give many exams? Yes, s/he does. S/He gives exams every week. / No, s/he doesn't.
4. Are you often late to class? Yes, I am. I'm always late to class. / No, I'm not.
5. Does the teacher check your homework? Yes, s/he does. / No, s/he doesn't. We check it together in class.
6. Do you study enough? Yes, I do. I study every night. / No, I don't. I need to study more.

E. Simple Present Tense: Information Questions and Answers

Read the information above the chart. Put some *-wh* questions on the board and have students make information questions with them. Ask students if they can answer these questions with *yes* or *no*. Have students respond to the questions on the board. Write a corresponding *yes / no* question below one of your information questions such as *Where do you live? Do you live with your family? Is your home near to the school?* Have students compare the structure and placement of the verbs *do* and *be* in each question. Write the answers and repeat the procedure. Have students read each question while other students read the possible answers. Have students read the notes. After each set of notes, have students provide additional examples of their own. Read the note below the chart, giving examples as necessary.

6 Page 28.

Read the instructions. Go over the example. Ask students if there could be any other questions for the response given. Tell students for some of the items there will be more than one possible question. Less advanced students might appreciate doing the first five together as a group. Put students in pairs to take turns asking and answering the questions.

Sample Answers:
1. Who's she / Ms. Kramer?
2. How do you get to school? / What do you do in the mornings?
3. Who is Mr. Sommers? / What does Mr. Sommers do?
4. When is the last class? / When will the test be?
5. Why can't you go with me / on the cruise?
6. Where's the milk / cheese?
7. What color is his hair / car?
8. Who is that man?
9. Where's your English class / apartment?
10. How's that?

7 Page 29.

Read the instructions. Go over the example. Have students provide a follow-up question of their own for the example. Tell students to add questions of their own when they come to them. Put students in pairs to do the exercise. To go over the exercise, have volunteer students share their exchanges with the class.

Answers: 1. is 2. do 3. is 4. does 5. do 6. is 7. do 8. do 9. does 10. do

Video Activities: Exchange Students

Before You Watch

Read the instructions and the questions. Check that all students know what exchange students are. Put students in groups to discuss the questions. Have groups share the highlights of their conversations.

Watch [on video]

Have selected students read the questions aloud. Tell students to watch the video without trying to answer the questions. Play the video. Tell students to answer the questions. Replay the video to check the answers.

Answers:
1. Turkey
2. Answers will vary
3. California
4. the prom
5. sad

Watch Again [on video]

Read the instructions. Have selected students read the statements aloud. Check students' comprehension of each statement. Tell students to write T or F while they are watching. Play the video. Check students' answers as a class.

Answers:
1. F
2. T
3. F
4. F
5. F

After You Watch

Read the instructions. Have students read the list of topics silently. Ask students if they have any other topics to add. If necessary, model the activity with another student. Put students in pairs to write and role-play the phone conversation.

Experiencing Nature

Part 1 Listening to Conversations

Before You Listen

1 Prelistening Questions. Page 32.

Ask students to identify the young people in the picture. (Ming, Jack, and Peter) Then point to the thought bubbles above Ming's, Jack's, and Peter's heads. Ask students to describe what they see. Then read the questions aloud and call on volunteers to answer. You may wish to note on the board the activities students mention and invite them to write them down in a vocabulary list in their notebooks for later use.

2 Vocabulary Preview. Page 32.

Explain that the words in the left-hand column will appear in the recording and that this exercise will make it easier for them to understand what they are going to hear. Read the words and have students circle any of them that they don't know. Discuss these words with the whole class, giving sample sentences to illustrate the meaning of each.

Answers:
Meanings:
1. It's raining very hard.
2. annoyed because something has continued so long   3. to allow the sun to darken the skin
4. like something very much   5. very cold
6. a measure of temperature   7. a prediction about what the weather will be like
8. possibility of

Fill-ins: 1. It's raining cats and dogs
2. crazy about   3. to get a tan   4. chance of
5. degrees   6. sick of   7. weather forecast
8. freezing

Listen

3 Listening for Main Ideas. Page 33. [on tape/CD]

Read the introduction to the exercise aloud. Then ask a confident student to read aloud the instructions and the questions. Prompt students to ask about any questions they don't understand. Remind them that they won't understand every word and that that isn't the goal of the exercise: they should be listening for main ideas. Ask students to look back at the picture on page 32 and explain that this picture illustrates what is happening in the recording they are going to hear. Then play the tape or CD and have the students answer the questions. Then have them go over the answers in pairs. You may wish to play the recording again and go over the answers together to provide confirmation and allow students to ask questions about anything they don't understand.

Answers:
1. It's raining hard outside.
2. It's raining.
3. It's October.
4. They want to go to Florida or Hawaii because those places are sunny and dry.
5. They can swim, snorkel, and get a tan.
6. Ming wants to go to the mountains so she can go skiing and snowboarding.
7. It will be cloudy and cold with a 90% chance of rain.

Tapescript
Peter: Hey, look outside. It's raining cats and dogs—again! I hate this weather. When does winter break start?
Jack: Winter break? It's only October.
Peter: I know, but I'm sick of studying. I want to go someplace warm and lie on the beach for a week. Someplace where it's sunny and dry. Florida or Hawaii, maybe?
Jack: Yeah. We can go swimming and snorkeling and get a great tan. Now that's my idea of a perfect vacation.

Ming: Not mine. I can't swim very well, and I don't like lying in the sun. I prefer the mountains, especially in winter. I'm crazy about skiing and snowboarding. In fact I'm planning to go to Bear Mountain with some friends in December. Do you want to come?

Jack: No thanks. I went there last year. I was freezing the whole time. Anyway, I don't know how to ski very well. I fell about a hundred times.

Ming: How about you, Peter?

Peter: Sorry, I agree with Jack. I don't want to go anyplace where it's below 70 degrees.

Jack: By the way, what's the weather forecast for tomorrow?

Ming: The same as today. Cloudy, cold, and a 90% chance of rain.

Jack: Oh, no! How am I going to go to the library?

Ming: Take an umbrella!

Stress

4 Listening for Stressed Words. Page 34. [on tape/CD]

Read the instructions and point out the list of words at the top. Ask students to read through the list and circle any words they aren't sure of. Discuss these words in class, encouraging students who know the words to explain them to their classmates. Remind students that after each pause in the recording they must do two things: repeat after the speaker and write in the missing words. There is enough time for both, so make sure students repeat audibly before writing. Then play the tape or CD again and ask students to fill in the missing words using the list at the top. After that, have students correct their own work using the tapescript at the back of the student book. Then have students find partners and do the second part of the exercise—reading the conversation with a partner while taking care to stress the words correctly. You might also invite a pair of students to present the conversation to the class.

Reductions

This section focuses on the reductions native speakers often produce when combining the words *and*, *want*, *to*, *can*, *going*, *about*, *you*, and *don't* with other words. Remind them that although the reduced forms are written out in the book for teaching purposes, they are never used in normal writing.

5 Comparing Long and Reduced Forms. Page 35. [on tape/CD]

Play the tape or CD and have students follow along in their books. Then have students repeat the sentences after the recording. If you hear a number of students making the same error, point it out and help them correct it.

6 Listening for Reductions. Page 35. [on tape/CD]

Read the directions for item 1. Remind students that the recording leaves enough time for students to repeat each sentence. Make sure students repeat audibly before writing. Remind them that they will have to write the full forms because the reduced forms are never written. Play the tape or CD. Then write the correct answers on the board and have them correct their own exercises. For item 2, have students read the sentences to a partner for pronunciation practice. Move around the room checking their progress and modeling pronunciation as needed.

Answers: Do you want to come? What are you going to do there? We can swim and lie in the sun. Thanks, but I don't want to go. How about you, Peter? I have to stay at home and study.

Tapescript

Jack: Hi, Ming, Hi, Peter.

Ming and Peter: Hey, Jack.

Ming: What's happening?

Jack: I'm going to the campus recreation center. D'you wanna come?

Ming: What are you gonna do there?

Jack: Well, it's a nice day. We kin swim 'n' lie in the sun.

Ming: Thanks, but I dowanna go. I'm too tired.

Jack: How bouchou, Peter?

Peter: I can't. I hafta stay at home 'n' study.
             Maybe tomorrow.

After You Listen

7 Vocabulary Review. Page 36.

This exercise reinforces vocabulary already introduced. Review the instructions with the class and do the first item as an example. The answer might be: *No, I enjoy studying English* or *I'm a little tired of studying English*. When the pairs finish work, ask volunteers to share some of their responses.

Pronunciation

Can vs. *Can't* [on tape/CD]

Read through the information on the differences in pronunciation with the class. Then play the tape or CD or read the examples again. Invite students to make up sentences with *can* and *can't* and say them aloud to demonstrate the correct pronunciation of the two words.

8 Distinguishing between *Can* and *Can't*. Page 36. [on tape/CD]

Read and discuss the instructions. Explain to students that they will have to listen very carefully to hear the differences. Play the tape or CD and have students repeat the sentences and mark their answers. If you feel it is appropriate, you can play the recording a second time so that students can check their answers. Then put the correct answers on the board and have students correct their work.

Answers: 1. No 2. Yes 3. Yes 4. No
5. No 6. Yes 7. No 8. Yes 9. No
10. Yes

Tapescript

1. She can't swim very well.
2. Mike can drive.
3. The boys can cook.
4. I can't find his phone number.
5. Kenji can't speak Spanish.
6. He can speak Japanese.
7. I can't understand him.
8. Pete can come with us.
9. She can't take photographs in the rain.
10. Herb can play tennis very well.

Using Language

Talking about Abilities

Explain that students are going to practice talking about things they are and aren't able to do. Read aloud the various expressions used to express ability and invite students to ask questions about any words or phrases that are confusing to them.

9 Talking about Abilities. Page 37.

Read the instructions and brainstorm a list of the types of abilities that students can use to get ideas for their lists. For example: *speaking languages, engaging in sports, doing strenuous exercise, cooking, sewing, making things out of wood, using computers,* and *taking care of children*. Then ask students to complete the chart individually. As they work, move around the room making suggestions to individual students as needed. Remind them to use all of the expressions from the explanation box. You might want to have students discuss their completed lists with a partner before going over the answers together in class.

Part 2 Recalling Main Ideas

Before You Listen

1 Prelistening Questions. Page 38.

Read and discuss the instructions and questions with the whole class. Then help them form pairs and complete the activity. Set a time limit of about five minutes. Then review their responses with the whole class. Encourage students to describe interesting or unusual things that happened to them when they were camping out.

2 Vocabulary Preview. Page 38.

Read the instructions and have students complete the activity individually. As you review the answers with the class, ask students to raise their hands if they are still having difficulty with any of the terms. Invite other students to explain these terms in their own words.

Answers: 1. d 2. e 3. b 4. f 5. g 6. c 7. a

Listen

3 Listening for Main Ideas. Page 38. [on tape/CD]

You may wish to go back and review *Hints for Remembering* in the *Listen* section of Chapter 1.

Possible Answers: 1. It started to rain very hard. 2. Two bears stole their clothes.

Tapescript

Manager: You're all wet and muddy. What happened to you?

Woman: You're not going to believe this! It's the most incredible thing! It all started when we decided to go hiking this morning.

Man: Yeah, the weather was sunny and clear when we got up. So we put on shorts and t-shirts and started up the mountain. Half an hour later it started raining cats and dogs!

Woman: So we hiked back to our tent as fast as we could. We couldn't wait to change into dry clothes.

Man: Right. But when we went into our tent, we couldn't find our clothes! So we went back outside to look around. And then we saw the craziest thing. Two great big brown bears came out of the woods, and guess what? They were wearing our clothes!

Manager: Aw, come on. That's impossible! What do you mean, the bears were wearing your clothes?

Man: Well, one bear had my t-shirt around his neck. And the other one had Mary's pants over his head. We still don't know where the rest of our clothes are!

Manager: [laughing]

Woman: I know it sounds funny, but we were so scared! Those bears were big! And now we have a big problem.

Manager: What's that?

Man: We don't have any dry clothes to wear!

4 Taking Notes on Specific Information. [on tape/CD]

Review the instructions with the class. Then play the tape or CD and have them fill in the information. Ask two or three students to write their notes on the board. Discuss the differences in the ways the students took notes and point out effective note-taking strategies.

Possible Answers: 1. hiking 2. sunny and clear 3. rain 4. tent, clothes 5. their clothes 6. outside 7. two bears, their clothes 8. scared 9. They have no dry clothes.

After You Listen

5 Summarizing Main Ideas. Page 39.

Read and discuss the instructions and help students form groups of three. As the groups work, move around the room offering assistance if needed. If time permits, have one or more of the groups present their role-play to the class.

6 Vocabulary Review. Page 39.

Have students complete this activity on their own. Go over the answers together in class.

Answers: 1. b 2. g 3. a 4. d 5. c 6. f 7. e

Talk It Over

Read aloud the instructions for the Truth or Lie game. Demonstrate how students use the "Truth" and "Lie" cards to express their opinions about the story. If a lot of students wish to tell stories, you may have to set up a lottery in order to choose who will get to speak. It's probably best to allow no more than five or six speakers in order to keep interest level high. Alternatively, small groups could play the game and then choose one story to be presented to the class.

Read the instructions for the role-play activity and point out how the pictures illustrate what happened. Discuss the two questions in the first part of the role-play activity with the whole class. Then set up groups and give them about 15 minutes to practice role-playing the situation. Remind them to make use of the expressions at the bottom of the page. Invite volunteer groups to perform their role-plays for the class.

Part 3 Reading

Before You Read

1 **Vocabulary Preview. Page 41.**
As you read the words aloud, have students circle the ones they don't know. Tell students to look for these words in the next reading selection. After reading the selection, students can return back to this list and check their understanding of the circled words. Encourage students to use context clues or look up the meanings of the words in a dictionary.

Read

2 **Global Climate Changes. Page 41.**
[on tape/CD]
Read the instructions together. Then play the tape or CD as students follow along in their books. Stop the tape or CD after every paragraph and ask volunteers to read the title they chose and identify the topic sentence. You may also want to

ask some comprehension questions and point out key vocabulary words in each of the paragraphs.

Answers:
Paragraph Titles:
1. Climate in Regions of the Globe
2. General Changes in the Nature of Weather
3. Global Warming and the "El Niño" Effect
4. The Powerful Effect of People on Nature

Topic Sentences:
1. In different areas of the globe, the climate generally stays the same from year to year.
2. According to some meteorologists (weather researchers), the earth's climate is changing slowly.
3. Global warming and El Niño are having major effects of the earth's atmosphere, the weather, and the changing world climate.
4. Probably, human beings are the main cause of the extreme effects of weather and climate changes.

After You Read

3 **Summarizing Paragraphs. Page 42.**
Review what a summary is. Read the instructions and call attention to the summary of the first paragraph. Arrange students in groups of four to practice summarizing and assign paragraphs to the groups. Allow 10-15 minutes for groups to read and summarize their paragraphs. Remind students that the topic sentence gives the main idea of a paragraph and the other sentences give details. Have a volunteer from each group read aloud its summary. If several groups have summarized the same paragraphs, compare and contrast the different versions. Discuss any differences.

Sample Answers:
2. Some people think the earth's climate is changing. The weather is becoming more extreme with longer times of very cold weather and longer times of very hot

weather. There are more storms, and the storms are stronger and more powerful.

3. Global warming and El Niño have affected the weather and climate. Global warming has made the temperature increase around the world. El Niño causes more rain and storms in the Americas. It also causes drought in parts of Asia. Northern regions have more cold weather and snow storms.

4. People also cause changes in weather and climate. Cars and factories create carbon dioxide. Coal and oil are burned which makes carbon dioxide. Plants and trees can use carbon dioxide, but people are cutting down many trees. The carbon dioxide affects the atmosphere and the weather.

Discussing the Reading

4 Small Group Discussion. Page 43.

Arrange students in groups of four to discuss the questions. Set a time limit of 15-20 minutes. Circulate among the groups, giving assistance as needed. Have a volunteer from each group summarize the most interesting points discussed.

Answers will vary.

Talk It Over

This activity gives students a chance to give their own opinions and to explain their beliefs. Read together the instructions. Model expressing opinions. For example: *I believe that ... I think that... I'm certain that ... I don't believe that... I'm not sure that...*

Arrange students in groups of four to talk about their own opinions about nature and weather statements. Allow 15-20 minutes for discussion. You may want to have groups report their findings. Were all their answers the same? For which topics were the answers similar? For which topics were the answers different? Students may write about their own beliefs and opinions using the answers they circled on the chart and adding supporting details from their own experiences.

Part 4 Writing

Before You Write

Exploring Ideas

1 **Page 44.**
   Sample Answers:
   1. Watson and the Shark. A shark is a marine animal that eats other marine animals. Sharks are known to attack humans on rare occasions.
   2. Watson is the drowning man in the foreground of the painting.
   3. In the painting, there are nine men on board a small lifeboat. One man has fallen overboard. Or, perhaps he is stranded and the others have come to rescue him. He is completely naked. The other men are trying to save him from the shark. One man is aiming a harpoon at the shark. The painting has a very dramatic feeling to it. There is a sense of urgency and fear.
   4. There are a good number of other ships in the background, so this could be taking place in the harbor of a major city.
   5. The action probably took place in the near the turn of the nineteenth century, judging by the clothing of the characters and the types of ships.
   6. This could have happened, because the painting is painted in a very realistic manner.

Organizing Ideas

Ordering Information in a Paragraph

2 **Page 45.**
   Answers:
   Sentences with general information:
   A Sunday on La Grande Jatte is a picture of a park on a warm and sunny day.

   It seems very peaceful.

In the park there are very many large trees.

There are people in the park. They might be European.

Many of the people are looking at the lake.

The people in the park are wearing old-fashioned clothes.

Sentences with specific information:

On the left you can see a lake with some small sailboats.

Some people are walking, and some are lying or sitting on the grass.

The women are wearing long dresses, and some of them are carrying umbrellas.

In the middle of the painting there is a small child. She is walking with her mother.

Point out to students that many sentences which provide general information are followed by sentences that give specific details.

3 Page 46.

Answer: 4. *Watson and the Shark,* by John Singleton Copley, shows a dramatic rescue.

4 Page 46.
Sample Answers:
1. the rowboat
2. the sea
3. the harbor
4. the shark
5. the drowning man
6. the man with the harpoon

Write

Developing Cohesion and Style

Adding Details: Adjectives

5 Page 46.
Sample Answers:
1. the boat: small, overloaded
2. the men in the boat: tense, scared
3. the weather: dark, gray
4. the shark: huge, frightening
5. the man in the water: pale, lifeless
6. the water: glassy, cold

6 Page 47.
Sample Answers:
1. The small, overloaded boat is in the water.
2. There is a huge, frightening shark in the water.
3. The men in the boat are tense and scared.
4. The man in the water seems pale and lifeless.
5. The weather looks dark and gray.

Adding Details: Prepositional Phrases

7 Page 47.

Answers: Phrases in the passage that show location: *In the park; On the left; in the park; on the grass; in the park; In the middle of the painting*

8 Page 47.
Sample Answers:
1. There are several men in a small boat.
2. A man is drowning in the water.
3. A huge shark is near the drowning man.
4. A man is holding aiming a spear at the shark.
5. Two men in the boat are trying to pull the drowning man on board.

Using Articles: *a/an* and *the*

9 Page 48.

Answers: There is a large tree in the middle. Two children are standing under the tree, and two children are climbing in the tree. The children are waving. On the left is a man and a woman in a boat. The man is fishing. The woman is holding a child. A large bird is flying over the boat. To the right is a smaller tree. Two people are sitting under the tree at a table. On the table is a plant.

Writing the First Draft

10 Page 48.

Have students write their first drafts of a paragraph about the painting *Watson and the Shark*. Remind them to use their notes from Activities 4 and 8 and to use the present continuous to tell what is happening.

Edit and Revise

Editing Practice

11 Editing for Content and Organization. Page 49.

Sample Answer: *The Starry Night* is a painting by Vincent Van Gogh, a Dutch artist. In the front of the painting are some tall, curved trees. In the background you can see rolling mountains with gently curving slopes. Between the trees and the mountains, in the center of the painting, is a valley. There is a small town or village in the valley, and in the center of the village is a church with a tall steeple. The most striking part of the painting is the sky. It is filled with bright, colorful stars. The stars, trees, and mountains look like they are moving. Our eyes follow their shapes up, around, down, and back again, like a ride on a roller coaster.

12 Editing for Form. Page 50.

See the paragraph above in the answer key for Activity 11. You may use this as an example of the passage edited for form.

Editing Your Writing

13 Editing Using a Checklist. Page 50.

Have students use items 1 and 2 in the Editing Checklist to conduct editorial passes on their paragraphs. In these passes, students should focus on content and organization. Tell students to make sure that their paragraphs "make sense" and that the ideas are well organized. Have students use items 3, 4, and 5 to conduct the final editorial passes on their paragraphs. In these passes, students are to focus on cohesion, style, and form.

14 Peer Editing. Page 50.

Use the suggestions in the student book to conduct peer conferences. Give pairs of students time to exchange papers and read each other's work. Students can write comments and suggestions in the margins of their partners' papers. Pairs can then reconvene and give each other verbal feedback, explaining the main points of their written comments. Afterwards, students can rewrite their paragraphs, incorporating the feedback as appropriate.

Writing the Second Draft

15 Page 50.

Have students rewrite their descriptions of *Watson and the Shark* using correct form and grammar. Their edits should reflect the suggestions of their peers and teacher, as well as their own edits from Activity 13. Then have them compare their paragraphs with those from Chapter 1. Are there any improvements?

Part 5 Grammar

A. *There is/There are*

Read the explanation above the chart. Have students read the examples and notes in the affirmative and negative statements chart. Have students look around the room and make statements about what *there is, there are, there isn't* or *there aren't any* of in the classroom. Write one of their affirmative statements on the board and then ask students to make it into a *yes/no* question. Write the question on the board. Point out the inversion of the *there* and the *is* or *are*. Have students read the affirmative and negative questions chart to themselves.

1 Page 51.

Read the instructions and the example. Have students read the conversation first without filling in the blanks. Then, ask students what Harold wants to do (go camping). Have students reread the conversation to fill in the blanks individually. Put students in pairs to check their answers.

Answers: 2. there aren't 3. there are
4. there is 5. there's 6. there are 7. is there
8. there is 9. there are 10. there aren't
11. Are there 12. there are 13. Is there
14. there is 15. There's

2 Page 52.

Read the instructions. Go over the examples. Put students in pairs to describe the picture while you circulate to answer individual questions.

Sample Answers: There's a river. There are two people by the river. There's one man standing in the water. There's one woman sitting on a rock. There's a bear standing near the people. There are many pine trees. There are mountains behind the pine trees. There are flowers behind the deer. There are fish in the river.

Optional Activity: Put students in pairs. Tell them to draw an X over one of the things in their picture without letting their partners see. Then have students try to guess what their partners crossed out of their picture by asking *yes/no* questions starting with *Is/Are there*.

B. Possessive Nouns

Ask students again one of the questions you wrote on the board. Write the answer on the board. Point out the use of the apostrophe -*s*. Have students read the chart. Check students' comprehension of the notes by asking *whose* questions that elicit answers with singular and plural nouns that end in -*s* and don't end in -*s*. Write an example of each on the board but leave off the apostrophe. Ask students to tell you where the apostrophe goes while you add it to your sentences.

3 Page 53.

Read the instructions and the example. Have students fill in the blanks individually. Then check answers as a class.

Answers: 2. Today's 3. Sarah's parents'
4. women's 5. boyfriend's 6. brothers'
7. campers' 8. wife's 9. birds'
10. fishermen's

C. The Present Continuous Tense

Put the following sentences on the board: *He teaches English. He's teaching English right now.* Ask students to say what the differences between the two sentences are. Read the explanation above the chart. Have students read the examples and notes for the statements. Have students make sentences of their own first for actions happening at the moment of speaking, and then with actions currently in progress. Change the sentence you put on the board to: *Is he teaching English right now?* Ask students to say what the changes in structure are. Contrast that with the following: *Does he teach English?* Have students read the examples and possible answers in the Yes/No Questions chart. Finally, change the *yes/no* question to the following information question by first erasing or crossing out the word

English and then writing on the board: *What is he teaching right now?* Ask students once again to say what the changes are. Contrast this with: *What does he teach?* Have students read the examples and possible answers in the Information Questions chart. Put the following verbs on the board: *have, die, get, begin, happen, carry.* Ask students to make sentences or questions in the present continuous tense with each one. Write one sentence or question for each verb on the board. Illustrate the spelling rules when adding the *-ing* to each one. Have students read the Spelling Rules for *-ing* Verbs chart on page 287.

4 Page 54.

Read the instructions and the example. Have students describe what they see in the pictures. Then put students in pairs to complete the exercise.

Answers:

1. Is the sky getting cloudy? Yes, it is.
2. Who is sleeping? Anita is.
3. What is the bear doing? It's chasing the hikers.
4. What is Paul wearing? He's wearing a bathing suit.
5. Are the hikers having trouble? Yes, they are.
6. What is the deer doing? It's running away.
7. What is happening to the tents? They are falling down.
8. What is Gil doing? He's running without his boots on / He's carrying his boots.
9. Is the weather changing? Yes, it is.
10. What are the hikers doing? They are running away from the bear / back to the tents.
11. Who is carrying an extra backpack? Rafael is.
12. What is Paul doing? He's shivering / standing.
13. Is anyone swimming? No, they aren't.
14. What is happening to Anita's book? It's floating away / down the river.
15. Why is Gil carrying the boots? Because they hurt him.
16. What is Anita doing? She's sleeping.

D. Modal Auxiliaries: *Can, May, Might, and Will*

Read the information above the chart to the students. Have students read the modals, meanings, and examples in the chart. Then have them make example sentences showing the meaning of each modal.

5 Page 55.

Read the instructions and the first sentence of the paragraph. Have students look at the picture to say what they see. Tell them to make *there is/are* sentences, present continuous sentences, and modal sentences. You may want to have less advanced students read the paragraph to themselves before circling the correct answers.

Answers: 2. will rain 3. will be 4. might catch 5. might be 6. might be 7. can't 8. see 9. might 10. be 11. may not 12. save 13. 'll 14. can 15. swim

Optional Activity: Put students in pairs to write quizzes with five questions to exchange with another pair. Tell students to use modals, present continuous tense, and *there is/are* in their questions. Circulate to answer questions and monitor for accuracy. As pairs finish, have them exchange quizzes with another pair. Have pairs close their books and answer the quiz questions from memory. When each pair is finished, have them return the quiz to the original pair to grade. Tell students to give each correct answer 20 points and to write the scores on the quizzes and then show each other what they did right and what their mistakes were.

Video Activities: Winter Storm

Before You Watch

Display a map of the United States and use it to introduce students to the major U.S. regions. Point to the cities mentioned in the Student Book. Ask students what they know about the seasons and weather commonly associated with these cities and regions. Confirm or modify students' answers as necessarily, and tell the class they will watch a video clip about extreme weather conditions in these places.

Watch [on video]

Read through the questions with students and then have students watch the video once straight through. When the video is over, give students two minutes to mark their answers. Discuss the answers with the class. If it seems appropriate, play the video again and suggest that students confirm or correct their answers.

Answers: 1. d 2. snow, storm, icy, freezing, wind

Watch Again [on video]

Ask students to read over the list of weather conditions in the second column. Then play the video again and have them fill in the answers in the first column. Review the answers together.

Answers: 1. d, e 2. c 3. a 4. f 5. b

After You Watch

In order to help students concentrate on what they are doing, it's usually a good idea to set a time limit for this activity. At the end, ask students to tell about any activities that no one had ever done. Invite students to explain why they think no one had done the activities.

Living to Eat or Eating to Live?

Part 1 Listening to Conversations

Before You Listen

1 Prelistening Questions. Page 58.

As students read the questions and look at the picture, help them figure out what is going on. You can use leading questions such as: *How long does it take to pay for two boxes of diapers? How long does it take to pay for a cart with 30 or 40 items in it? What is the purpose of an "Express Line?"* Then go over the answers to the three questions.

2 Vocabulary Preview. Page 58.

Ask students to read the Language Tip silently. If necessary, explain that noncount nouns are nouns that can't be preceded by a number. For example, *water* and *money* are noncount nouns because you can't say *one water* or *one money*. Then discuss the quantity words with the class and ask them to think of some other words that are used in this way. For example: *a liter, a kilogram, a package*. Point out that numbers can precede these words.

Then read aloud the words students will write in the sentences. Have them complete the activity and then go over it immediately.

Answers: 1. pound 2. gallon 3. take checks 4. produce 5. groceries 6. aisle 7. in line

Listen

3 Listening for Main Ideas. Page 59. [on tape/CD]

Read the instructions and remind students that in this activity they don't need to understand every word and that they should be listening only for the most important ideas. Ask students to look back at the picture on page 58 and explain that this picture illustrates what is happening in the recording they are going to hear. Have a student read aloud the questions before you play the tape or CD. Play the tape or CD and have the students answer the questions. Then have them go over the answers in pairs. Ask the pairs to point out any items they would like you to explain.

Answers:
1. They are talking about groceries that they are buying.
2. He's hungry.
3. $1.19
4. soap
5. They already have a gallon of ice cream at home.
6. They have too many items.

Tapescript

Mr. N: Well, dear, I got a few things that aren't on the grocery list.

Mrs. N: I can see that! You're not shopping for an army, you know.

Mr. N: You know I always do this when I'm hungry.

Mrs. N: Well, let's see what you have here.

Mr. N: Some nice, fresh strawberries for only a dollar nineteen a pound.

Mrs. N: Well, that's fine. They always have nice produce here. But why do you have all these cookies?

Mr. N: I don't know; don't you like them?

Mrs. N: Oh, I suppose. I hope you have a box of soap here.

Mr. N: Oops, I forgot. Where's the soap in this market?

Mrs. N: Aisle 3.

Mr. N: I'll go get it.

Mrs. N: Wait – This steak you got looks really expensive!

Mr. N: Well, it isn't. It's on sale for just $3.99 a pound.

Mrs. N: And what's this? More ice cream? We already have a gallon at home. Go put it back. Meanwhile, I'll get in line.

Chapter 3

Cashier: I'm sorry, ma'am; this is the express line. You have too many groceries, and we don't take checks here.

Stress

4 Listening for Stressed Words. Page 60. [on tape/CD]

Read the instructions and point out the blanks below where students will fill in the missing stressed words. Then point out the words they will use to fill in the blanks and go over the list together. You might have a different student read aloud each of the six columns. Answer any questions they may have about meaning or pronunciation.

Explain that after each pause in the recording students must do two things: repeat after the speaker and write in the missing words. Then play the tape or CD again and ask students to fill in the missing words using the list at the top. After that, have students exchange books and correct each other's work using the tapescript in the back of the student book as a guide. Discuss any items that more than five people got wrong. Then have students practice reading the completed dialogue with partners.

Reductions

5 Comparing Long and Reduced Forms. Page 61. [on tape/CD]

Play the tape or CD and have students follow along in their books. Then have students repeat the sentences after the recording.

6 Listening for Reductions. Page 61. [on tape/CD]

Read the directions for item 1. Remind students that the recording leaves enough time for students to repeat each sentence. Make sure students repeat audibly before writing. Play the tape or CD. Then ask a student to write the answers on the board for the others to use as an answer key. For item 2, have students read the sentences to a partner for pronunciation practice.

Move around the room checking their progress and modeling pronunciation as needed.

Answers: 1. what you 2. Do you 3. lots of 4. do you 5. don't know 6. don't you

Tapescript

Customer:	Waiter?
Waiter:	Yes sir. Do you know whatcha want?
Customer:	D'ya have the spaghetti with mushroom sauce tonight?
Waiter:	Yes, we do.
Customer:	Well, are the mushrooms fresh or canned?
Waiter:	We get lotsa fresh from the produce market every day.
Customer:	Great, I'll have that.
Waiter:	What kind of wine d'ya want with that?
Customer:	I dunno. Why doncha recommend something?
Waiter:	Our California wines are excellent.

After You Listen

7 Vocabulary Review. Page 62.

Review the instructions with the class and do the first item as an example. The answer might be: *I do all the grocery shopping in my family.* When students finish, ask volunteers to share some of their responses.

Pronunciation

Teens or Tens? [on tape/CD]

Read through the information on the difference between the pronunciation of *-ty* and *-teen*. Then go back and work on each of the pairs of words. First play the tape or CD or read the examples and have students listen to the words. Point out that although people sometimes think they should listen for the N sound at the end of *teen* as a way of telling the difference, in reality it is very difficult to hear that sound in ordinary conversation. Syllable stress is a much more reliable guide.

26 Interactions 1 Integrated Skills Instructor's Manual

8 Distinguishing between Teens and Tens. Page 63. [on tape/CD]

Read and discuss the instructions. Explain to students that they will have to listen very carefully and pay attention to which syllable is stressed. Play the tape or CD and have students mark their answers. If you feel it is appropriate, you can play the recording a second time so that students can check their answers. Then put the correct answers on the board and have students correct their work.

Answers: 1. 30 2. 14 3. 15 4. 60
5. 70 6. 18 7. 90

Tapescript

1. We waited in line for 30 minutes.
2. My sister is 14 years old.
3. We've lived in this city for 15 years.
4. Sixty people came to the party.
5. The groceries cost seventy dollars.
6. There are 18 students in the class.
7. I live 90 miles from my parents.

9 Listening for Teens and Tens. Page 63.

Read the instructions and then ask students to complete the activity with a partner. You may wish to do one or two items with the whole class to get them started. To review answers, call on volunteers to answer each question. You may wish to write the key words with *-s* endings on the board followed by the appropriate phonetic symbol.

Answers: 1. 14 2. 10:30 3. $40
4. 13 5. 1.90 6. 15 7. 30 8. 15
9. 70 10. 19

Tapescript

1. This turkey weighs 14 pounds.
2. The market is open until 10:30.
3. We spent $40 on groceries yesterday.
4. This milk is good until November 13th.
5. Those peaches cost $1.90 a pound.
6. Everything in this store is about 15 percent cheaper today.
7. My daughter is getting married. I need 30 bottles of champagne.
8. Please hurry up. The store will close in 15 minutes.
9. By using this coupon, you can save 70 cents on this ice cream.
10. Canned vegetables are on aisle 19.

Talk It Over

Read the instructions and review briefly the difference between a count noun and a noncount noun. (Count nouns can have numbers in front of them and noncount nouns can't.) Then have students do step 1 in small groups. For step 2, answer all questions honestly, but try to include quantity words as often as possible. Ask students if they understand how to proceed and answer any questions they may have. As the groups do step 3 together, move around the room monitoring their conversations. When everyone is through, invite students to tell the class about any interesting facts they learned while doing this activity. For example, they may have discovered that one student drinks ten cups of coffee a day or that another never eats breakfast.

Culture Note

Americans generally feel comfortable talking about how much money they spend on everyday items such as food or clothing or gasoline. However, most are not comfortable talking about how much they earn at their jobs, how much rent they pay, or how much they have in the bank.

Part 2 Recalling Main Ideas

Before You Listen

1 Prelistening Questions. Page 65.

Read and discuss the instructions and questions with the whole class. If one is available, show students the food pyramid that shows graphically which foods the U.S. government thinks are healthiest and the relative amounts of various types of foods they suggest that people eat. Then help students form pairs and complete the activity. Set a time limit of about five minutes. Review the responses with the whole class.

2 Vocabulary Preview. Page 65.

Have students complete the activity individually. As you review the answers with the class, ask students to raise their hands if they are still having difficulty with any of the terms. Invite other students to explain these terms in their own words.

Answers: 1. d   2. f   3. a   4. b   5. h   6. g   7. e   8. c

Listen

Culture Note

Weight-loss diets are an important part of popular culture in the United States. Not a month goes by without one or more articles about the topic in women's magazines, men's magazines, and even news magazines. Although millions seem to be obsessed with the topic of weight loss, statistics show that not many are successful in doing anything about it.

3 Listening for the Main Idea. Page 66. [on tape/CD]

Read the instructions and the question students are to listen for. Then play the tape or CD and call on volunteers to answer the question.

Answers: The best way to lose weight is to eat right, exercise, and be patient.

4 Taking Notes on Specific Information. Page 66. [on tape/CD]

Point out the *Do* and *Don't* columns. Then play the tape or CD and ask students to take their own notes under these headings in the chart. Mention that the recording is quite long and that students should make short notes like the sample

notes shown. Otherwise, they may get bogged down in writing and miss important points.

Tapescript

Announcer: Do you think you're overweight? Are you thinking of going on a diet? Here are some things you should and shouldn't do if you want to lose weight. First, the best way to lose weight safely is to lose it slowly. This means about 2 pounds, or one kilogram, a week, no more. If you lose weight too quickly, you'll probably gain it back anyway. So how do you lose weight slowly? First, eat right. Stay away from fast food and prepackaged foods—you know, canned and frozen foods. They may save you time, but they're bad for your health because they're high in fat and salt. In addition to changing your eating habits, you should also exercise regularly. To lose 1 pound, you must burn about 3,500 calories. You can do this by exercising just one hour, three times a week. Finally, to lose weight safely, don't take diet pills and don't go on crash diets. Diet pills can be very dangerous. They can hurt your muscles, bones, and heart. They can even cause death. Crash diets promise quick results in a very short time. For example, they say you can lose five pounds in two days if you just eat grapefruit. But crash diets are bad because the weight you lose always comes back. Don't try them. Remember, the best way to lose weight is to eat right, exercise, and be patient.

After You Listen

5 Summarizing Main Ideas. Page 66.

Read the Part 1 instructions and example with the class. Then help students find partners and practice summarizing the recording As they work, listen to different pairs, helping them with any aspects of the task that are proving difficult for them. If time permits, have one or more students present their summary to the class. For Part 2, brainstorm with the whole class a list of other dos and don'ts and discuss which weight-loss strategies have proved successful for class members.

6 Vocabulary Review. Page 67.

This is an open-ended oral activity that reviews key vocabulary words and provides listening and speaking practice. If possible, match up students of differing ability. You may wish to have less fluent students focus on only two or three of the questions so that they have time to receive plenty of feedback from their partners. More fluent students can try answering all the questions.

Talk It Over

Read the instructions and discuss the examples supplied in the chart. Next give students about ten minutes to write their own personal information on the chart. Then help students form small groups and begin comparing their eating habits.

Part 3 Reading

Before You Read

1 Discussing Pictures. Page 68.

Arrange students in small groups. Ask them to look at the pictures on page 68 and answer the questions. After the groups have finished their discussions, have a volunteer from each group report their responses. List vocabulary on the board as students describe the pictures. Help summarize the responses. Encourage students to identify specific items in the illustrations and to talk about items they have eaten and/or like.

Sample Answers:
1. The first picture is a food stand in an Asian community. There are people eating with chopsticks, chopping/preparing food, and ordering food. The second picture is a supermarket or convenience store with food products. There are some frozen foods, international foods, and convenience/packaged foods. In the third picture, a family is preparing food at home and eating. They are probably in the kitchen. The mother is offering food. Others are eating, cooking, and preparing vegetables.

2. The foods are similar because they are all ready to eat or need very little preparation. The foods are different because they are representative of different ethnic groups, different methods of serving the food.

2 Thinking about the Answers. Page 69.

Point out the title of the reading selection, "The Changing Global Diet," and the illustrations on page 68. Then read the questions aloud and call on volunteers to suggest any ideas they have. Remind students that these questions will help guide them as they read the selection and work on the exercises. Point out key vocabulary: *fast foods, diet, convenience foods, nutritious.* As students suggest answers, record students' responses and ideas on an overhead projector or on a large piece of paper. Encourage students to develop their own pre-reading questions about the reading selection. You may want to review these questions and responses later after students have read the selection.

Sample Answers:
1. A diet is a plan for eating.

2. The same or similar types of fast foods can be found around the world.

3. People might like quick and convenient eating places because you can get food quickly, you don't need to prepare it, you don't need to clean up afterwards, you can get a variety of different types of food. People might not like these places because the food is not always good for you and it might be more expensive than preparing your own food.

4. Fast foods are becoming more nutritious because of better rules about foods and food preparation. People want more salads and fruits which are more nutritious.

5. Eating customs are changing because people are more concerned about health and nutrition.

3 Vocabulary Preview. Page 69.

As you read the words aloud, ask students to circle the ones they don't know. You may want to have volunteers suggest the meanings of the new words. Encourage students to look for the words in the following reading. After completing the reading selection, have students come back to this list and check their understanding of the circled words.

Read

4 The Changing Global Diet. Page 69. [on tape/CD]

Play the tape or CD as students follow along in their books. You may want to stop the tape after every paragraph to ask comprehension questions and to point out key vocabulary words. Listen a second time as students read along.

After You Read

5 Recognizing Paragraph Topics. Page 71.

Read the instructions aloud. Point out the example. Then have students complete the rest of the exercise. Go over the answers together. Then have volunteers change the topic statements into questions. Write the questions on the board or overhead projector.

Answers: 1. e 2. c 3. d 4. b 5. a
1. e. In what ways is the global diet changing?
2. c. Why do people choose to stay away from fast food?
3. d. How are convenience foods becoming more nutritious?
4. b. How is fast food the same around the word?
5. a. What are some definitions of the word *diet*?

6 Understanding the Main Idea. Page 71.

Read the instructions. Review the questions that the class wrote in Exercise 5. Point out that the five main idea statements in this exercise answer the questions. Read the question about paragraph A (What are some definitions of the word *diet*?). Ask students if the statement is true or false. Then have students complete the exercise. Discuss the answers with the whole class.

Answers: 1. F 2. F 3. T 4. F 5. F

Ask students to point out the information that is incorrect in the false statements. Students can look back in the reading selection for the correct information. Ask volunteers to restate the false statements to make them true.

Sample Answers:
1. The word diet has three basic definitions- "usual food choices," "an eating plan," and "go on a diet."
2. Fast food has a lot of variety around the world. Some examples are hamburgers, tacos, pizza, schnitzel, falafel, eggrolls, and sushi. The style of the nourishment and the atmosphere of the eating places don't differ much.
4. Fast foods and convenience foods are becoming more healthful. Restaurant items are sometimes grilled and there are more vegetables. Packaged items now contain less fat, sugar, salt, and so on.
5. The global diet is changing mostly in good ways. Many people buy fresh, natural foods at markets. More families cook at home. Many meals contain the necessary food elements There is a larger variety of food choices and preparation methods.

7 Getting Meaning by Using Punctuation Clues. Page 72.

After reading the instructions together, have students look for examples of the punctuation and italics in the reading selection. Tell students to work individually to write the words or phrases to complete the sentences in Exercise 7. Go over the answers with the group.

Answers:
1. diet 2. diet 3. fast food 4. universal
5. fast-food chains 6. fiber, vitamins, minerals
7. convenience foods 8. junk food 9. nutrition bars 10. natural food

Students can look back at the reading on pages 69-70 for definitions of other vocabulary words.

Model asking questions about the vocabulary words and responding with a complete sentence answer. Point out the examples on the bottom of the page. Have students practice asking and answering questions about the meanings of the vocabulary words in Exercise 7.

8 Recognizing Supporting Details. Page 73.
Read together the instructions. Remind students that details support or are examples of the main idea. Have students complete the exercise. Go over the answers together.

Answers: 1. a 2. c 3. d 4. a 5. b

You may want to have students answer the questions in Exercise 2 page 69 by giving details or examples from the reading selection.

Discussing the Reading

9 Small Group Discussion. Page 74.
This activity allows students to use the vocabulary from the reading to talk about their own opinions and preferences about food. Arrange students in groups of four. Set a time limit for the small group discussions. As groups talk about their answers together, circulate among the groups, listening, and giving assistance as needed. When all groups are finished, ask a volunteer from each group to summarize their ideas.

Answers will vary.

Part 4 Writing

Before You Write

Exploring Ideas

1 Describing Holiday Foods. Page 74.
Give students five minutes to write in their journals about typical foods in their home countries. Remind them to write as much as they can in the given amount of time without worrying about spelling or grammar.

2 Page 75.
Students should have no trouble thinking of a special holiday and related foods from their home countries. To get them started, you may want to share about one of your own favorite holidays.

3 Page 75.
To make the passage more interesting, encourage students to write about specific foods and dishes that they eat on holidays.

Organizing Ideas

Ordering Information in a Paragraph

4 Page 76.
Answers:
1. 7
2. 4
3. 5
4. 1
5. 3
6. 2
7. 6

5 Page 76.
Answers will vary.

Chapter 3

Writing Topic Sentences

6 Page 77.
Answers:
1. c
2. (not complete)
3. c
4. (not complete)
5. c

7 Page 77.
Answer: Topic Sentence: Thanksgiving is a family celebration.

8 Page 77.
Have partners use the questions to hold a short pre-writing conference. Students should give each other feedback on their topic sentences. Can it be expanded upon? Is it interesting enough to be the basis for a paragraph?

Write

Developing Cohesion and Style

Giving Examples with *such as*

9 Page 78.
Answers:
Italian: ravioli, cannoli, minestrone
Chinese: dim sum, spring rolls, moo shu pork
Mexican: tacos, enchiladas, tamales
Indian: samosas, curry, mulligatawny soup

10 Page 78.
Answers:
1. Italian restaurants serve many wonderful dishes such as ravioli, cannoli, and minestrone soup.
2. In Chinese restaurants you can try delicious dishes such as dim sum, spring rolls, and moo shu pork.
3. Mexican dishes such as tacos, enchiladas, and tamales have become very popular in the United States.
4. Many Indian dishes such as curry and mulligatawny soup are very spicy.

Writing the First Draft

11 Page 79.
Have students write the first draft of a paragraph describing holiday foods for one specific holiday. They should include the name of the holiday in the title. Remind them to use appositives and to give examples using *such as.*

Edit and Revise

Editing Practice

12 Editing a Paragraph. Page 79.
Sample Answer:
Food is an important part of Christmas. The holiday season would not be complete without the many special treats that are typically prepared at this time of year. Some of these treats, such as fruitcake and eggnog, originally come from Great Britain. In North America, fruitcake is made with fruit, nuts, and liquor. Eggnog is a drink of eggs, milk, and a liquor such as rum. Americans also eat a lot of Christmas cookies. I love all the special Christmas foods.

Editing Your Writing

13 Editing Using a Checklist. Page 80.
Have students use the items in the Editing Checklist to conduct editorial passes on their paragraphs. Students should focus on content and organization in their first passes. Tell students to make sure that their paragraphs "make sense" and that the ideas are well organized. After they are satisfied with the flow of ideas, they should conduct passes to focus on grammar and form.

14 Peer Editing. Page 80.

Use the suggestions in the student book to conduct peer conferences. Give pairs of students time to exchange papers and read each other's work. Students can write comments and suggestions in the margins of their partners' papers. Pairs can then reconvene and give each other verbal feedback, explaining the main points of their written comments. Afterwards, students can rewrite their paragraphs, incorporating the feedback as appropriate.

Writing the Second Draft

15 Page 80.

Have students rewrite their paragraphs describing holiday foods using correct form and grammar. Their edits should reflect the suggestions of their peers and teacher, as well as their own edits from Activity 13.

Part 5 Grammar

A. Count and Noncount Nouns

Read the explanation above the chart. Have students read the examples and notes. Have students look around the room and point to count and noncount nouns they see saying, *there's a pencil, there are some books, there is some chalk.*

B. *Some and Any*

Read the explanation above the chart. Have students read the examples and the notes in the chart. Then, have students make sentences with *some* and *any* about things that are and aren't in the classroom.

1 Page 82.

Read the instructions and the example. Have students fill in the blanks individually. Then have students read out the sentences.

Answers: 2. any 3. some, any 4. some, any 5. any 6. any 7. some, some 8. any, some 9. any 10. any

C. *A lot of / Many / Much*

Put some sentences with *much* and *many* on the board. Ask students to deduce which type of nouns, count or noncount, go with *much* and which with *many*. Substitute *a lot of* in both types of sentences to illustrate that it can be used with count or noncount nouns. Read the explanation above the chart. Have students read the examples and notes in the chart.

2 Page 82.

Read the instructions and the example. You may want to have less advanced students label each of the nouns in the pictures count or noncount nouns before doing the exercise. Have students write their questions and answers individually. Put students in pairs to check their answers by taking turns asking and answering their questions.

Sample Answers:
2. Are there a lot of cookies on the plate? No, there aren't a lot. There are only two.
3. Is there much milk in the refrigerator? Yes, there is a lot of milk in the refrigerator.
4. Are there many apples in the basket? yes there are a lot of apples in the basket.
5. Are there many pancakes on the plate? Yes, there are a lot of pancakes on the plate.
6. Is there a lot of rice in the bag? Yes, there's a lot of rice in the bag.
7. Is there much water in the glass? No, there isn't much water in the glass.
8. Is there much salad in the bowl? Yes, there's a lot of salad in the bowl.

D. Asking Questions with *How many* and *How much*

Read the explanation above the chart and have students read the examples and possible answers. Point out the note below the chart.

3 Page 84.

Read the instructions and the example. Put students in pairs to do the exercise.

Sample Answers:

3. How much milk is in the refrigerator? (*or* How many cartons of milk are there in the refrigerator?) There's a lot of milk in the refrigerator. (*or* There are twelve cartons of milk in the refrigerator.)

4. How many apples are in the basket? There are a lot of apples in the basket.

5. How many pancakes are on the plate? There are eight pancakes on the plate. (*or* There are a lot of pancakes on the plate.)

6. How much rice is there in the bag? There's a lot of rice in the bag.

7. How much water is in the glass? There isn't much water in the glass.

8. How much salad is in the bowl? There's a lot of salad in the bowl.

E. Modal Auxiliaries: Requests, Offers, and Permission

Read the explanation above the chart. Have students read the examples, the possible answers, and the notes for each of the three functions. Put on the board the following sentences with *can* and *may*, and *will: Can you speak French? I may stay home tonight. I'll finish that tomorrow.* Then contrast these with the following: *Can I use your phone? May I sit here? I'll get that for you.* Ask students to say which sentences or questions express making a request, ability, future possibility, making an offer, future, and requesting permission.

4 Page 85.

Read the instructions. Have students look at the first picture and say what they see happening. Read the example. Have students read all the examples for A. Then, put them in pairs to take turns making appropriate requests, offers, or requests for permission. Have students look at the second picture and say what they see happening. Ask them to say who they think these people are. Then have them continue doing the exercise in their pairs. Have selected pairs share their

requests, offers, or requests for permission with the class.

Answers:

A. 2. May I have a second helping of rice?
3. Can I have the last piece of bread?
4. Could you give me your recipe?
5. Can I start clearing the table?

B. 1. Would you like to join us? 2. Could you bring another cup of tea, please? 3. Can I pour you a cup of tea? 4. Will you pass me the sugar? 5. Could you bring the check, please?

Video Activities: Treat Yourself Well Campaign

Before You Watch

Arrange students in small groups. Read the questions aloud and ask students to discuss their opinions about various types of food. Have students report to the class their answers.

Watch [on video]

Ask them to read two questions. Then play the video and have them write their answers. Review the answers together.

Answers: 1. fast food, fattening food 2. salmon with black bean sauce, low-fat pizza with extra vegetables

Watch Again [on video]

Have students read the statements and choices. Then replay the video and have students circle the correct answers. Go over the answers.

Answers: 1. b 2. c 3. d

After You Watch

Have students bring in menus from the local area or from the Internet. Ask students to prepare a brief description of the food choices and the types of food offered on their menus. In small groups, students can compare and contrast the menus and prices.

In the Community

Part 1 Listening to Conversations

Before You Listen

1 Prelistening Questions. Page 88.

Ask students to discuss the first two questions with a partner. As you go over their responses together in class, you may wish to note on the board key vocabulary items that come up, such as *drugstore, Laundromat,* and *ATM (automated teller machine)* and have students write them down in their notebooks for later use. Point out the boy running in the picture. Then read the third question aloud and call on volunteers to tell what they think is happening.

2 Vocabulary Preview. Page 88.

Explain that the expressions in the left-hand column of the chart will appear in the recording and that this exercise will make it easier for them to understand what they are going to hear. Read the expression aloud and have students fill in the sentences below on their own. Discuss the correct completions with the whole class. Then ask students to go back and fill in the meanings in the right-hand column of the chart.

Possible Answers:

Meanings: 1. drive me somewhere in your car   2. do several small tasks around the community   3. let someone get out of your car   4. where clothes that can't be washed are cleaned   5. wash clothes   6. easy to find or get to   7. convert a check into paper money   8. must   9. crossing the street in the middle of the block

Fill-ins: 1. run, errands   2. do laundry   3. convenient   4. give me a ride   5. have got to   6. dry cleaners   7. cash a check   8. drops off   9. jaywalking

3 Listening for Main Ideas. Page 89. [on tape/CD]

Read aloud the instructions for item 1. Remind students that the goal of the exercise is to listen only for main ideas. Ask them to look back at the picture on page 88 and explain that this picture illustrates one thing that happens in the recording they are going to hear. Have a student read the questions. Prompt students to ask about any questions they don't understand. Have a student read aloud the questions before you play the tape or CD. Play the tape or CD and have the students answer the questions. Then have them go over the answers in pairs.

Answers:

1. to give him a ride
2. at the corner of King Boulevard and Second Avenue
3. go to the bank, go to the dry cleaner's, drop off some film, pay a traffic ticket
4. pay a traffic ticket
5. he could cross the street and not worry about jaywalking

Tapescript

Kenji: Peter, are you going downtown today?

Peter: Uh-huh. Why?

Kenji: Can you give me a ride? I have to run some errands.

Peter: Where do you need to go?

Kenji: Uh, a lot of places. First, I've got to go to the bank. Could you drop me off at the corner of King Boulevard and Second Avenue?

Peter: King and Second? Oh, sure. I know where that is. But why are you going to the bank? Why don't you use the ATM on campus?

Kenji: 'Cause I need to cash a check my dad sent me. And the cleaner's is next door to the bank. I have to pick up some clothes there anyway.

Peter: There's a laundry room right here on the first floor. You can do your laundry there much cheaper.

Kenji: I'm not picking up laundry. It's dry cleaning. By the way, is there a photo shop near there? I need to drop off some film to develop.

Peter: A photo shop? Oh, yeah. There's probably one in the drugstore, across the street from the bank.

Kenji: Oh, that's convenient. So what are *you* gonna do downtown?

Peter: I'm going to the courthouse. I've got to pay a traffic ticket.

Kenji: No kidding! I'm going there, too. I also got a ticket.

Peter: But, Kenji, you don't drive!

Kenji: I know. I got a ticket for jaywalking!

Peter: Really?!

Kenji: Yeah. MAN, sometimes I miss living in Japan. I could cross the street and not worry about stupid rules like "jaywalking"!

Stress

4 Listening for Stressed Words. Page 90. [on tape/CD]

Read the instructions and ask students to read through the list and circle any words they don't know. Discuss these words and have students who know the words explain them to their classmates. Remind students that after each pause in the recording they should repeat after the speaker and write in the missing words. Play the tape or CD and ask students to fill in the missing words. Correct them in class or have students use the tapescript to correct their own work. Then have them do the second part of the exercise in pairs.

Reductions

This section focuses on the reductions native speakers often produce when combining the words *can, you, give, me, do, have, to, got, could, lot, of, are,* and *going* with other words. Remind them that the reduced forms are never written out in normal writing.

5 Comparing Long and Reduced Forms. Page 91. [on tape/CD]

Play the tape or CD and have students follow along in their books. Then have students repeat the sentences after the recording. If you hear a number of students making the same error, point it out and help them correct it.

6 Listening for Reductions. Page 91. [on tape/CD]

Read the directions for item 1. Remind students that the recording leaves enough time for students to repeat each sentence before they fill in the answer. Play the tape or CD. Then write the correct answers on the board and have students correct their own exercises. For item 2, have students read the sentences to a partner for pronunciation practice. Move around the room checking their progress and modeling pronunciation as needed.

Answers: 1. Do you 2. have to 3. Could you 4. because, got to, lot of 5. can you , give me 6. Are you

7 Reductions Game. Page 92.

Read the introductory material to the class and ask questions to make sure that students understand the situation being described. Then read and discuss the instructions. Role-play the first two or three rounds of the game in which students repeat the earlier statements and add one of their own. Review the items in the Word Bank at the bottom and explain any terms that are new to students. Also point out the list of reductions at the top and remind students to use them in their responses. If you have a large class, you may wish to have several groups play the game simultaneously.

After You Listen

8 Vocabulary Review. Page 92.

This exercise reinforces vocabulary already introduced. Review the instructions with the class and do the first item as an example. The answer might be: *Yes, I dropped off my laundry on the way to school on Tuesday*. When the pairs finish work, ask volunteers to share some of their responses.

Part 2 Recalling Main Ideas

Before You Listen

1 Prelistening Questions. Page 93.

Read and discuss the instructions and questions with the whole class. Point out the pictures and invite students to describe what they see in each one. Then help them form pairs and complete the activity. Set a time limit of about five minutes. Then review their responses with the whole class.

2 Vocabulary Preview. Page 93.

Read the instructions and have students complete the activity individually. As you review the answers with the class, ask students to raise their hands if they are still having difficulty with any of the terms. Invite other students to explain these terms in their own words.

Answers: 1. d 2. e 3. b 4. a 5. c

Listen

3 Listening for Main Ideas. Page 94. [on tape/CD]

This main idea exercise is different from others in the book. Students are asked to choose a title for a conversation. Give students about three minutes to do step 1. Then allow the discussion in step 2 go on for as long as it is productive. You may wish to have students review *Hints for Remembering* in the Listen section of Chapter 1 before beginning this exercise.

Tapescript

Peter: Phew...I'm glad I don't live in the city. The traffic is terrible. I have a headache from the noise and all the smog.

Ming: You think cities here are bad? Ask Kenji

about Tokyo.

Kenji: Yeah, Tokyo is noisier and much more crowded than the cities here.

Ming: Yeah, and I hear the smog's worse, too.

Kenji: That's right.

Peter: So, I guess you don't miss that, huh?

Kenji: Well, I don't miss those things. But a big city like Tokyo can be very exciting.

Peter: Yes, I'm sure that's true. But I prefer the peace and quiet of a small town like ours.

Kenji: Well, I like it here, too. The people are friendlier and things are cheaper.

Ming: Well, you know, I come from a small town, and it can be so conservative and boring. When I graduate, I want to live in a big city like New York or Chicago. You can make more money there, too.

Peter: Yeah, but it's more dangerous there.

Ming: Yeah, that's a disadvantage. But there are also lots of advantages.

Peter: Yeah? Like what? The long lines at the bank or in the stores?

Ming: Waiting in line doesn't bother me. I really love shopping in the city. You can find anything.

Kenji: Great! Then next time we need something downtown, we'll send you.

4 Taking Notes on Specific Information. Page 94. [on tape/CD]

Review the instructions with the class. Then play the tape or CD and have them fill in the information. Ask two or three students to write their notes on the board. Discuss the differences in the ways the students took notes and point out effective note-taking strategies.

Possible Answers:

Big Cities		Small Towns	
Good things	Bad things	Good things	Bad things
1. exciting	1. traffic	1. peace	1. conser-
2. can make more money	2. noise	2. quiet	servative
3. good shopping	3. smog	3. friendly	2. boring
	4. crowded		
	5. dangerous		
	6. long lines		

After You Listen

5 Summarizing Main Ideas. Page 94.
Read and discuss the instructions and help students find partners. As they work together, move around the room offering assistance as needed.

6 Vocabulary Review. Page 94.
This is an open-ended activity in which students describe familiar situations and express their own feelings about them. Have students complete this activity with a partner. Invite volunteers to share some of their opinions with the class.

Part 3 Reading

Before You Read

1 Discussing the Picture. Page 95.
Arrange students in small groups to answer the questions about the picture on page 95. After the groups have finished their discussions, ask a volunteer from each group to report the group's responses. As students describe the pictures, list vocabulary on the board. Guide students to summarize the responses. Encourage students to talk about their own experiences related to asking directions and being in a new city or place.

Sample Answers:
1. The two travelers are visiting a new place. They are looking at maps and a brochure about the city. They don't understand the map or brochure or they can't find the place(s) they want to visit. They look confused.
2. The other people are explaining the directions and pointing in different directions. It looks like the people don't agree with each other because they look angry.
3. This situation happens to me. I prefer to use a map for directions. People sometimes ask me for directions. I tell them "I don't know."

2 Thinking about the Answers. Page 95.
Point out the title of the reading selection "How Can I Get to the Post Office?" Then read the questions aloud and call on volunteers to suggest possible answers and to make predictions about the reading. Remind students that these questions will help guide them as they read the selection and work on the exercises. Call attention to key vocabulary: *directions, body language, community*. Record students' responses and ideas on an overhead projector or on a large piece of paper. Encourage students to develop their own pre-reading questions about the reading selection. You may want to review these questions and responses later after students have read the selection.

Sample Answers:
1. People can make a map. They can tell you the directions. They can take you there. They can show you a map. They can point out the way.
2. If a person doesn't know the answer, he or she might not answer. The person might tell you to ask another person, or he or she might just walk away.
3. Body language can help you find directions because people can point out the direction with their hands.

3 Vocabulary Preview. Page 95.
As you read the words aloud, ask students to circle the ones they don't know. Ask volunteers to suggest the meanings of the new words. Tell students to look for the words as they complete the reading. Later, have students come back to this list and check their understanding of their circled words.

Read

**4 How Can I Get to the Post Office?
Page 96. [on tape/CD]**
Play the tape or CD as students follow along in their books. Pause the tape or CD after every paragraph to ask comprehension questions and to point out key vocabulary words. Listen a second time as students read along again.

After You Read

5 Recognizing Paragraph Topics. Page 97.

Read the instructions aloud. Point out the examples. Then have students complete the rest of the exercise. Go over the answers together.

Answers:

C. Directions in the American Midwest

D. Directions in Los Angeles, California

E. Directions in Greece

F. Directions in Yucatan, Mexico

G. The Conclusion: Body Language and Gestures

b. The reading tells about people giving directions in different cities and countries.

6 Understanding the Main Idea. Page 97.

Read the instructions. Read the question about paragraph A (*What is the point of the introduction to the reading material?*) Review question words and question formation as needed. Then ask students to complete the exercise. Discuss the answers with the whole class.

C. *How do people give* directions in the region of the American Midwest?

D. *How do people give* directions in the city of Los Angeles, California?

E. *How do people give* directions in the European country of Greece?

F. *How do people give* directions in some areas of Mexico like Yucatan?

G. *What is the point of* the conclusion to the reading material?

In what ways *do people give* directions in various cultures around the world?

7 Correcting Information. Page 98.

Read the instructions aloud before having students complete the exercise. Encourage students to look back at the reading selection as they correct the statements.

Sample Answers:

1. If you don't carry a map when you travel, you have to ask for directions.

2. In Japan, people most often use landmarks in their directions.

3. In the flatlands of the American Midwest, people will tell you directions and distances.

4. In Los Angeles, California, the most common way to give directions is with times (minutes).

5. Even if visitors to Greece don't understand the Greek language, the people will usually understand because the Greeks give directions with motions or gestures.

6. In some parts of Mexico, people are very polite, so they don't want to say "I don't know" in answer to questions about directions.

7. All over the world, body language is easier to understand than words in sentences.

8. In various cultures around the world, people give directions to travelers and tourists in various ways and by pointing.

8 Finding Illustrations of Word Meanings. Page 98.

After reading aloud the directions and example, have students complete the exercise. Go over the answers together.

1. landmarks: the corner, the big hotel with the sushi bar, the fruit market, the bus stop, the fast-food fried chicken place, and so on.

2. directions: straight north, turn right, go another mile, in a northeast direction, and so on.

3. distances: 2 miles, another mile, about 5 minutes, kilometer, block, and the like.

4. body language: facial expressions, gestures, motions, movements, pointing, and so on.

Chapter 4

9 Recognizing the Relationship of Detail to the Point. Page 99.

After reading the instructions together, have students look for examples of the colons, commas, and quotation marks in the reading selection. Tell students to work individually to complete the exercise 9. Go over the answers with the group.

Sample Answers:

1. The writer's rule is: "Never carry a map."
2. Some advantages are you practice a new language, you meet new people, and you learn new customs.
3. Tourists are often confused in Japan because there are no street names.
4. Some illustrations of Japanese directions are: "Turn left at the big hotel." "Go past the fruit market."
5. In the American Midwest, people might give directions like: go north for 2 miles, turn right and go another mile.
6. People in Los Angeles don't give directions in miles, kilometers, or blocks because they don't know directions or distance.
7. Greeks seldom give foreigners directions in words and sentences because most tourists don't understand Greek.
8. A person in New York City will say, "Sorry, I have no idea," if he or she doesn't know the location of a place.
9. A polite resident of Yucatan doesn't say "I don't know" because it is more polite to stay and talk to a person.
10. A person gives directions with body language such as: facial expressions, gestures, motions, and movements.

You may want to have students answer the questions in Exercise 9 by giving details or examples from the reading selection.

Discussing the Reading

10 Small Group Discussion. Page 100.

Encourage students to talk about their own experiences with directions and being lost. Arrange students in groups of four. Set a time limit for the small group discussions. As groups talk about their answers together, circulate among the groups, listening and giving assistance as needed. When all groups are finished, ask a volunteer from each group to summarize their ideas.

Answers will vary.

Part 4 Writing

Before You Write

Exploring Ideas

Describing Places, Things to Do, and Directions

1 Page 101.

You might want to begin this activity as a class and then have students continue independently.

2 Building Vocabulary. Page 101.

Have several volunteers share their lists with the class. Encourage students to ask questions about these lists and to comment on them as well.

3 Page 101.
Sample Answers:

1. go sightseeing
2. go for a walk
3. go shopping
4. go for a drive
5. go on a trip

4 Page 101.

Ask students to label each element of their maps and to create legends for their maps as well.

Organizing Ideas

5 Page 102.
   Answers:
   a. 1
   b. 2
   c. 1
   d. 2
   e. 3
   f. 2
   g. 1
   h. 1
   i. 3

Write

Developing Cohesion and Style

Using Prepositions

6 Page 103.
   Answers: Take Route 44 south <u>to</u> Exit 12. Turn right <u>at</u> the first light. You will be <u>on</u> Maple Avenue. Go straight <u>down</u> Maple Avenue <u>for</u> two miles. <u>At</u> the corner of Bryant and Maple you will see an elementary school. Turn right <u>at</u> the first street <u>after</u> the school. The name of the street is Roosevelt Drive. Go straight <u>for</u> five blocks. Then make a left turn <u>onto</u> Broadmoor. My apartment building isn't difficult to find. It's <u>on</u> the left, Number 122. You can park your car <u>behind</u> the building.

7 Page 103.
   Answers: I live <u>in</u> the old part of the city. Take the number 5 bus. Get off <u>at</u> Franklin Street. You will see a large church down the street. Walk <u>to</u> the church and turn right. Walk two blocks and turn left <u>at</u> Smith's drugstore. You will be <u>on</u> Ames Avenue. Go straight <u>on</u> Ames Avenue for two blocks. Then turn left <u>at</u> the corner of Ames and Findlay. My house is the third one <u>on</u> the left.

Writing the First Draft

8 Page 103.
   Have students write letters to a friend who is coming to visit. In the first paragraph, they should describe what they are going to do during the friend's visit. In the second paragraph, they should give directions to their homes. In the third paragraph, they should say good-bye and how excited they are about the visit. Remind them to use prepositions when giving their friend directions.

Edit and Revise

Editing Practice

9 Using Correct Form in an Informal Letter. Page 105.
   Answer:
   June 15, 20xx

   Dear Mary,

   I'm very glad that you are going to visit me next week. We will have such a good time.

   It's easy to find my house. Make a left turn at the corner of Broadway and Fifth Street. Drive down Fifth for two blocks. Then make a right turn on Henry Street. There is a park on the corner. My house is on the left side. It is number 150. The weather is warm so we might go hiking and swimming. Please bring your photo album. I want to see pictures of your family.

10 Addressing an Envelope. Page 106.
Sample Answer:
Michael Ryall
150 Henry Street
Monterey, CA 93940

Mary Pirewali
256 Rose Avenue
San Jose, CA
51947

Editing Your Writing

11 Editing Using a Checklist. Page 106.
Have students use the items in the Editing Checklist to conduct editorial passes on their paragraphs. Students should focus on content and organization in their first passes. Tell students to make sure that their letters "make sense" and that the steps are well organized. After they are satisfied with the flow of ideas, they should conduct passes to focus on grammar and form.

12 Peer Editing. Page 106.
Use the suggestions in the student book to conduct peer conferences. Give pairs of students time to exchange papers and read each other's work. Students can write comments and suggestions in the margins of their partners' papers. Pairs can then reconvene and give each other verbal feedback, explaining the main points of their written comments. Afterwards, students can rewrite their letters, incorporating the feedback as appropriate.

Writing the Second Draft

13 Page 106.
Have students rewrite their letters to the friend who is coming to visit using correct form and grammar. Their edits should reflect the suggestions of their peers and teacher, as well as their own edits from Activity 11.

Part 5 Grammar

A. The Future with *be going to*
Have students look at the first picture on page 108. Ask the students to say what the man is doing (*weighing himself; standing on a scale*). Ask how he looks (*worried; concerned*). Ask what he's thinking (*he's thinking about exercising/joining a gym*). Say, "*He's thinking about joining a gym. Tonight after work, he's going to going a gym. He's going to start exercising.*" Write the sentences "He's weighing himself" and "He's going to join a gym" on the board and ask the students to compare them structurally. Read the two sentences aloud. Read the "going to" sentence with the reduced pronunciation, *gonna*. Point this out to the students. Have the students read the explanation above the charts. Then have them practice saying the future sentence you wrote on the board. Encourage them to use *gonna*. Have students read the purposes and examples in the charts. Ask students to make statements about other things they think the man is going to do to lose weight. For example, *go on a diet, start running in the morning, stop eating fatty foods*.

1 Page 108.
Read the instructions and the example. Have students look at all the pictures and ask any questions they may have about vocabulary. Have students do the exercise individually. Then have students read out their sentences.

Sample Answers: 2. The woman is going to start riding her bike to work. 3. The man is going to recycle his garbage. 4. The man is going to get a haircut and shave his beard.
5. The couple are going to go on a trip.
6. The woman is going to visit her mother.

B. The Future with *will*
Say to the students, "*I think I'll go shopping this afternoon.*" Then say, "*I'm going to go out to eat this evening.*" Ask students when you decided to do each of the activities. Read the explanation above the chart. Have students read the purposes

and examples in the statements chart. Have students make more statements of their own for each purpose. Then have students to read the examples and possible answers in the *yes/no* questions and information questions chart.

2 Page 109.

Read the instructions. Have students pronounce the names Chiara and Angela. Tell students to read the complete dialogue before choosing their answers. Have students do the exercise individually. Then, put students in pairs to read the dialogue together with their choices. Have students tell each other why they chose their answers.

Answers: 1. 'll 2. 'm going to 3. 'll 4. Will you 5. will you / are you going to 6. 'm going to 7. ' ll 8. are going to 9. 'll 10. 'm going to 11. 'll 12. 'll

3 Page 110.

Read the instructions. Read the example. Put the students in groups to do the exercise.

C. The Future Using The Present Continuous and the Simple Present

Tell students what you are planning to do on the weekend using the present continuous. Write two or three of your plans on the board. Then tell them about a trip you plan to take saying what you do each day using the simple present. Write two or three of these weekend and vacation plans on the board. Read the explanation above the charts. Have students say what the specific situations are of the sentences on the board. Have students read the examples and notes in the two charts.

4 Page 111.

Read the instructions and the examples. Have students fill in the blanks individually. Put students in pairs to compare answers.

Answers: 3. Are / going 4. is leaving 5. leaves, arrives 6. opens 7. are / meeting 8. are / doing 9. am taking 10. does / begin 11. does / arrive 12. am / going

D. Prepositions of Place and Time

Ask students to call out *place* and *time* prepositions while you write them on the board in place and time lists. Have students read the prepositions, the examples, and the notes in the two charts.

5 Page 113.

Have students look at the picture and say what stores they see. Read the instructions and the example. Put students in pairs to complete the exercise. Have selected students share their answers with the class.

Sample Answers: 1. The movie theatre is at the end of the street. It is near the bookstore and next to the gym. It is across from the grocery. 2. The dentist's office is between the pet supply store and the grocery. It's across from the gym and the bookstore. 3. The ballet school is on Maple Street. It's next to the bookstore and over the café. It's across from the pet supply store. 4. The pet shop is between the bank and the dentist. It's near the subway and across from the café. It's on Maple Street. 5. The bank is on Maple Street between the heath food store and the pet store. It's across from the ballet school and near the corner. 6. The subway is on Elm Street at the corner of Elm and Maple. It's near the heath food store and the bank. 7. The bookstore is between the gym and the café. It's across from the dentist. 8. The café is under the ballet school and next to the bookstore. It's across from the bank. 9. The health food store is on the corner of Elm and Maple. It's under the video store and next to the bank. 10. The grocery store is next to the dentist. It is across the street from the gym. 11. The florist is on the corner of Elm and Maple. It's across from the subway and the health food store. 12. The gym is between the movie theatre and the bookstore. It's near the ballet school and the café and across from the grocery store.

6 Page 113.

Answers: 1. during, at 2. on 3. from, to, during (or in) 4. on, until 5. until 6. In (or During), on

Video Activities: A Homeless Shelter

Before You Watch

Arrange students in small groups. Read the questions aloud and ask students to talk about their thoughts about homeless people in their small groups. Have students report to the class their answers.

Answers will vary.

Watch [on video]

Ask them to read three questions. Remind them to think about the questions as they view the video. Allow students to discuss their answers to the questions in small groups. Then, review the answers together with the whole class.

Answers: 1. because there are no emergency shelters 2. like a big temporary white dome 3. trying to raise $50, 000 by organizing fund-raising events

Watch Again [on video]

Have students read the statements. Then replay the video and have students fill in the correct answers. Go over the answers.

Answers: 1. 1,200 2. 58 3. $20,000 4. 100 5. motels 6. volunteer

After You Watch

You can help students organize a fund-raising campaign for a homeless shelter, as suggested in the student book, or any other charitable organization or event in your community. Many newspapers have a section which lists volunteer opportunities. You can consult this section of your local newspaper for ideas.

Home

Part 1 Listening to Conversations

Before You Listen

1 Prelistening Questions. Page 116.

As students read the questions and look at the picture, help them figure out what is going on. You can use leading questions such as: *Who are these two women?* (Ming and Jennifer) *What does "vacancy" mean?* (empty apartment) *Why is the woman on the left looking down at the ground and holding her chin?* (She's thinking about something.) Then go over the answers to the three questions.

2 Vocabulary Preview. Page 116.

Read aloud the instructions and the list of words at the top. You may wish to have students repeat the words after you. Then have them complete the exercise on their own.

Answers: 1. landlord 2. closet
3. studio 4. unfurnished 5. pretty 6. raised
7. vacancies 8. fireplace 9. move out
10. stressed out

Listen

**3 Listening for Main Ideas. Page 117.
[on tape/CD]**

Read aloud the instructions for item 1. Remind students that the goal of the exercise is to listen only for main ideas. Ask them to look back at the picture on page 116 and explain that this picture illustrates what is happening in the recording they are going to hear. Have a student read the questions. Prompt students to ask about any questions they don't understand. Play the tape or CD and have the students answer the questions. Then have them go over the answers in pairs. Ask the pairs to point out any items they would like you to explain.

Answers:

1. The landlord raised the rent.
2. She suggests that Jennifer move into her building.
3. She's not happy. The landlord raised the rent.
4. Jennifer needs a studio apartment.
5. The one-bedrooms come with a bathroom, a kitchen, a fireplace and pretty big closets.
6. She's going to stop by and talk to the landlord.

Tapescript

Jennifer: I'm so stressed out. My landlord just raised my rent. I think I'll have to move.

Ming: Really? My building has some vacancies. It's a pretty nice place and it's just ten minutes from campus.

Jennifer: Oh? How much is the rent for a studio?

Ming: There're no studio apartments in our building. My neighbor just moved out of a one-bedroom. He paid $850 a month, I think.

Jennifer: That's not bad. Tell me more.

Ming: Well, one-bedrooms come with a bathroom, a kitchen, a fireplace in the living room, pretty big closets and uh… Are you looking for a furnished or unfurnished place?

Jennifer: Unfurnished. I have all my own stuff. What about parking and laundry?

Ming: There's no garage. You have to park on the street. But there is a laundry room downstairs.

Jennifer: Hmm. I think I'm interested. Could you give me the address?

Ming: Sure. It's 1213 Rose Avenue. The manager's name is Jerry Kohl. Call him up or stop by and talk to him.

Jennifer: Thanks, Ming. I'm gonna do that tomorrow for sure.

Stress

4 Listening for Stressed Words. Page 118. [on tape/CD]

Read the instructions and point out the blanks below where students will fill in the missing stressed words. Then point out the words they will use to fill in the blanks and go over the list together. Remind students to do two things: repeat after the speaker and write in the missing words. Then play the tape or CD again and ask students to fill in the missing words. After that, have students exchange books and correct each other's work using the tapescript in the back of the student book as a guide. Discuss any items that more than five people got wrong. Then have students practice reading the completed dialogue with partners.

Reductions

5 Comparing Long and Reduced Forms. Page 119. [on tape/CD]

Play the tape or CD and have students follow along in their books. Then have students repeat the sentences after the recording.

6 Listening for Reductions. Page 119. [on tape/CD]

Read the directions for item 1. Remind students that the recording leaves enough time for students to repeat each sentence. Play the tape or CD. Then ask a student to write the answers on the board for the others to use as an answer key. For part 2, have students read the sentences to a partner for pronunciation practice. Move around the room checking their progress and modeling pronunciation as needed.

Answers: 1. have to, have   2. Could you
3. Could you, him   4. lot of, him   5. him
6. Are you   7. give me, him   8. give me

Tapescript

A: Mr. Kohl, I have to talk to you. I have another problem.
B: Could you call me later? I'm busy now.

A: No, I need the plumber again. Could you call him right now?
B: I have a lot of things to do. I'll call him tomorrow morning, okay?
A: No, I need him right now!
B: Are you having trouble with the toilet again?
A: Yes. Look, just give me the plumber's phone number. I'll call him.
B: All right, all right. Just give me a minute and I'll do it.

After You Listen

7 Vocabulary Review. Page 120.

Review the instructions with the class and do the first item as an example. The answer might be: *I get stressed out when my children fight with each other.* When students finish, ask volunteers to share some of their responses.

Pronunciation

The *-ed* Ending [on tape/CD]

Read through the information on pronouncing the *-ed* ending with the class. Then go back and work on each of the different pronunciations individually. First play the tape or CD or read the examples and have students listen to the lists of sample words. Focus on an ending, for example */id/*, and have students repeat it in several times in isolation. Then ask them to try to think of other words that feature that particular pronunciation of the *-ed* ending.

8 Distinguishing between *-ed* Endings. Page 120. [on tape/CD]

Read and discuss the instructions. Explain to students that they will have to listen very carefully to hear the differences among the three endings. Play the tape or CD and have students mark their answers. If you feel it is appropriate, you can play the recording a second time so that students can check their answers. Then put the correct answers on the board and have students correct their work.

Answers: 1. turned /d/   2. rented /id/
3. mixed /t/   4. asked /t/
5. recommended /id/   6. walked /t/
7. tested /id/   8. followed /d/
9. moved /d/   10. changed /d/

Tapescript

1. turned
2. rented
3. mixed
4. asked
5. recommended
6. walked
7. tested
8. followed
9. moved
10. changed

9 Using *-ed* Endings. Page 121.

Review the instructions and help students find partners. Ask them to work on their own and raise their hands if they have any questions they can't figure out. Review the answers by calling on different pairs of students to present to the class dialogues based on the various pictures. Point out both the strong points in the conversations and review the pronunciation of the *-ed* verbs.

Possible Answers: 1. Jennifer moved in on Monday. The movers carried the boxes inside. Jennifer watched them.   2. She called her family. They asked about the apartment. She described it to them.   3. Jennifer looked for a place to put the dishes. She decided to unpack them later.   3. She unpacked the dishes on a shelf.   5. She washed the dishes. She dropped two cups.   6. She dusted the counter. She sneezed several times.   7. She painted the living room walls.   8. She worked in the yard. She planted flowers.   9. She ordered pizza for dinner.   10. She rested after dinner.

Part 2 Recalling Main Ideas

Before You Listen

1 Prelistening Questions. Page 122.

Read and discuss the instructions and questions with the whole class. Then help students form pairs and complete the activity. Set a time limit of about five minutes. Review the responses with the whole class.

2 Vocabulary Preview. Page 122.

Have students complete the activity individually. As you review the answers with the class, ask students to raise their hands if they are still having difficulty with any of the terms. Invite other students to explain these terms in their own words, or use a bilingual or learner's dictionary to find definitions.

Answers: 1. d   2. a   3. b   4. e   5. c

Listen

3 Listening for Main Ideas. Page 122. [on tape/CD]

Read the instructions and go over the questions students are asked to answer after this first time listening to the conversation.

Answers: 1. living room, kitchen, bedroom, bathroom   2. No, it isn't.   3. She needs to think about it more and she has more questions.

Tapescript

Manager: So, here's the living room. Oh, and please don't touch the walls; we just painted them. I hope you like green.

Jennifer: Well, green is not my favorite color...

Manager: As you can see, there's lots of light in here. And here's the fireplace. It's great in the winter.

Chapter 5

Jennifer:	Whew, it's warm in here, isn't it? Is there any air conditioning?
Manager:	No, there isn't. Just keep this window open. Oh, it's almost never this noisy.
Jennifer:	I'm sorry, what did you say?
Manager:	Come this way. Here's your kitchen, all electric, a dishwasher... This big refrigerator is included; and there's room for a breakfast table here...
Jennifer:	That's nice. Could I see the bedroom?
Manager:	Sure, it's over here. We just put in new carpeting, so...uh...we raised the rent $25.
Jennifer:	Oh, really? Hmm...the bedroom looks a little small.
Manager:	But look at all the closet space! And here is the bathroom, with a shower and bathtub.
Jennifer:	Oh, what about that leak?
Manager:	Hmm. I can't believe it. The plumber just fixed it last week.
Jennifer:	Uh, if I decide to take this apartment, when can I move in?
Manager:	It's available on the first of the month. That's actually the day after tomorrow.
Jennifer:	I see. And, uh, do I have to sign...I mean, is there a lease?
Manager:	It's up to you. You can sign a 1-year lease or you can pay month-to-month. So, uh, are you interested?
Jennifer:	Possibly. I need to think about it a little more. And I have a few more questions.
Manager:	No problem. Let's go to my office and talk.

4 Taking Notes on Specific Information. Page 123. [on tape/CD]

Point out the *Good things* and *Bad things* columns. Then play the tape or CD again and ask students to take their own notes under these headings in the chart. Remind students that they should take short notes so they don't get bogged down in writing and miss important points.

Possible Answers:

Good things: just painted, lots of light, fireplace, dishwasher, big refrigerator, room for breakfast table in kitchen, new carpeting, lots of closet space, shower and bathtub

Bad things: green walls, no air conditioning, noisy street, raised rent, small bedroom, leak in bathroom

After You Listen

5 Summarizing Main Ideas. Page 123.

Read the instructions and help students find partners to complete the activity with. As they work, listen to different pairs, helping them with any aspects of the task that are proving difficult for them. If time permits, have one or more students present their summary to the class.

6 Vocabulary Review. Page 123.

This is an open-ended oral activity that reviews key vocabulary words and provides listening and speaking practice. If possible, match up students of differing ability. You may wish to have less fluent students focus on only two or three of the questions so that they have time to receive plenty of feedback from their partners. More fluent students can try answering all the questions.

Using Language

Making and Answering Requests

Ask students to study the chart containing language they can use to make and answer requests. Review the information with the class, including the footnote about *Would you mind*. Point out and explain the difference between the polite requests and the strong requests. Then invite volunteers to make up some requests using the language in the first column.

7 Role-Play. Page 124.

This activity allows students to practice the language and functions they have studied in a practical situation. As students work, move around the room offering language support as needed. Invite volunteers to present one of their conversations to the class.

48 Interactions 1 Integrated Skills Instructor's Manual

Part 3 Reading

Before You Read

1 Discussing Pictures. Page 124.

Point out the four pictures and ask students to identify the people, places, and activities. Then read the questions aloud and call on volunteers to answer. Encourage students to talk about things that are the same and things that are different from the pictures and their own family life. List vocabulary on the board as students describe the pictures.

Sample Answers:
1. The first picture is at the front door of a home and the husband and wife are saying good-bye and kissing before leaving for work in the morning. The second picture is in a living room with a large extended family relaxing together in the evening. The third picture is a small nuclear family sitting around the TV in the evening. The last picture is a mother and son eating dinner in the kitchen.
2. Answers will vary.
3. Family life is changing because there are so many different types of families now. Families don't do the same activities or live the same way because of jobs and economic conditions and life styles. Family life might change in the future by children spending more time away from school. Families will also probably become smaller with people having fewer children.

2 Thinking about the Answers. Page 125.

Read the questions aloud and call on volunteers to answer. Point out key vocabulary: *family, extended family, nuclear family, marriage.* As students suggest answers, record their responses and ideas on an overhead projector or on a large piece of paper. Review these responses after students have read the selection.

Sample Answers:

1. An extended family includes more relatives than a nuclear family.
2. Families today include two-parent families, single-parent families, combined families (when parents marry after divorce), no-children families, and so on.
3. Families changed in the 20th century because of World War II and social changes. Families became smaller.
4. The 1930s and 1940s were difficult years for most families because of the Great Depression and World War II.
5. After World War II, people married and created families again and there were more traditional families.
6. The most common family forms around the world today are extended families and nuclear families although single-parent families are becoming more common.

3 Vocabulary Preview. Page 125.

Read the words aloud and have students circle the ones they don't know. Students can look for the words they don't know in the reading. Have students check their understanding of the circled words after they complete the reading selection.

Read

4 A Short History of the Changing Family. Page 125. [on tape/CD]

Play the tape or CD as students follow along in their books. Stop the tape or CD after every paragraph to check understanding and point out vocabulary words. Listen a second time as students read along.

After You Read

5 Recognizing Paragraphs in Time Order (History). Page 127.

Read the instructions. Have students look back at the reading on to complete the exercise. Go over the answers together.

Answers:

A. family

B. different kinds of families

C. present changes in the structure of the family

D. in the 1930s and 1940s

E. in the 1950s (the next decade)

F. changes in family structure

G. continue to change in the future

6 Topic of the Whole Reading. Page 127.

After reading the instructions, have students choose the best statement of topic. Have students give reasons for their choices.

Answer: d

7 Understanding the Main Idea. Page 127.

Read together the instructions. Have students work individually in pairs to complete the questions. Go over possible answers with the group.

Sample Answers:

A. What are the definitions

B. What are

C. Why have there been

D. What happened to

E. What happened to

F. between 1960 and the end of the twentieth century

G. What will families be like; will family structure change

8 Correcting Information. Page 128.

Be sure students understand the instructions. Students can look back at the reading as they complete the exercise. Go over the answers together.

Sample Answers:

1. The extended family is different from the nuclear family: it consists of many relatives (grandparents, parents, children, cousins, etc.) living in the same house.

2. There are many kinds of families on planet earth today including traditional nuclear family, single-parent family, foster family, etc.

3. In the early 1900s in the United States (and later in other countries), the divorce rate began to rise and the birthrate began to decline; couples were staying married for fewer years and having fewer children.

4. Before and during World War II, families faced more financial problems in the industrialized world, so women had to work outside the home. Families were not "perfect."

5. After the war, family structure changed back in the other direction: there were fewer divorces and more stay-at-home mothers; children began living at home longer.

6. From the 1960s on, there were more new changes in the structure of the family around the globe.

7. Some people want the traditional two-parent nuclear family—with a working father and a mother at home; however, this structure will probably not come back and more family forms will appear on the earth.

8. In the twentieth century, there were many changes in the structure of the family; in

the next century, there will probably be more changes, too.

9 Using Punctuation and Phrase Clues. Page 128.

As you read through the instructions, ask students to locate examples of the various types of punctuation and phrases in the reading selection on pages 125-126. Have volunteers identify the punctuation in the example. Then have students complete the exercise with their own definitions. If students finish early, have them create their own definitions of the additional vocabulary items. Go over the answers together.

Answers:

1. groups of people that are not close relatives
2. from the distant past
3. living in the same house or close together on the same street or in the same area
4. parents and their biological or adopted children
5. stays at home
6. one parent
7. divorced or widowed men and women who marry again and live with the children of their previous or earlier marriages
8. legal endings compared to the number of marriages
9. husbands were away at war
10. ten years

10 Recognizing Time Details (Facts). Page 129.

Read together the instructions. Students can look back at the reading for examples of the time expressions. Then have students match the events with the time expressions. Go over the answers. You may want to have students practice asking and answering *When* questions about the events. *When did many families have money problems, so more women began to work outside the home?*

Answers: 1. e 2. a 3. c 4. g 5. d 6. b 7. f 8. h

Discussing the Reading

11 Small Group Discussion. Page 130.

Arrange students in groups of four. Give the groups about 15-20 minutes to discuss the questions. Circulate among the groups, listening and giving assistance as needed. When all groups are finished, ask reporters from each group to share the most interesting information from their groups.

Answers will vary.

Part 4 Writing

Before You Write

Exploring Ideas

1 Using a Lifeline. Page 131.

To get students started, if may be helpful if you model how to do this activity on the board. Draw a timeline as shown in the student book. Then, write in the ages of important events and turning points in your life. Write a brief caption explaining why that age is important to you. Verbalize as you fill in each part of the graphic. Then ask students to create their own timelines.

Organizing Ideas

Limiting Information

2 Page 132.

Ask students how they would organize the information shown into different paragraphs and why. Remind students that a paragraph is typically organized around related information. A common way of organizing autobiographical information in a short essay is to write paragraphs about each major period of one's life. Make sure that students understand that the activity is asking them to focus on one period of their lives. They can use the questions to help them evaluate their choice of topic.

Writing Topic Sentences

4 Page 133.

Answers will vary. Review students' work to make sure that their topic sentences capture the main idea of the various ideas they have gathered for their paragraph.

5 Page 133.

Students' answers will vary.

Write

Developing Cohesion and Style

6 Page 134.

Encourage students to check each other's work for variation in verb choice and correct tense.

Combining Sentences with Time Words and *because*

7 Page 134.

Answers:
1. but
2. when
3. Before
4. as soon as
5. and
6. Because
7. so
8. but
9. because

Punctuating Sentences with Dependent Clauses

8 Page 135.

Answers:
1. I got a scholarship because I was a good student.
2. I graduated from high school before I was sixteen.

3. My mother went to work after my father died.
4. I found a job as soon as I finished high school.
5. I was unhappy when I stopped studying.

9 Page 136.
Sample Answers:
1. I went to college in my hometown because I didn't want to leave my family.
2. I started college before I was eighteen years old.
3. I got my first job as a journalist after I finished school.
4. I was very happy when my first story got published.
5. I bought my own home as soon as I could afford to.

Writing the First Draft

10 Page 136.

Have students write the first draft of a paragraph about a part of their lives. Remind them to use the topic sentence that they wrote in Activity 5 and the notes they wrote in Activities 2 and 3. They should combine some sentences with time words and *because, and, but,* and *so.* They should also use the past tense to write about completed actions.

Edit and Revise

Editing Practice

11 Editing a Paragraph. Page 136.
Answer:
How I Became a Jazz Musician
I fell in love with jazz when I was five years old. I always heard jazz in the streets, but for my fifth birthday, my brother took me to a concert. That was the first time I saw a great saxophonist, and I decided to play the saxophone. First I needed a saxophone, so I

asked my father. My father said he had no money for a saxophone, so I worked for my brother, uncles, and cousins. I made a little money and my father saw that I was working hard, so he gave me some money. I listened to recordings, and my brother gave me lessons. I practiced every day, and now I am a good saxophone player.

Editing Your Writing

12 Editing Using a Checklist. Page 137.

Have students use the items in the Editing Checklist to conduct editorial passes on their paragraphs. Students should focus on content and organization in their first passes. Tell students to make sure that their paragraphs make sense and that the steps are well organized. After they are satisfied with the flow of ideas, they should conduct passes to focus on grammar and form.

13 Peer Editing. Page 137.

Use the suggestions in the student book to conduct peer conferences. Give pairs of students time to exchange papers and read each other's work. Students can write comments and suggestions in the margins of their partners' papers. Pairs can then reconvene and give each other verbal feedback, explaining the main points of their written comments. Afterwards, students can rewrite their paragraphs, incorporating the feedback as appropriate.

Writing the Second Draft

14 Page 137.

Introduce students to the practice of effectively using feedback from peers and the teacher to improve their writing. Then hand out the students marked up paragraphs and have them write second drafts considering the questions on the checklist.

Part 5 Grammar

A. The Simple Past Tense: Statements

Ask students what the family pictured on page 139 are doing. Then ask them to say what the father's family used to do at nights. Write the answers on the board and have students compare the use of the present continuous to describe what they are doing now, and the past tense to describe what they used to do. Read the explanation above the chart. Have students read the examples and notes. Ask students to make statements about things the father's and the mother's families didn't do that the family pictured does now. Have students read the spelling rules for forming the past tense of regular verbs. Then have them think of more examples for each rule. Have students review the Pronunciation of *-ed* on page 120. Have them practice pronouncing the three different endings. Review the expressions of past time with the students.

1 Page 138.

Have students look at the picture and say what they see happening. Ask them to say if they think this picture is about the present or the past. Have them give reasons for their decisions. Read the instructions and the example. Have students fill in the blanks individually. Have different students read individual sentences of the passage aloud to go over the answers. You may want to practice the pronunciation of the verbs and have students write their answers on the board to check their spelling.

Answers: 2. didn't own 3. stayed
4. played 5. looked 6. relaxed 7. smoked
8. tried 9. visited 10. stopped 11. discussed
12. argued 13. washed 14. joined
15. talked 16. peeled 17. helped
18. finished 19. handed 20. enjoyed

Chapter 5

Optional Activity: Put students in pairs to compare how their family spent hot summer evenings in the past with the way the family in the passage spent them. Start them off by saying, *When I was younger, we often went for walks after dinner in the summer.*

B. The Simple Past Tense: *Yes/No Questions and Short Answers*

Ask the students *yes/no* questions about the activities in Exercise 1. For example, ask *Sami, did you play games when you were young?* Write some of your questions and some of the answers on the board. Ask students to note what happens to the *-ed* ending. Compare a *yes/no* question to a negative past tense statement. Read the explanation above the chart on page 139. Have students read the examples and the possible answers in the chart.

2 Page 140.

Read the instructions and the examples. Point out the additional information in the affirmative answer. Have less advanced groups read the list of activities before doing the exercise. Answer any questions they may have. Put students in pairs to do the exercise.

Sample Answers:
1. Did you clean your room last night? No I didn't. I went out instead.
2. Did you play any sports last week? Yes, I did. I played baseball with some friends.
3. Did you listen to the radio last weekend? Yes, I did. I listened to the radio Sunday morning.
4. Did you watch TV last weekend? No, I didn't.
5. Did you cook anything last weekend? Yes, I did. I cooked a meal for some friends.
6. Did you telephone anyone last weekend? Yes, I did. I telephoned my boyfriend.
7. Did you visit your friends last weekend? No, I didn't, but some friends visited me.
8. Did you wash your clothes last weekend? No, I didn't. I'm going to wash them tomorrow.

9. Did you study at home last weekend? Yes, I did. I studied for a test all day Saturday.
10. Did you finish your homework last weekend? Yes, I did. I finished it on Sunday.
11. Did you receive any letters or packages last weekend? No, I didn't.
12. Did you mail any letters or packages? Yes, I did. I mailed a letter to my friend.
13. Did you use a computer last weekend? Yes, I did. I spent Saturday and Sunday mornings emailing friends.
14. Did you surf the Internet? Yes, I did.
15. Did you stay up late last weekend? No, I didn't. I went to bed early both nights.
16. Did you enjoy yourself? Yes, I did. I had a great time.

C. The Simple Past Tense: Information Questions

Ask students some information questions about some of their answers to Exercise 2, for example, *"Juana, How late did you stay up on Friday night? Miko, where did you go on the Internet?"* Write a few of your questions on the board. Point out the use of *did*. Read the explanation above the chart. Have students read the examples, possible answers, and notes in the chart.

3 Page 141.

Read the instructions. Have students read the question words and the incomplete questions. Have them write their questions individually while you circulate to check for accuracy. Put students in pairs to take turns interviewing each other. When students are finished, have selected students choose something interesting to tell the class about their partners.

Answers: 1. Where did you live?
2. Who/what did you play with? 3. What games or sports did you play?
4. When/where did you start school?
5. How did you like school?
6. Why/where/when did you want to study English?

Optional Activity: Put students in pairs. Tell them to imagine they are going to interview a specific favorite celebrity or sports figure. Have students write the questions and answers they imagine this person would give. Have them practice their interview and then perform it for the class. Tell them not to tell the class who they are interviewing to see if the class can guess who it is from the interview.

D. Irregular Past Tense Verbs

Read the explanation above the chart. Have students read the list of irregular past tense verbs and the notes in the chart. Have students practice pronouncing the different groups of verbs. Then put them in pairs to practice the verbs by making sentences of their own.

4 Page 142.

Read the instructions. Have less advanced students read the passage first while you circulate to answer individual questions. Have students complete the exercise individually. To go over the answers, have selected students read segments of the passage.

Answers: 1. sent 2. let 3. read 4. were 5. was 6. slept 7. took 8. had 9. went 10. cost 11. spent 12. left 13. threw 14. was 15. rang 16. got 17. drove 18. caught 19. thought 20. began 21. got 22. took 23. bought 24. knew 25. had 26. began 27. read 28. made 29. told 30. went 31. paid 32. gave 33. found 34. met 35. made

Video Activities: Asthma and Dust Mites

Before You Watch

You can discuss these questions with the whole class, or have students divide into pairs or small groups to discuss them and then later share their findings with the class. If anyone in the class has asthma or knows someone who does, he or she might tell the class something about the causes and effects of the disease.

Sample Answers:

1. Asthma is chronic disease. It affects the nasal passages and makes it very difficult to breath at times. Asthma attacks are brought about by contact with dust and pollen. It can sometimes be treated with steroid injections or other drugs.

2. Mites are very small spiders. They live in sheets, clothing, foodstuffs, and carry disease.

3. People can reduce house dust by keeping their homes clean and dusting regularly. You can also water the ground outside your house when it is very dry to keep the dust from rising and floating in through the windows.

Watch [on video]

Read through the questions with students and suggest that they take notes as they watch the video. Then play the video once straight through. When it is over, have students collaborate on a complete list of answers to the five questions.

Answers: 1. clean, bare 2. very small 3. c 4. uses plastic mattress covers, washes the bedding, doesn't have carpets, doesn't have curtains 5. hang the bedding out in the sun to dry

Watch Again [on video]

Read the questions to the class and discuss any meaning of any specific words students don't know. Then help them form small groups to discuss the answers to the three questions.

Possible Answers:

1. The phrase "part genetic and part environment" refers to a disease or condition that is inherited at birth. This condition may or may not become a problem later in life. The presence of other factors in one's home, job, and environment may trigger the disease. If these factors aren't present, you might not even know you have the disease.

2. Answers will vary.

3. Answers will vary. Ask students to think about all the things in their house that are made of cloth and all the different surfaces that they would have to constantly clean.

After You Watch

Read the instructions. Have students fill in the blanks individually. Put students in pairs to compare answers.

Possible Answers:

Getting Rid of Dust Mites

When/Because some children are exposed to dust mites, they get asthma. _If/When_ they already have asthma, dust mites make it worse. Therefore, you should cut down the number of dust mites in the home _if_ your child has allergies or asthma. How can you do this?

Dust mites love warm, humid areas filled with dust, _so/and_ pillows, mattresses, carpets, and furniture are great places for them to live. You should wash your sheets and blankets in very hot water every week. If possible, dry them in the sun _because_ heat kills dust mites. You should also wash your pillow every week _and/or_ put a plastic cover on it. Vacuuming your carpets every week can help, _but_ the best thing to do is to remove all the carpets. Finally, _because_ dust mites love warm, humid places, it helps to run your air conditioner and keep the air dry.

Cultures of the World

Part 1 Listening to Conversations

Before You Listen

1 Prelistening Questions. Page 146.

Ask students to discuss the first two questions with a partner. Before they begin, you might ask the group which of the words in question 2 they don't understand so that you can have other students explain what they mean and use them in sample sentences. If time permits, create a master list on the board showing all the countries the students in your class have visited. Then take a poll to find out which of the feeling words in question 2 were circled by the most students. Ask one or two volunteers to tell the class how they responded to question 3.

2 Vocabulary Preview. Page 146.

Explain that the words and expressions in the left-hand column of the chart will appear in the recording they are going to hear. Read the words and phrases aloud and have students write what they think each one means in the second column. Discuss the correct definitions with the whole class.

Possible Answers: 1. first idea
2. familiar with something that was strange at first 3. very unusual (behavior) 4. strange and unfamiliar 5. a container used to take left over food home from a restaurant (supposedly for the family dog) 6. surprised 7. up until this point 8. the portion of food left at the end of a meal

Listen

3 Listening for Main Ideas. Page 147. [on tape/CD]

Read aloud the instructions for item 1. Remind students that the goal of the exercise is to listen only for main ideas. Have a student read the questions. Prompt students to ask about any questions they don't understand. Play the tape or CD and have the students answer the questions. Then have them go over the answers in pairs. Ask the pairs to point out any items they would like you to explain.

Answers:
1. the streets are very clean, and the people are friendly
2. yes
3. a bag to take leftovers home in
4. she couldn't finish all the food
5. outside
6. When you are in another culture, try to follow its customs.

Tapescript

Kenji: Is this your first trip to the U.S., Simone?
Simone: Yes, it is.
Kenji: What's your impression so far?
Simone: Well, the streets are very clean, and the people are so friendly. But the food is not so good.
Kenji: That's what I thought too, when I first got here. But I'm used to it now. I really love hamburgers and french fries.
Simone: French fries? What is that?
Jennifer: You know, fried potatoes. I think you call them "pommes frites" in France. But we call them french fries, for some reason. And a lot of people eat them with ketchup.
Simone: Ketchup! That is very bizarre. We eat our pomme frites with salt, or maybe mustard.
Jennifer: Last night I took Simone to a Mexican restaurant. I wanted her to try something exotic.

Kenji: Did you like it?

Simone: The food was delicious, but it was too much. I couldn't finish it all.

Jennifer: Simone was amazed when I said she could take the leftovers home in a doggie bag.

Kenji: Yes, that's funny, isn't it? They call it a doggie bag but it's for people. Was there anything else that surprised you?

Simone: Yes. The restaurant was so cold! We don't use air conditioning so much in France. And the water had ice in it too. I had to put on my sweater!

Waiter: Excuse me miss, but there's no smoking here.

Simone: Oof, I forgot, you can't smoke in restaurants here. That is the strangest thing of all for me. In France you can smoke almost everywhere, and almost everybody smokes. It's normal for us.

Kenji: It's not normal here. Most Americans don't smoke, and it's illegal to smoke in most public places. If you want to smoke in someone's home, you'd better ask for permission first.

Simone: I know. Last night Jennifer made me smoke outside.

Jennifer: I'm sorry Simone.

Simone: It's OK. When in Rome, do as the Romans do.

Stress

Remind students that the stressed words usually give the most important information in a sentence. Focusing on the stressed words can help the listener understand the meaning.

4 Listening for Stressed Words. Page 147. [on tape/CD]

Read the instructions and read the word list aloud. Ask students to fill in as many of the answers as they can on the first listening, and offer to discuss any questions they may have after they have filled in all the responses they can. Remind students that after each pause in the recording they should repeat after the speaker

before they write in the missing words. Play the tape or CD. Correct the answers in class or have students use the tapescript to correct their own work. Answer any questions at this time. Then have students do the second part of the exercise in pairs.

Reductions

This section focuses on the reductions native speakers often produce when combining the words *this, your, what, is, your, them, her, to,* and *for* with other words. Remind them that the reduced forms are never written out in normal writing.

5 Comparing Long and Reduced Forms. Page 148. [on tape/CD]

Play the tape or CD and have students follow along in their books. Then have students repeat the sentences after the recording.

6 Listening for Reductions. Page 149. [on tape/CD]

Read the directions. Remind students that the recording leaves enough time for students to repeat each sentence before they fill in the answer. Play the tape or CD. Then write the correct answers on the board and have students correct their own exercises.

Answers: 1. this your 2. for 3. to, them 4. want to 5. her, for 6. don't know, them, you

Tapescript

Anita: Well, it's time to get back to the office. I'll see you soon, Brenda.

Brenda: OK, see you... Wait, Anita, is this your cell phone?

Anita: Oh my goodness, yes, thanks. By the way, I almost forgot: My parents are coming for a visit next week.

Brenda: Really? I'd love to meet them.

Anita: Well, do you want to have lunch with us on Saturday?

Brenda: Saturday? Hmm...I told my roommate I'd

go shopping with her that day. Could we get together for a drink later in the afternoon?

Anita: I don't know, they might be busy. I'll ask them and let you know.

After You Listen

7 Vocabulary Review. Page 149.

This exercise reinforces vocabulary already introduced. Review the instructions with the class and do the first item as an example. The answer might be: *Yes, I am. I want to go to Australia.* When the pairs finish work, ask volunteers to share some of their responses.

Part 2 Recalling Main Ideas

Before You Listen

1 Prelistening Questions. Page 150.

Read and discuss the instructions and questions with the whole class. Point out the picture and invite students to describe what they see. Then help them form pairs and complete the activity. Set a time limit of about five minutes. Then review their responses with the whole class.

2 Vocabulary Preview. Page 151.

Read the instructions and have students complete the activity individually. As you review the answers with the class, ask students to raise their hands if they are still having difficulty with any of the terms. Invite other students to explain these terms in their own words.

Answers: 1. e 2. g 3. b 4. a 5. f 6. d 7. c

Listen

3 Listening for Main Ideas. Page 151. [on tape/CD]

Read the instructions and remind students that this time the task is just to write down the names of the five cultures that are discussed in the listening passage.

Answers: 1. North American Indian culture 2. Jewish culture 3. Japanese culture 4. United States mainstream culture

Tapescript

At what age does a child become an adult? The answer depends on your culture or religion. Here are a few examples.

First, in some North American Indian cultures, a boy became a man around the age of 13. At that time, he would go into the woods alone, without food or water, for several days. When he returned safely, he became an adult man. Girls became adult women as soon as they were old enough to have babies, also around the age of 12 or 13.

To give another example, in the Jewish religion, children spend years studying their history and religion. Then, at age 13 for boys and 12 for girls, they go through an important religious ceremony called a *bar mitzvah* for boys and *bat mitzvah* for girls. From that day, they are adults, and they become responsible for their own religious development.

In Japan today, young people become legal adults at age 20. Each year on January 15, they celebrate "Coming of Age Day," when all the twenty-year-olds in a town are invited to attend a special ceremony. They wear traditional clothes, listen to speeches, and visit with old friends.

Finally, in the United States, the passage into adulthood takes several years. American teenagers look forward to their 16th birthday, because in most states that is the age when can get a driver's license. The legal age of adulthood is 18, when Americans can vote, get married, and work full-time. However, they must wait until age 21 to buy alcohol. Many people celebrate their 21st birthday by having a drink with friends in a bar.

4 Taking Notes on Specific Information. Page 151. [on tape/CD]

Review the instructions with the class. Then play the tape or CD and have them fill in the information. Ask two or three students to write their notes on the board. Discuss the differences in the ways the students took notes and point out effective note-taking strategies.

Possible Answers:

1. North American Indian, 12-13,
   Boys = when they go into woods alone,
   Girls = when they can have babies

2. Jewish religion, Boys = 13, Girls = 12,
   Boys = bar mitzvah, Girls = Bat Mitzvah

3. Japanese, Age = 20, special "coming of age day" ceremony

4. American culture, legal adulthood = 18, many celebrate when they are 21—can buy alcohol

After You Listen

5 Summarizing Main Ideas. Page 152.

Read and discuss the instructions and help students find partners. As they work together, move around the room offering assistance as needed.

6 Vocabulary Review. Page 152.

This is an open-ended activity in which students describe familiar situations and express their own feelings about them. Have students complete this activity with a partner. Invite volunteers to share some of their opinions with the class.

Talk It Over

This activity helps students examine some of the laws of their own country and reflect on what it might be like to make some changes. Encourage them to experiment with new ideas, even if they aren't absolutely certain that they would like to

see these changes take place. If time permits, hold a class discussion on some of the points students seem most interested in talking about.

Part 3 Reading

Before You Read

1 Discussing the Picture. Page 153.

Arrange students in small groups to discuss the picture. Have a volunteer from each group report their responses to the questions. List vocabulary on the board.

Sample Answers:

1. There are people from several different cultural/ethnic groups sitting around a table talking about important parts of their cultures. There are some business men (or professors) and some students. Different types of architecture are pictured. The people are eating different ethnic foods.

2. There's an American, an Egyptian, a Hispanic, and an Indian. The first person on the left might be French (because there's a glass of wine). The second person might be German (because of the beer stein). The third might be Indian (because he's thinking of the Taj Mahal and wearing a Nehru jacket and has a calm, serene expression). The fourth is probably American (because of his causal clothes and casual position on the chair). The fifth might be American but could also be Japanese (because of the skyscrapers and the hamburger and fries and food in front of him). The fifth might be Mexican (because of the tacos and fiesta). The sixth could be Egyptian (because of the pyramids and espresso coffee).

3. The people are probably all talking about the good points of their cultures. Everyone's culture is different.

2 Thinking about the Answers. Page 153.

Read the questions aloud and point out key vocabulary: *cultural legacy, achievements, ancient cultures, universal*. Encourage students to make guesses based on the topic of the chapter (cultures) and clues within the questions. Record students' responses and ideas on an overhead projector or on a large piece of paper. You may want to review these responses later after students have read the selection.

Sample Answers:
1. A "cultural legacy" from the past is the ideas, traditions, and customs that come from past or ancient cultures. It might include architecture, art, religion, philosophy, customs, traditions, food, dance, music, folk stories, medicine, etc.
2. Technical achievements from ancient cultures include transportation, aqueducts (water systems), weapons, tools, writing methods, time keeping (clocks, calendars), etc. Scientific achievements include medicine, astronomy, etc.
3. Culture might be universal because ideas and inventions are exchanged around the world. There is more contact between different cultural groups than in the past. Most cultures want modern communication and industrialization.
4. Modern cultures vary around the world in language, gestures, social rules, and customs.
5. "Culture" can be viewed as being cultural history, ancient traditional culture, global culture, and cultural diversity.

3 Vocabulary Preview. Page 153.

As you read the words aloud, tell students to circle the ones they don't know. Ask volunteers to suggest the meanings of the new words. Encourage students to look for the words in the following reading. After completing the reading selection, have students check their understanding of the circled words.

Read

4 Cross-Cultural Conversation. Page 155. [on tape/CD]

Play the tape or CD as students follow along in their books. Stop the tape or CD occasionally to ask comprehension questions and to point out key vocabulary words. Listen a second time as students read along again.

After You Read

5 Recognizing Conversation in Paragraph Form. Page 156.

Read the instructions aloud. If needed, point out the words that the different speakers say in the conversation. Then have students complete the exercise. Go over the answers together.

Answers: 1. the long cultural legacy of the arts in European history 2. humanity's scientific and technological discoveries and achievements 3. the cultural sameness and similarities among modern peoples 4. cultural diversity—how groups vary in their styles and customs 5. different cultural ways of discussing ideas and telling opinions

Topic or subject of the whole reading: c

6 Understanding the Point. Page 157.

Read the instructions and have students complete the exercise. Then discuss the answers with the whole class.

Sample Answers: 2. included; achievements and discoveries 3. want; modern; everybody 4. more significant; appreciate and enjoy 5. cultures; different; a variety of

7 Figuring Out New Vocabulary from Context. Page 158.

After reading the instructions together, have students work individually using context clues to define the vocabulary words. Go over the answers with the group.

Answers:

1. Some examples of architecture are cathedrals and castles. Features of modern architecture include design and building styles. A

2. Civilization began in the Middle East and Africa over five thousand years ago. Ancient civilizations had astronomy, mathematics, medicine, and government. C

3. A legacy comes from the past. A legacy might include cities, governments, tools, and weapons. B

4. Modern things can be part of culture. People that like classical art and music will not agree with him. Kevin and Jade have very different opinions. A

5. Some examples of the worldwide media are movies, TV, CDs, the Internet, newspapers, and magazines. The media gives people around the world the same information, music, and jokes. C

Students can look back at the reading on pages 155-156 for definitions of other vocabulary words.

8 Recognizing the Details of Opinions. Page 160.

Read together the instructions. Remind students that there are several answers for each question. Have students complete the exercise. Go over the answers together. Have students find specific references from the reading selection to support the answers.

Answers: 1. b, c, e, f 2. b, c, d, e 3. c, e, f 4. a, b, c, d, e, f 5. a, b, c, d, e, f

Discussing the Reading

9 Small Group Discussion. Page 161.

This activity allows students to use the vocabulary from the reading to talk about their own experiences related to the content. Arrange students in groups of four. Set a time limit for the small group discussions. As groups talk about their answers together, circulate among the groups, listening and giving assistance as needed.

When all groups are finished, ask a volunteer from each group to summarize their ideas.

Answers will vary.

Part 4 Writing

Before You Write

Exploring Ideas

Folktales

1 Page 162.

Model pronunciation and intonation by reading the folktale aloud. Then invite volunteers to take turns reading parts of the folktale aloud for the class. Check comprehension by asking students to retell the folktale in their own words. Point out that the folktale is incomplete as presented here. The ending will be revealed later in the chapter.

2 Page 163.

Have students look at the illustration to imagine how the folktale might end. Tell them that the bald man is the poor miner's brother, and that the illustration shows three different scenes in sequence.

3 Page 163.
Sample Answers:
1. The brother decided to give the king his best horse.
2. No, the king was not happy. He thought the brother was being greedy.
3. The king gave the miner's brother a bushel of corn for his horse.
4. The brother felt cheated.

Organizing Ideas

Using a Time Sequence

4 Page 164.

Answers:

The time words and phrases in the passage are:

once; late at night; at last; when; Then; quickly; Early the next morning; then; Then; As soon as; Then; last night; When

Limiting Information

5 Page 164.

Have students use the questions in the student to book help them evaluate each other's work during a peer writing conference.

Write

Developing Cohesion and Style

Using *as soon as*

6 Page 164.

Answers:

1. The brother decided to give the king a better gift as soon as he heard the story.

2. As soon as the king talked to the brother, he knew that he was a liar.

3. The king fell asleep as soon as he ate dinner.

4. As soon as the miner got the farm, he quit his job.

7 Page 165.

Answers will vary.

Using *then*

8 Page 165.

Answers:

1. The king washed in the river. Then he thanked the woman and left.

2. The woman gave the king a plate of potatoes. Then she gave him a blanket.

3. The king gave the woman a coin. Then he gave the miner a house and a farm.

4. The brother found a bushel of potatoes. Then he took them to the king.

Using Quotations

9 Page 166.

Answer:

The following shows how students should mark the story which appears on pages 162-163 of the student book.

A powerful king was once lost in a forest. It was late at night. He was tired, cold, and hungry. He at last reached the hut of a poor miner. The miner was working and his wife was home alone. She was cooking potatoes on the fire when she heard someone at the door.

The king asked her for help. "We are very poor," she explained, "but we can give your potatoes for dinner and a blanket on the floor for a bed." The king gratefully accepted the kind old woman's offer. He sat down to dinner with her and ate a large plate of potatoes. "These are better than the best beef," he exclaimed. Then he stretched out on the floor and quickly fell asleep.

Early the next morning, the king washed in the river and then returned to the hut. He thanked the woman for her kindness and gave her a gold coin. Then he left.

As soon as the miner returned home, his wife told him about the visitor. Then she showed her husband the gold coin. The husband realized that the visitor was the king. However, he felt that the gold coin was too generous. He decided to take a bushel of potatoes to the king.

The miner went to the palace to see the king. "Your majesty," he said, "last night you gave my wife a gold coin for a hard bed and a plate of potatoes. You were too generous. Therefore, I have brought you a bushel of potatoes, which you said were better than the best beef. Please accept them."

The miner's words pleased the king. He wanted to reward him for his honesty, so he gave him a beautiful house and a small farm. The miner was very happy and he returned to tell his wife the news.

The poor miner had a brother. His brother was rich but greedy and jealous of anyone who had good luck. When he heard his brother's story, he as very upset.

Students' answers will vary for the second half of the activity, which asks students to write a conversation between the king and the miner's brother. Remind students to use the tips in the box on page 165 to punctuate the dialogue correctly.

Writing the First Draft

10 Page 166.

Have students write a first draft of an ending to the folktale. Remind them to follow these three guidelines:

1. Use time words where necessary, including *when, while, as soon as,* and *then.*
2. Limit the information to 100–150 words.
3. Use quotations.

Edit and Revise

Editing Practice

11 Using Editing Symbols. Page 167.

Answer: While he was riding through the forest, he thought of a plan. "I'll give the king my best horse," he thought, "then he will have to give me an even better gift!" As soon as he finished breakfast the next day, he went to the palace. The guard immediately took him to see the king. "Your majesty," the brother said, "I have brought you my finest horse as a gift."

The king knew that this was not an honest gift. He smiled and said, "Thank you, my dear friend. I accept your kind gift. Now I am going to give you a gift in return. Do you see that bushel of potatoes in the corner? Well, those potatoes cost me a house and a farm. I am sure that they are the most expensive potatoes in the land. I would like you to have them." What could the greedy brother do? He lifted the heavy bushel and sadly left the room. As he was leaving, he heard the king laughing.

Editing Your Writing

12 Editing Using a Checklist. Page 168.

Have students use the items in the Editing Checklist to conduct editorial passes on their paragraphs. Students should focus on content and organization in their first passes. Tell students to make sure that their paragraphs "make sense" and that the ideas are well organized. After they are satisfied with the flow of ideas, they should conduct passes to focus on grammar and form.

13 Peer Editing. Page 168.

Use the suggestions in the student book to conduct peer conferences. Give pairs of students time to exchange papers and read each other's work. Students can write comments and suggestions in the margins of their partners' papers. Pairs can then reconvene and give each other verbal feedback, explaining the main points of their written comments. Afterwards, students can rewrite their paragraphs, incorporating the feedback as appropriate.

Writing the Second Draft

14 Page 168.

Have students rewrite their endings to the folktale, based on the suggestions of their peers and teacher, as well as their own edits from Activity 12. Have students assess whether they feel their writing is improving.

Part 5 Grammar

A. The Present Perfect Tense

Put the following two sentences on the board: *The boys have just arrived. The girls arrived a few days ago.* Ask the students what the differences between the two sentences are in structure and meaning. Point out the use of the auxiliary verb *have* in the first sentence. Read the explanation above the chart. Have students read the purposes and examples in the statements chart. You may want to have students make sentences of their own for each purpose. Then have them read the examples and possible answers in the two questions charts.

1 Page 170.

Have students say what they see in the pictures. Ask them what they know about Madame Tussaud's and playing darts. Read the instructions and the example. Have students fill in the blanks individually. Explain that there could be more than one answer. Then, put them in pairs to read sections of the letter to each other to compare answers. Tell students when they disagree to give reasons for their choices. Then go over the answers as a class, having students explain their choices.

Answers: 2. haven't had 3. is / has been 4. have met / met 5. have done 6. have been / went 7. have visited / visited 8. ridden 9. have eaten 10. have lost 11. have spoken 12. have taught 13. have learned / learned 14. have been 15. have played 16. have watched 17. have discovered / discovered 18. am / have been 19. have tried 20. haven't been 21. hasn't been 22. haven't seen 23. have caught / caught 24. have taken 25. have bought 26. told / have told 27. have begun

2 Page 171.

Read the instructions and the examples. Have students write their questions individually. Then put students in pairs to compare questions.

Answers:
A. 1. Has she taken a lot of photographs?
   2. How many pictures has she taken?
   3. What has she taken pictures of?
B. 1. Have you spent a lot of money on transportation?
   2. How much money have you spent?
   3. How have you gotten around?

Video Activities: Chinese New Year

Before You Watch

Read the questions aloud and have students discuss their answers in groups. Have students report to the class their answers.

Watch [on video]

Ask them to read three questions. Then play the video and have them write their answers. Review the answers together.

Answers: 1. winter 2. a visitor celebrating the Chinese New Year 3. fireworks, the red lion dance

Watch Again [on video]

Have students read the statements and choices. Then replay the video and have students choose the correct items in 1 and fill in the missing words in the other items. Go over the answers.

Answers: 1. eat, see dancing, light firecrackers 2. merchants, merchant, red, money 3. the noise wards off evil spirits 4. 10

After You Watch

Read together the instructions. You may want to read aloud the sound words as clues. Have students complete the exercise and then go over the answers. Have students suggest feelings they associate with the different sounds. For example: *a baby crying: I feel worried and concerned. A boom of thunder makes me feel scared.*

Answers: 1. j 2. d 3. b 4. g 5. h 6. i 7. c 8. a 9. f 10. k 11. e

Entertainment and the Media

Part 1 Listening to Conversations

Before You Listen

1 Prelistening Questions. Page 174.

Ask students to look at the pictures and tell what is happening in each one. Then review the four pictures again and ask them to tell whether the person is or is not making good use of the television program. Encourage students to explain the reasons for their opinions. At this point, help students express their ideas by offering language support as needed, but put off any detailed feedback until students get to the Using Language section of the chapter.

2 Vocabulary Preview. Page 175.

Explain that the words and expressions in the left-hand column of the chart will appear in the recording they are going to hear. Read the words and phrases aloud and have students write what they think each one means in the second column. Discuss the correct definitions with the whole class.

Possible Answers: 1. g 2. f 3. i 4. c
5. d 6. b 7. a 8. j 9. e 10. h

Listen

**3 Listening for Main Ideas. Page 175.
[on tape/CD]**

Read aloud the instructions for item 1. Remind students that the goal of the exercise is to listen only for main ideas. Ask them to look back at the picture on page 174 and explain that this picture illustrates one thing that happens in the recording they are going to hear. Have a student read the questions. Prompt students to ask about any questions they don't understand. Have a student read aloud the questions before you play

the recording. Play the tape or CD and have the students answer the questions. Then have them go over the answers in pairs.

Answers: 1. TV watching habits 2. He always has the TV on when she comes over. 3. Ming says TV is a waste of time. Jack disagrees. 4. They both hate commercials. 5. Jack suggests that next time Ming visits, Ming gets to choose the station. 6. Ming suggests turning off the TV.

Tapescript

Ming: Hey, listen to this. The average American family watches six hours of TV a day.

Jack: A day? You're joking.

Ming: No, it says so right here in this magazine. Hmm, I guess *you're* an average American, Jack. When I come over to your place, you always have your TV on.

Jack: Come on. Are you saying I'm a couch potato?

Ming: Yeah. I really think watching TV is a waste of time.

Jack: Well, I disagree. Some programs are bad, like those soap operas. But what about sports or the news? You watch those sometimes, don't you?

Ming: Well, actually, for the news, I prefer the newspaper. Or the Internet.

Jack: Why?

Ming: First, because they give you a lot more information. And I can read them any time I want. Plus, I hate all the TV commercials.

Jack: I know what you mean. That's why, when the commercials come on, I just turn down the volume or change channels.

Ming: Yeah, I noticed that. Channel surfing drives me crazy.

Jack: Well, then, next time you come over I'll let you have the remote control.

Ming: That's so sweet. But I have a better idea. Next time I come over, let's just turn the TV off.

Culture Note

Americans express a wide variety of opinions about the value of television in the culture. Sociologists blame TV programs for everything from the poor physical health of Americans (They watch TV instead of exercising) to the high crime rate among adolescents (They are inspired to commit crimes because of watching violent TV programs). Other people see television as innocent entertainment. And some educators are trying to use television as an instructional medium to help raise the level of literacy among the nation's poor.

Stress

4 Listening for Stressed Words. Page 176. [on tape/CD]

Read the instructions and read the word list aloud. Then ask students to fill in as many of the answers as they can on the first listening, and offer to discuss any questions they have at that point. Remind them that after each pause they should repeat after the speaker before they write in the missing words. Play the tape or CD and have students write their answers. Correct the answers in class or have students use the tapescript to correct their own work. Then have students do the second part of the exercise in pairs.

Reductions

This section focuses on the reductions native speakers often produce when combining the words *are*, *you*, *don't*, *what*, and *let* with other words. Remind them that the reduced forms are never written out in normal writing.

5 Comparing Long and Reduced Forms. Page 177. [on tape/CD]

Play the tape or CD and have students follow along in their books. Then have students repeat the sentences after the recording. If you hear a number of students making the same error, point it out and help them correct it.

6 Listening for Reductions. Page 177. [on tape/CD]

Read the directions. Remind students that the recording leaves enough time for students to repeat each sentence before they fill in the answer. Play the tape or CD. Then write the correct answers on the board and have students correct their own exercises. Then have students read the sentences to a partner for pronunciation practice. Move around the room checking their progress and modeling pronunciation as needed.

Answers: 1. Are you calling 2. Don't you want to 3. you, can, Do you, what you want to 4. let you 5. going to

Tapescript

B: Are ya calling the movie theater?

A: Uh-huh. Why, what's wrong? Don'tcha wanna go to the movies tonight?

B: To tell you the truth, I'm pretty tired. But we can go to an early show. D'ya know whatcha wanna see?

A: Not really. I'll letcha choose. Terminator III is playing at 8:00 and James Bond is at 10:00.

B: Let's see Terminator. I'm tired now and by 10 o'clock I'm gonna be dead.

After You Listen

7 Vocabulary Review. Page 178.

Read over the statements in Activity 2 together and lead a discussion on which ones are true and not true for various class members. Pause to have students define vocabulary words for each other or paraphrase sentences if necessary.

Using Language

Expressing Opinions, Agreeing, and Disagreeing

Read aloud the introduction in the box and ask two students to read the dialogue to the class. Then review the sentence starters in the speech bubbles and ask different students to add a logical completion for each one. For example, *I think that children should play outdoors instead of watching TV* or *I feel that movies are getting too expensive.* If some students are puzzled by a certain expression, you might wish to invite other students to explain it to them and give a sample of how it is used in a conversation.

8 Expressing Opinions. Page 179.

Ask students to read the instructions and example at the beginning of the exercise and have a group of three read aloud the example in the book. Then ask three volunteers to choose one of the topics from the list and role-play the three-way exchange for the class. If it seems appropriate for your class, have several groups do this before putting students on their own to finish the activity.

Part 2 Recalling Main Ideas

Before You Listen

1 Prelistening Questions. Page 179.

Read and discuss the instructions and questions with the whole class. Then help students form pairs and complete the activity. Set a time limit of about five minutes. Then review their responses with the whole class.

Answers: 2. What happened? Where did it happen/crash? When did it happen/crash? How many people were on board/were injured? Who was injured?

2 Vocabulary Preview. Page 180.

Read the instructions and have students complete the activity individually. As you review the answers with the class, ask students to raise their hands if they are still having difficulty with any of the terms. Invite other students to explain these terms in their own words.

Answers: 1. e 2. g 3. a 4. d 5. f 6. c 7. b

Listen

3 Listening for Main Ideas. Page 180. [on tape/CD]

Read the instructions and remind students not to include details and not to write complete sentences. They should concentrate on writing down the most important ideas as single words or short phrases.

Possible Answers: 1. Airplane crash Route 1 Passengers injured Almost hit two cars Blocked traffic for an hour 2. c

Tapescript

Radio Announcer: Good evening. Our top story tonight: About an hour ago, a small airplane carrying six people landed safely in traffic on Highway 1. Two of the passengers received back injuries and one of the passengers suffered a broken leg. Here's reporter Larry Jones at the scene of the crash.

Reporter: Good evening, Mark. I'm standing here on Highway 1 with two drivers who almost hit the plane as it landed. Could you tell me what you thought as you watched the plane coming down?

Witness 1: Well, at first I wasn't scared. But then I saw it was flying very low. So I drove to the side of the road in a hurry.

Reporter: And you, sir?

Witness 2: I almost didn't see the plane at all. It happened so fast. When I finally heard the plane's motor, I knew something was wrong. And then I hit my brakes. Phew...it was real close. I'm still shaking.

Reporter: Fortunately, no one on the ground was hurt, but the plane blocked traffic for over an hour. Officer John McNamara of the local highway police thinks the plane ran out of gasoline. A complete investigation will begin tomorrow. Back to you, Mark.

4 Taking Notes on Specific Information. Page 181. [on tape/CD]

Review the instructions with the class. Then play the tape or CD and have them fill in the information. Ask two or three students to write their notes on the board.

Answers: 1. Highway 1   2. six   3. three
4. back injuries and a broken leg   5. none
6. ran out of gas

After You Listen

5 Summarizing Main Ideas. Page 181.

Read and discuss the instructions and help students find partners. As they work together, move around the room offering assistance as needed.

6 Vocabulary Review. Page 181.

Have students complete this activity with a partner. When they finish, invite volunteers to share their answers with the class.

Talk It Over

Summarizing News Reports

This activity gives students an opportunity to pull together the new vocabulary and summarizing skills taught in this chapter, as well as the listening skills and speaking skills they are working on. Encourage them to choose a story that interests them and to be sure to include the answers to the *who, what, where, when,* and *why* questions in their summaries.

Part 3 Reading

Before You Read

1 Vocabulary Preview. Page 182.

Read the words aloud. Students can underline words they already know and circle the ones they don't know. Tell students to look for these words in the next reading selection. Students can return back to this list and check their understanding of the circled words after completing the reading selection.

Read

2 Classifying Stories and Putting Events in Order. Page 182. [on tape/CD]

Read the instructions together. Explain the purpose of skimming in this exercise—to determine the kind of story for each of the different movies. Play the tape or CD and have students classify each story and choose the best movie title or name of the TV show. Go over the answers.

Answers:
   A: suspense or horror; 1. *Psycho*
   B: adventure or action; 3. *Tarzan, the Ape Man*
   C: science fiction; 3. *Star Trek: The Next Generation*
   D: comedy; 2. *Friends*

Replay the tape or CD and have students follow along again in their books. Ask comprehension questions and point out key vocabulary words in each of the paragraphs.

After You Read

3 Learning to Summarize. Page 187.

Read the instructions together before arranging students in groups of four to practice summarizing. You may want to assign stories to the groups. Allow 10-15 minutes for groups to read and summarize their stories. Then, ask a volunteer from each group to read aloud its summary. If several groups have summarized the same stories, compare and contrast the different versions. Discuss any differences.

Sample Answers:

B. A baby boy is adopted and raised by a gorilla after his parents were killed by wild animals. A professor arrives in the jungle with his daughter, Jane, and a hunter, Clayton. They discover the apeman and find out that he is human. The apeman wants to be with the humans, but doesn't want to leave his gorilla family. The white people are captured and the apeman saves them. Jane stays with the apeman in the jungle after her father and Clayton return to England.

C. The Bynars (computerized beings) are doing the repairs on the star ship Enterprise. They order the other crew members of the Enterprise to leave the ship. Captain Picard and Riker do not leave and the star ship Enterprise disappears. The captain and Riker find the Bynars dying and asking for help. They go to the planet Bynarus to restore the data from the planet's center computer. The planet is saved and the star ship returns to the starbase.

D. Six friends (three men and three women) are friends and roommates in New York City. Chandler plans to ask Monica to marry him, so he takes her to a restaurant. Unfortunately, Monica's old boyfriend sees Monica at the restaurant, so Chandler doesn't propose to Monica. The next day, Monica's old boyfriend proposes to her. She is confused and decides to go to stay with her parents to decide. Chandler goes to her and proposes. She accepts. The other friends decide that they will all marry each other if they are still single when they are forty years old.

Discussing the Reading

4 Small Group Discussion. Page 187.
Allow 15-20 minutes for students to work in groups of four to discuss their answers to the questions. Circulate among the groups, giving assistance as needed. Ask a volunteer from each group to summarize the most interesting points discussed.

Answers will vary.

Talk It Over

Read aloud the instructions. Point out that answers may vary. Ask students to explain their reasons for their responses. Invite students to share with the class their favorites and preferences. Model expressions and phrases for talk about preferences. *I prefer _____ because. I really like _____, but I don't like _____. My favorite _____ is _____.*

Answers will vary.

Part 4 Writing

Before You Write

Exploring Ideas
Describing and Categorizing Movies
1 Page 189.
   Answers:
   1. action
   2. comedy
   3. science fiction
   4. musical
   5. drama
   6. horror

2   Page 190.

Use the questions to lead students in a discussion about movies. Share about your own favorite movies to get the discussion started.

3   Building Vocabulary. Page 190.

Answers will vary. Explain the meaning of vocabulary items as necessary or have students use bilingual dictionaries.

Organizing Ideas

Summarizing a Movie Plot

4   Page 191.

Answers will vary. Tell students to focus on key events in the movie—those events which establish the problem, the obstacles faced by the main characters, and the resolution.

Including Important Information in a Summary

5   Page 192.

Answer:

The first summary is the better of the two, because it describes the most important events and gives interesting details about the action and characters. The second summary is too brief and choppy.

6   Page 192.

A good way for students to test whether the events they have selected will communicate the plot of the movie is to share them with their classmates. If the classmates cannot understand what the movie is about, then more details should probably be provided.

Writing a Title

7   Page 193.

Answers:

1. You should see *The Seven Dwarfs,* a classic Disney film.
2. The Chinese actor Chow Yun Fat was in *Anna and the King.*

3. The Italian movie *Life Is Beautiful* won several awards.
4. Sandra Bullock starred in *While You Were Sleeping.*
5. One of the most famous horror movies of all time is *The Exorcist.*

Write

Developing Cohesion and Style

Using Adjectives

8   Page 193.

Answers:

1. *Star Wars* is a realistic science-fiction movie.
2. *Dracula* is a frightening horror movie about an evil vampire.
3. *Titanic* is a touching love story about a couple on a sinking ship.
4. *Schindler's List* is a well-directed drama about a German who saved the lives of many Jews.

9   Page 193.

Answers will vary.

Using the Historical Present Tense

10 Page 194.

Answers: *It's a Wonderful Life* <u>is</u> a heartwarming drama. In this movie, James Stewart <u>plays</u> an ordinary family man who <u>lives</u> in a small American town. When he is about to lose his business because of a serious mistake, Stewart <u>becomes</u> very depressed. He <u>tries</u> to jump off a bridge, but an angel <u>shows</u> him how important he <u>is</u> to his friends, family, and the community. He then <u>decides</u> not to kill himself.

Writing the First Draft

11 Page 194.
Have students write their first drafts of a paragraph about their favorite movie. Remind them to use important events and information, and to combine sentences to show the relationship between events. They should also include adjectives and appositives to describe the movie and characters. They can write the paragraph in the historical present tense and use the title they wrote for Activity 7.

Edit and Revise

Editing Practice

Using Two or More Adjectives

12 Page 195.
Answers:
1. *Gandhi* is the story of a wise, kind man who leads India to freedom.
2. In *It's a Wonderful Life*, James Stewart plays a hard-working, ordinary man.
3. *The 400 Blows* tells the story of a lonely, unhappy boy.
4. *Women on the Verge of a Nervous Breakdown* contains many colorful, comic characters.

13 Page 195.
Answers:
1. *Gandhi* is about a gentle but powerful leader.
2. *Frankenstein* is the story of a destructive but tragic monster.
3. *The Godfather* is about an evil but loyal man.
4. The lead characters in *Thelma and Louise* are vulnerable but brave.

Editing Your Writing

14 Editing Using a Checklist. Page 195.
Have students make different editorial passes on their paragraph, using the checklist in the student book.

15 Peer Editing. Page 196.
Use the suggestions in the student book to conduct peer conferences. Give pairs of students time to exchange papers and read each other's work. Students can write comments and suggestions in the margins of their partners' papers. Pairs can then reconvene and give each other verbal feedback, explaining the main points of their written comments. Afterwards, students can rewrite their paragraphs, incorporating the feedback as appropriate.

Writing the Second Draft

16 Page 195.
Have students rewrite their paragraphs about their favorite movie, based on the suggestions of their peers and teacher, as well as their own edits from Activity 14. Have students assess whether they feel their writing is improving.

Part 5 Grammar

A. The Past Continuous Tense
Write this sentence on the board.

I watched television last night from 7 to 9.

Ask the students *What was I doing at 8:30? (You were watching television.)* Write their responses on the board. Prompt them with part of the answer if no one is sure. Ask various students *What were you doing last night at 8:30?*

Call on students to read the examples and the notes in the Grammar Charts on page 196.

1 **Page 197.**

Read the instructions and the examples. Have students work on their own or in pairs.

Answers:

Interview 1: 3. was sitting 4. was cashing
5. were filling out

Interview 2: 1. were you doing 2. were watching 3. was working
4. were doing 5. was knitting

B. The Simple Past Versus the Past Continuous

Write these sentences on the board. Tell the class that this is a list of the things that you did yesterday. All of these things began and ended in the past.

> *Yesterday, I cleaned the house. I taught class. I cooked dinner.*

However, we can also look at each event while it was happening.

> *While I was cleaning house, the telephone rang. (The telephone interrupted the cleaning.)*

> *I was teaching class when the electricity went out. (I started teaching before the lights went out.)*

> *I wasn't eating at 6. I was cooking dinner. (I started cooking before 6.)*

Call on students to read the examples and the notes in the Grammar Chart on page 198.

2 **Page 198.**

Read the examples. Have the students work individually or in pairs. Then call on different pairs of students to read the dialog aloud.

Answers: 1. did you do 2. woke up
3. was raining 4. stayed 5. read
6. Were you reading 7. was 8. did you do
9. watched 10. Didn't you go 11. were you doing 12. was returning 13. watched
14. did you do 15. played 16. were you doing 17. did you call 18. was walking
19. didn't want

C. *When* and *While* with the Simple Past and the Past Continuous Tenses

Write these sentences on the board.

	1st action	2nd action
when	*When* we left class,	we went to the library.
		same time
while	*While* I was surfing the Internet,	Don was looking for a book.
	action in progress	interrupting action
when or	*While* we were working,	Gina came in.
while	We were working,	*when* Gina came in.

Call on students to read the examples and the notes. Then put them in pairs and ask each pair to think of an example sentence using *when* or *while*. Give them two minutes to think of a sentence. Then call on two or three pairs to write their sentences on the board.

3 **Page 199.**

Read the instructions and the example. Have students write their answers individually. Then put students in pairs to compare answers.

Suggested Answers: 2. When 3. while
4. When 5. while 6. while 7. while
8. When

Video Activities: Quiz Shows

Before You Watch

Ask students to complete this section with a partner. Move around the room offering language support as needed.

Watch [on video]

Read through the questions with students and then have students watch the video once straight through. Then discuss the answers with the whole class.

Answers: 1. answer questions 2. They are inexpensive to produce. 3. b

Watch Again [on video]

Ask students to read the questions to themselves. Then play the video again and have them fill in the true and false answers. Review the answers together.

Answers: 1. T 2. F 3. F 4. T 5. T 6. F 7. F

After You Watch

Read the instructions. Put students in pairs to take turns asking and answering their questions. Have pairs share some of their more interesting answers with the class.

Answers:
1. started 2. jumped 3. clone, are doing
4. is 5. are making 6. are 7. found out, lost, is bringing 8. don't have to 9. will, last

Social Life

Part 1 Listening to Conversations

Before You Listen

1 Prelistening Questions. Page 202.

Ask students to read and discuss the questions with a partner. If they don't know, have them guess the meaning of the terms "reunion" (a meeting which happens when people haven't seen each other for a long time) and "stay in touch" (stay in contact). Use the picture to help explain what "run into an old friend by accident" means.

2 Vocabulary Preview. Page 202.

Read aloud the instructions and the list of words in the left-hand column. You may wish to have students repeat the words after you. Then have them complete the exercise on their own.

Answers:

	Expressions	**Meanings**
graduation	graduation day	the day someone finishes high school or college.
be up to	What have you been up to?	What have you been doing?
make(s) sense	That makes sense.	I can understand that.
terrific	That's terrific.	wonderful
(to be) good at	You were good at math.	are able to do well
sales rep	I'm a sales rep.	a traveling salesperson
on the road	I'm on the road a lot.	travel
nurse	I'm a nurse in a hospital.	person who gives medical care
keep in touch	Let's keep in touch	continue to communicate with each other

Fill-ins: 1. terrific 2. been up to
3. good at 4. on the road 5. nurse
6. keep in touch 7. graduation 8. make
sense 9. sales rep

Listen

**3 Listening for Main Ideas. Page 203.
[on tape/CD]**

Read aloud the instructions for item 1. Remind students that the goal of the exercise is to listen only for main ideas. Ask them to look back at the picture on page 202 and explain that this picture illustrates one thing that happens in the recording they are going to hear. Have a student read the questions. Prompt students to ask about any questions they don't understand. Have a student read aloud the questions before you play the tape or CD. Play the tape or CD and have the students answer the questions. Then have them go over the answers in pairs.

Answers: 1. b 2. on graduation night
3. They don't think he's really studying hard.
4. He's a computer science major. 5. Karen
works in a hospital. 6. stay in touch

Tapescript

Karen:	Yolanda, look! I can't believe it! It's Peter Riley. Hey Peter! How are you?
Peter:	Karen? Yolanda? Wow! I haven't seen you guys since graduation night!
Yolanda:	I know. You look great!
Peter:	Thanks. So do you.
Yolanda:	So what have you been up to?
Peter:	Well, I go to Faber College.
Karen:	Really? Do you like it?
Peter:	Yeah, so far. But I've been studying really hard.
Yolanda:	Sure you have…
Karen:	What's your major—body building?
Peter:	No, actually it's computer science.
Yolanda:	Ah-h-h. That makes sense. You always *were* good at math and science.
Peter:	Thanks. Anyway, what have *you* guys been up to?
Yolanda:	Well, I'm a sales rep for a publishing company.

Peter: No kidding! How do you like that?
Yolanda: Oh, I love it! I'm on the road a lot, but I get to meet some interesting people.
Peter: That's terrific. And how about you, Karen?
Karen: I'm a nurse in a hospital.
Peter: You always were good at science too. Well, it was great seeing you both. We should be sure to keep in touch from now on.

Stress

4   Listening for Stressed Words. Page 204. [on tape/CD]

Read the instructions and point out the blanks below where students will fill in the missing stressed words. Then point out the words they will use to fill in the blanks and go over the list together. Remind students to do two things: repeat after the speaker and write in the missing words. Then play the tape or CD again and ask students to fill in the missing words. After that, have students exchange books and correct each other's work using the tapescript in the back of the student book as a guide. Discuss any items that more than five people got wrong. Then have students practice reading the completed dialogue with partners.

After You Listen

5   Vocabulary Review. Page 205.

Have students complete this activity with a partner. When they finish, invite volunteers to share their answers with the class.

Pronunciation

Intonation with Exclamation

Play the tape or CD of the exclamations. Then read the explanation with the class and demonstrate the strong emphasis and falling intonation used with exclamations. You may wish to have students repeat them after you.

6   Pronouncing Exclamations. Page 205. [on tape/CD]

Play the tape or CD and have students follow along in their books. Then ask students to close their books as they listen to the pairs of sentences again. After that, have them repeat the sentences after the recording.

7   Matching Statements and Responses. Page 206. [on tape/CD]

Read the directions and play the tape or CD. Review the correct answers at the end.

Answers: 1. a   2. b   3. e   4. c   5. h   6. f   7. d   8. g

Tapescript

1. My sister just had triplets.
2. Guess what? I'm getting married next month.
3. Would you like a job for a dollar an hour?
4. I've been exercising a lot and I've lost 30 pounds.
5. Someone hit my car yesterday. It's going to cost $1,000 to repair.
6. I met the President of the United States yesterday.
7. My sister likes to eat peanut butter and banana sandwiches.
8. I locked the keys in the car.

8   Practicing Exclamations. Page 206.

Read the instructions and designate pairs. Remind students to look at only one of the boxes and stress the importance of students' not looking at the other one while doing the exercise. Do one item together as an example. Circulate among the pairs answering questions if necessary.

Possible Answers:
Student A: 1. Congratulations!   2. Yes. You look great!   3. Oh no! That's awful!   4. I can't believe it!

Student B: 1. Oh no! That's awful!   2. That's terrific!   3. It's disgusting!   4. Congratulations!

Part 2 Recalling Main Ideas

Before You Listen

1 Prelistening Questions. Page 207.
Read the instructions and the six sentences to the class. Explain the term *blind date* if necessary. (It's a date in which the two people have never met before. Blind dates are usually arranged by a mutual friend.) Have students complete the activity in pairs. Invite volunteers to describe to the class any unusual experiences they have had on a blind date.

Listen

2 Listening for Main Ideas. Page 207.
[on tape/CD]
Read the instructions and go over the questions students are asked to answer after this first time listening to the conversation.

Answers: 1. She wants to set up a blind date. 2. The blind date doesn't speak English.

Tapescript

Karen: Listen, a friend of mine is coming to town next week. I think you might like him.

Beverly: Well, I really don't like blind dates. But tell me about him anyway.

Karen: Well, he's very good-looking.

Beverly: Oh, yeah? Tell me more.

Karen: He's got dark hair and green eyes and a wonderful smile. He had a beard the last time I saw him. And he has his own business.

Beverly: That's nice. What kind of business?

Karen: Import/export. And he loves to travel.

Beverly: About how old is he?

Karen: He's almost thirty.

Beverly: Does he like dancing or music?

Karen: He loves jazz, and he's played the piano for years. I'm sure he likes dancing too.

Beverly: Wow, he sounds great! Maybe he could come with me to the football game next weekend.

Karen: Oh, I don't know if Franco would like that.

Beverly: Why is that?

Karen: Well, they don't play American football in Italy. They play soccer.

Beverly: Italy? You mean he's Italian?

Karen: Yes. So there is one small problem, I guess.

Beverly: Don't tell me...

Karen: Right. He doesn't speak English.

3 Taking Notes on Specific Information. Page 207. [on tape/CD]
Read the instructions and point out the five details students are going to listen for this time. Then play the tape or CD again and ask them to make notes after each heading. Remind students that they should take short notes so they don't get bogged down in writing and miss important points.

Possible Answers:
Appearance: tall, good-looking, dark hair, green eyes

Job: Import/export business

Interests: travel, jazz, piano, dancing

Age: almost 30

Problems: doesn't like American football, doesn't speak English

After You Listen

4 Summarizing Main Ideas. Page 207.
Read the instructions and help students find partners to complete the activity with. As they work, listen to different pairs, helping them with any aspects of the task that are proving difficult for them. If time permits, have one or more students present their summary to the class.

5 Discussing Dating Customs. Page 208.
This is an open-ended oral activity that reviews key vocabulary words and provides listening and speaking practice. Try to include students of various ability levels in each group. Set a time limit for the discussions. At the end, invite individuals from various groups to tell the class the most interesting thing they learned from the discussion.

Talk It Over

Videodating

Ask students to read the first paragraph. Then discuss how videodating works and answer any questions they may have. Then read through the six steps with the class and get them started on their applications. (You may wish to photocopy the application form and distribute copies to students.) When the forms are complete, post them on the wall and give students about 10 minutes to read them and choose the one they are most interested in. Suggest that they jot down the made-up name on that application. Then complete steps 4 through 6 of the activity. If time permits, have students prepare and present the role-plays outlined at the bottom of the page. (Alternatively, you could have some students prepare for the videodating activity while others prepare role-plays to be presented at the end of the class.)

Culture Note

The traditions that surround dating in American culture and the rules that parents set vary from place to place. In some places "dating" begins as early as age 11 or 12 when adolescents start inviting each other to school dances and to the movies. In other places, particularly in more conservative rural areas, teenagers don't usually go out as a couple until they are 16 or 17 years old. Often these first dates involve several couples going somewhere together.

Part 3 Reading

Before You Read

1 Discussing Pictures. Page 210.
Point out the eight pictures and ask students to describe the people and their expressions. Have students read what each person is saying. Read the questions aloud and call on volunteers to answer. Encourage students to talk about the different ways to meet boyfriends/girlfriends. List vocabulary on the board.

Answers will vary.

2 Thinking about the Answers. Page 210.
Read the questions aloud and call on volunteers to suggest possible answers. Point out key vocabulary: *marriage, boyfriend, girlfriend, meeting people.* As students suggest answers, record students' responses and ideas on an overhead projector or on a large piece of paper. You may want to review these responses later after students have read the selection.

Sample Answers:
1. A common kind of marriage in Korea in the past was an arranged marriage where the parents chose the mate for their child.
2. Young people around the world meet people through friends, going out to dances and parties, at school or work, at clubs, and on the Internet.
3. Answers will vary.

3 Vocabulary Preview. Page 211.
Read the words aloud and have students circle the ones they don't know. Students can look for the words they don't know in the reading. Have students check their understanding of the circled words after they complete the reading selection.

Read

**4 Meeting the Perfect Mate. Page 211.
[on tape/CD]**
Play the tape or CD as students follow along in
their books. You may want to stop the recording
after every paragraph to check understanding and
point out vocabulary words. Listen a second time
as students read along.

After You Read

**5 Recognizing the Structure of
Conversations. Page 212.**
Read the instructions together. Point out the
outline form on page 213 that students will
complete. Have students look back at the reading
on pages 211 and 212 to guide them as they
complete the outline. Go over the answers
together.

Answers:
I. Introduction: reasons for interviewing people

   A. I'm studying "Social Structure" in a
graduate seminar.

   B. I'm interviewing people about ways to
meet potential mates.

II. Arranged marriages

   A. Mates may meet for the first time on
their wedding day.

   B. Husbands and wives may learn to love
each other.

III. Meeting people in dance clubs

   A. You can talk or just listen to music.

   B. The women act unfriendly because a lot
of men are too aggressive

IV. Finding friends in cyberspace

   A. You can go online at home, in cafes,
and in other places.

   B. You don't know what is unreal or
dangerous about people you meet on
the Web.

V. Meeting in health clubs or the gym

   A. People with common interest in physical
exercise meet here.

   B. If you're not really interested in
exercise, there might be a problem.

There are <u>advantages</u> and disadvantages to the
various ways of <u>meeting potential mates</u>.

6 Understanding the Main Idea. Page 214.
After reading the instructions, have students change
the underlined words and phrases to complete the
summary of the reading selection. Have students
explain the reasons for their answers.

Answers:
Ex. advantages and disadvantages; mates;
  1. A disadvantage; love each other
  2. dance; women; a lot of men
  3. convenient; everywhere; difficult
  4. something in common; loses interest

**7 Supplying Left-Out Words and References.
Page 214.**
Read together the instructions. Have students
work individually in pairs to complete the
statements with the missing words. Go over
answers with the group.

Answers:
  1. for meeting a possible mate
  2. match; can you match
  3. of arranged marriages
  4. they were upset
  5. women; to nightclubs

In the second part of the exercise, point out that
students will identify the idea to which the
underlined words refer. Go over the example and
clarify as needed. Then have students complete
this part of the exercise. Review the answers with
the class.

Chapter 8

Answers:
1. seminar
2. matched marriage
3. their children's, their children
4. meet
5. dance clubs seem great.
6. in cyberspace
7. The healthy atmosphere in the gym is continuing into the relationship. The idea sounds wonderful.
8. I hate to exercise.

You may want to arrange students in pairs to practice asking and answering the questions about references to previous ideas. Call attention to the sample question in the example on page 215.

Finally, have students complete the answers to the questions on page 210. Go over the answers with the group. Discuss any differences in the responses.

Sample Answers:
1. A common kind of marriage in Korea in the past was an arranged marriage where the parents chose the mate for their child.
2. Young people around the world meet people through friends, going out to dances and parties, at school or work, at clubs, on the Internet.
3. Answers will vary.

Discussing the Reading

8 Small Group Discussion. Page 216.
Arrange students in groups of four. Give the groups about 15-20 minutes to discuss the questions. Circulate among the groups, listening and giving assistance as needed. When all groups are finished, ask reporters from each group to share the most interesting information from their groups.

Answers will vary.

Part 4 Writing

Before You Write

Exploring Ideas
Interviewing Someone

1 Page 216.
   Sample Answers:
   Academic Life
   Religious Life
   Hobbies

2 Page 216.
   Sample Answers:
   1. What classes have you taken in this last year?
   2. What decisions have you made about your education and career?
   3. Have you taken any steps to pursue your goals? What are they?
   4. What do you do for fun?

3 Page 216.
   Answers will vary. Some students may not want to talk about their private lives for a variety of reasons, and their privacy should be respected.

4 Page 216.
   Give students about fifteen minutes to conduct their interviews. Encourage students to take good notes during the interview. They will need these notes to complete the writing project.

5 Building Vocabulary. Page 217.
   Sample Answers:
   Nouns: *preferences, education, goals, pursuits;*
   Verbs: *pursue, concentrate, plan;*
   Adjectives: *enjoyable, challenging, interesting*

Organizing Ideas

Writing Topic Sentences

6 Page 217.

Answer:

Sentences 1, 3, and 6 are the best examples of topic sentences because they are general and set the context for a detailed discussion.

7 Page 217.

Give students a few minutes to have a peer conference about their topic sentences.

Organizing Information in a Paragraph

8 Page 218.

Answers:

One possible arrangement of the sentences:

1. got married in June—a lot of responsibility
2. works in Uncle's factory—makes him tired
3. works evenings in gas station
4. goes to English classes—has no time to study
5. goes biking with his wife
6. plays soccer with friends

9 Page 218.

Have pairs of students exchange notes for their paragraphs and discuss the order of ideas. Partners should give each other suggestions to improve the flow of ideas when appropriate.

Writing a Concluding Sentence

10 Page 218.

Answers will vary. Ask students to share their final sentences and invite students to give feedback on why or why not these could be good concluding sentences.

Write

Developing Cohesion and Style

Using Transitional Words and Phrases

11 Page 219.

Answers:

1. Tony has been working very hard. In fact, he works from 8:00 in the morning until 9:00 at night.
2. Tony has been working very hard. However, he still finds time to play soccer every week.
3. Raúl has been doing well, and he likes his English class a lot. In fact, he's been studying so much that he isn't sleeping well.
4. Raúl has been doing well in his English class. In fact, he went from level 2 to level 4 last month.
5. Patricia enjoys going to school. However, she doesn't like going at night.
6. Patricia has been exercising a lot. In fact, she now runs about 30 miles a week.

12 Page 220.

Answers will vary. Help students to check their work for accuracy.

Writing the First Draft

13 Page 220.

Have students write their first drafts of a paragraph about a classmate. Remind them to use transitional expressions to unify their paragraphs. They should use their topic sentence from Activity 7 and their notes about the interview from Activity 9.

Edit and Revise

Editing Practice

Using Long Forms in Formal Writing

14 Page 220.
Answers:
1. He has been playing in a band.
2. They have not moved yet.
3. They are not having problems with Canadian customs.
4. Recently she has been planning a party.
5. It is difficult work.

15 Page 220.
Answer: Marta Duarte has had a very interesting year. Last June she graduated from a tourism development course in Mexico. She received a scholarship to study English and has been attending classes here at the University of Ottawa since September. Marta travels throughout Canada and the United States. She visits hotels to study the different management systems and has learned a lot. In fact, she says that one day in a hotel is better than ten days in a classroom. However, Marta hasn't spent all her time in Canada working. She loves to dance and goes dancing at least two nights a week. She has also found time to develop a close friendship with the manager of a big hotel here in Ottawa. She is hoping to get to know him better.

Editing Your Writing

16 Editing Using a Checklist. Page 221.
Have students make different editorial passes on their paragraph, using the checklist in the student book.

17 Peer Editing. Page 221.
Use the suggestions in the student book to conduct peer conferences. Give pairs of students time to exchange papers and read each other's work. Students can write comments and suggestions in the margins of their partners' papers. Pairs can then reconvene and give each other verbal feedback, explaining the main points of their written comments. Afterwards, students can rewrite their paragraphs, incorporating the feedback as appropriate.

Writing the Second Draft

18 Page 221.
Have students rewrite their paragraphs about a classmate, based on the suggestions of their peers and teacher, as well as their own edits from Activity 16. Have students assess whether they feel their writing is improving.

Part 5 Grammar

A. Time Expressions with the Present Perfect: *For, Since, All, Always*
Write this question on the board.

How long have you lived in (this town)?

Ask students to give you an answer with since.

I have lived in (this town) since (1998).

Ask another student to give you an answer with for.

I have lived in (this town) for (ten years).

Ask who in the class was born in this town. Write these sentences on the board.

Pablo has lived in (this town) all his life.
Pablo has always lived in (this town).

Call on students to read the examples and the notes in the Grammar Chart on page 222.

1 Page 222.

Read the instructions and the example. Have the class do items 1–4 together. Then have them complete 5–9 individually.

Answers: 1. always 2. since 3. always
4. all 5. always 6. for 7. for 8. since
9. since

2 Page 223.

Read the instructions and the example. Tell them that some sentences can use either *for* or *since* depending on the time phrase they use. Tell them to look at the example and give you an alternative with since. *(She has been a member of the soccer team since last year.)* Have the students work in pairs.

Answers: 1. Juanita has liked Daniel for three years. 2. Adrian has lived in Mexico since last year. 3. Angela has been tired since this morning. 4. Jong has had a cell phone since 1998. 5. They've been up since 8:00.
6. She has had the stereo on for an hour.
7. I haven't been hungry since last night.
8. My visitors have been here since last week.

B. Present Perfect: Time Clauses with *Since*

Draw this time line on the board. Substitute information that is true for you.

1998	*2001*
finished school	*got married*
began teaching English	*moved here*

Ask the students to make sentence in the present perfect with 1998.

> *You have taught since 1998.*

Then tell them that there is another way to say this.

> *You have taught English since you finished school.*

Ask the students to make a sentence in the present perfect with 2001.

> *You have lived here since 2001.*

Ask them to give you another way to say this.

> *You have lived here since you got married.*

Call on students to read the examples and the notes in the Grammar chart on page 223.

3 Page 223.

Read the instructions and the examples. Have the students work individually and check their answers in pairs.

Answers: 1. Hanna has met a lot of new people since she joined the tennis club.
2. Since Alfonso went to the concert last week, he has had a headache. 3. Since Taro went on vacation he has been much more relaxed.
4. I haven't seen Reiko and Yoko since they moved to an apartment off campus. 5. Patrick hasn't been in school since he broke his leg.

C. The Present Perfect Continuous Tense

Write these sentences on the board.

> *1. I've eaten sushi a few times.*
>
> *2. I've been eating sushi all week. I'm tired of it!*

Tell students that both sentences are correct. Ask students to guess why sentence 1 uses the present perfect and sentence 2 uses the present perfect continuous. *(Because 2 emphasizes the continual nature of the activity.)*

Call on students to read the information above the Grammar Chart on page 224. Then write these sentences on the board.

> *3. We've painted the house three times in five years.*
>
> *4. We've been painting the house for 2 days and we're only halfway done.*

Ask students to tell you which sentence shows that they are painting the house (#4). Tell them that although the people are painting the house, it doesn't mean that they are doing it at this minute. It is enough to show that the job is not done.

Call on students to read the information in the Grammar Charts on pages 224-225.

4 Page 225.

Read the instructions and the example. Let the class work together.

Answers: 1. I have been looking forward to this party for weeks. 2. The music has been playing all night. 3. Everyone has been dancing for hours. 4. That woman has been flirting with that man since the party began. 5. That couple has been fighting since the party began.

5 Page 225.

Read the instructions and the example. Have the students work individually.

Answers: 1. How long have they been arguing? 2. How long has she been flirting with Felipe? 3. How long has she been dyeing her hair? 4. How long has he been wearing a hairpiece? 5. How long has he been dieting? 6. How long has he been living downtown?

D. The Present Perfect Continuous Versus the Present Perfect

Write these sentences on the board.

>   1. *I've talked to Anna two times this week.*
>
>   2. *I've been talking to Anna for two hours.*

Ask the students to tell you the difference in meaning between sentences 1 and 2. *(In Sentence 2 the person is still talking to Anna.)*

Write these sentences on the board.

>   3. *They've owned that car for 3 years.*
>
>   4. *They've been owning that car for 3 years.*

Ask students to tell you which sentence is incorrect and why. *(Sentence 4 is incorrect because own is a nonaction verb. It cannot be used in the continuous.)* Draw a large X over sentence 4 to show that it is incorrect. Write these sentences on the board.

>   5. *He's lived here for two years.*
>
>   6. *He's been living here for two years.*

Ask the students if there is any difference in meaning between sentences 5 and 6. *(No)* Then tell them to look at the Grammar Chart on page 226 and find out why there is no difference.

Call on students to read the rest of the examples and the notes in the Grammar Chart.

6 Page 227.

Read the instructions and the example. Let the class work together.

Answers:
A: 1. been thinking 2. noticed
B: 1. been sleeping 2. been snoring 3. liked
C: 1. been acting 2. been doing 3. had been having 4. been 5. been calling 6. been studying
D: 1. been cleaning up 2. been helping 3. been thinking

Video Activities: Online Love Story

Before You Watch

Ask students to discuss the questions in small groups. Encourage them to give reasons for their answers. If anyone in the class has experience with online dating, ask them to share the pros and cons with the class.

Answers:
1. A "chat room" is a service provided by an Internet company. Visitors to a chat room can "talk" to each other by typing messages back and forth. The messages are received almost instantly so it is a virtual conversation.

2. Sample answer: The Internet can be a fun and easy way to meet new people, but it is difficult to know if people are really telling the truth about themselves.

3. Answers will vary.

4. Answers will vary.

Watch [on video]

Read through the questions with students and remind them to listen only for the sequence of the events listed. Then play the video once straight through. Review the correct answers with the class.

Answers: 2, 5, 1, 4, 3

Watch Again [on video]

Read the questions to the class and discuss any meaning of any specific words students don't know. Then help them form small groups to discuss the answers to the questions.

Possible Answers:

1. She meant that she wasn't ugly.
2. Because they met in an anonymous setting—an Internet chat room. And because they lived near each other.
3. 2 weeks
4. 6 months
5. that it wouldn't last
6. Patrick says she's his princess. Vesna says he's her soulmate.
7. an online dating service that they started

After You Watch

You can have students do the simulated chatroom activity in pairs and then invite volunteers to perform a role-play of their "chat" for the rest of the class.

Customs, Celebrations, and Holidays

Part 1 Listening to Conversations

This section of Chapter 10 focuses on the buying and giving of gifts. It features a variety of listening practice situations and introduces a wide range of vocabulary items related to gifts and gift-giving.

Before You Listen

1 Prelistening Questions. Page 230.

Ask students to discuss the questions with a partner. As you go over their responses together in class, you may wish to note on the board key vocabulary items that come up, such as *celebrate, romantic,* and *holiday.* Explain that the word "holiday" has different meanings in British and American English. In British English, it can mean "vacation"—time off from work. In American English, it generally means "a day of celebration," such as New Year's Day.

2 Vocabulary Preview. Page 230.

Explain that the words and expressions in the left-hand column of the chart will appear in the recording they are going to hear. Read the words and phrases aloud. Then have them fill in the blanks in the sentences below. Ask students to take turns reading the completed sentences. After that, have students write what they think each one means in the right-hand column of the chart. Discuss the correct definitions with the whole class.

Possible Answers:

Definitions: cologne: perfume; jewelry: rings, bracelets, necklaces; elegant: stylish, fashionable; romantic: related to love; bracelet: a chain or band worn on the wrist; else: additional, other

Fill-ins: 1. cologne 2. jewelry 3. elegant 4. romantic 5. bracelet 6. else

Listen

3 Listening for Main Ideas. Page 231. [on tape/CD]

Read aloud the instructions for item 1. Remind students that the goal of the exercise is to listen only for main ideas. Ask them to look at the picture on page 231 and explain that this picture illustrates one thing that happens in the recording they are going to hear. Have a student read the questions. Prompt students to ask about any questions they don't understand. Have a student read aloud the questions before you play the tape or CD. Play the tape or CD and have the students answer the questions. Then have them go over the answers in pairs.

Answers: 1. a Valentine's Day gift for a girl who's not his girlfriend yet   2. She's on a diet. 3. It's too expensive.   4. a card and a perfect red rose   5. give her the card and the rose

Tapescript

Clerk: Hello. Can I help you with anything?

Kenji: I'm looking for a Valentine's Day gift for my girlfriend. Well, actually, she's not my girlfriend yet, so I really don't know what to get her.

Clerk: How about some chocolate?

Kenji: Well, I think she's on a diet.

Clerk: Hmm, then how about some jewelry?

Kenji: Like what?

Clerk: Well, look at this bracelet. It's simple but very elegant, don't you think?

Kenji: It's pretty, but I really can't spend that much money.

Clerk: Okay. Let's see …What else? …Well, here's a nice bottle of cologne. I'm sure she'll like that.

Kenji: Actually she once told me that she doesn't like any kind of perfume. And anyway, I really wanted to give her something…unusual.

Clerk: I'm afraid something unusual might be expensive. Look, I have an idea. Why don't you get her a nice card and give it to her with one perfect red rose. Most women love to get flowers. Doesn't that sound romantic?

Kenji: Yeah, I guess so. Okay, that's what I'll do.

Clerk: Don't worry. I'm sure she'll like whatever you give her.

Kenji: Oh, I hope so. Thanks for your help!

Culture Note

In the United States most people only give gifts to people they know very well. It is especially unusual to give a new acquaintance something personal, such as jewelry or clothing. However, most people feel comfortable giving or receiving an inexpensive gift, such as flowers or a book, at the beginning of a relationship.

Stress

4 Listening for Stressed Words. Page 232. [on tape/CD]

Read the instructions and read the word list aloud. Then ask students to fill in as many of the answers as they can on the first listening, and offer to discuss any questions they have at that point. Remind them that after each pause they should repeat after the speaker before they write in the missing words. Play the tape or CD. Correct the answers in class or have students use the tapescript to correct their own work. Then have students do the second part of the exercise in pairs.

Reductions

Dropping the /h/ Sound [on tape/CD]

This section focuses on the places that American English speakers leave out the /h/ sound. Play the tape or CD and have students listen carefully to the contrasting sentences. Remind them that the reduced forms are never written out in normal writing.

5 Comparing Long and Reduced Forms. Page 233. [on tape/CD]

Play the tape or CD and have students follow along in their books. Then have students repeat the sentences after the recording. If you hear a number of students making the same error, point it out and help them correct it.

6 Listening for Reductions. Page 234. [on tape/CD]

Read the directions for item 1. Remind students that the recording leaves enough time for students to repeat each sentence before they fill in the answer. Play the tape or CD. Then write the correct answers on the board and have students correct their own exercises. Then have students read the sentences to a partner for pronunciation practice. Move around the room checking their progress and modeling pronunciation as needed.

Answers: 1. you 2. and, want to, him, Do you want to 3. have to, can you 4. Could you 5. his 6. going to, her, her, And, going to 7. you

Tapescript

Jane: Hi Helen. Are ya going out?

Helen: Yeah, I'm going downtown. It's my brother's birthday tomorrow, 'n' I wanna buy 'im a gift. D'ya wanna come with me?

Jane: I really can't...I hafta study for a big test. But kin ya do me a favor?

Helen: Okay.

Jane: Couldja buy me some film? My sister just had a baby boy...

Helen: Really? Congratulations! What's 'is name?

Jane: Jeremy. He's so cute, but my poor sister is so tired. I'm gonna visit 'er this weekend and give 'er a hand. 'N' while I'm there, I'm gonna take some pictures of the baby.

Helen: OK, no problem.

Jane: Thanks. See ya later.

After You Listen

7 Vocabulary Review. Page 234.

Help students find partners. Have them take turns asking and answering the questions. If one student in the pair is much less fluent than the other, you might ask the more fluent one to do all the answering the first time through. Then have them repeat the activity with the less fluent student answering the questions with the partner's help.

Talk It Over

American Holidays

Introduce the calendar and ask volunteers to tell what they know about the various holidays. Then explain that the class is going to form groups of eight people each, and that each person is going to research and report to their group on a different holiday using information in the back of the student book. Help the students form groups and then ask them to proceed on their own. When they finish, go on to the second part of the activity. Invite volunteers to tell about their favorite holiday. It can be one of the ones they have just researched, or they can describe a holiday from their own culture which might be interesting to the other students.

Part 2 Recalling Main Ideas

Before You Listen

1 Prelistening Questions. Page 236.

Invite students to describe holidays for giving thanks from their own culture or from other countries or cultures that they are familiar with. How is it similar to American Thanksgiving? How it is different?

2 Vocabulary Preview. Page 236.

Read the instructions and have students complete the activity individually. As you review the

answers with the class, ask students to raise their hands if they are still having difficulty with any of the terms. Invite other students to explain these terms in their own words.

Answers: 1. f 2. d   3. e 4. b 5. a
6. c

Listen

3 Listening for Main Ideas. Page 237. [on tape/CD]

Read the instructions and remind students not to include details and not to write complete sentences. They should concentrate on writing down the most important ideas as single words or short phrases.

Answers: 1. the Pilgrims and American Indians   2. their good luck

Tapescript

Kenji: Everything is delicious, Mrs. Riley. It really was nice of you to invite me.

Mrs. R: Well, nobody should have dinner alone today. Thanksgiving is a time for families and friends to be together. Is this your first Thanksgiving in the United States, Kenji?

Kenji: Yes. In fact, I don't really know much about it.

Mrs. R: Well ask Robbie. He'll tell you all about it.

Robbie: Ah, come on. What's this, a history lesson?

Kenji: No, I'm really interested. Come on, tell me.

Robbie: Well, see, these guys came over from Europe like maybe a thousand years ago …

Mr. R: Not exactly. It was more like four hundred years ago.

Robbie: Oh, yeah, that's right. Anyway, they made good friends with the Indians, and they tried planting corn and other stuff together. But it was really hard growing all that stuff, so when they had the first harvest …

Kenji: What's a "harvest?"

Robbie: You know, when they pick the food after it's done growing. So after the first harvest, the Indians and the Pilgrims had a big dinner together to thank God for their good luck.

Kenji: Wait. Who were the Pilgrims?

Mr. R: They were the first immigrants from Europe.

Mrs. R: And the foods we are eating now are the same kinds of things that they ate.

Kenji: Oh, so that's where turkey and corn and squash come from, right?

Robbie: Right!

Kenji: But why is Thanksgiving on November 27th?

Robbie: It's different every year. But it's always the fourth Thursday of November. Right, Dad?

Mr. R: Right. Except that in Canada they celebrate it in October.

4 Taking Notes on Specific Information. Page 237. [on tape/CD]

Review the instructions with the class. Then play the tape or CD and have them fill in the information. Ask two or three students to write their notes on the board.

Answers:

The first Thanksgiving:

Who? Indians and Pilgrims

Why? celebrate their good luck

When? 400 years ago

Special foods: turkey, corn, squash

Thanksgiving today:

When? fourth Thursday in November
(Canada celebrates it in October.)

Customs: families and friends get together

After You Listen

5 Summarizing Main Ideas. Page 237.

Read and discuss the instructions and help students find partners. As they work together, move around the room offering assistance as needed

6 Vocabulary Review. Page 238.

Have students complete this activity with a partner. When they finish, invite volunteers to share their answers with the class.

Using Language

Invitations

Ask students to study the chart containing language they can use to invite, to accept an invitation, and to refuse an invitation. Review the information with the class, pointing out that the refusals all begin with a positive comment followed by the word *but*.

7 Making Invitations. Page 238.

Read the instructions with the class and have a pair of students read the example. Then help students find partners. Pair less fluent speakers with more fluent speakers for this activity. Set a time limit of about 15 minutes and suggest that students finish as many role-plays as they can comfortably do in that amount of time. Assure them that it is more useful to do only one role-play and to understand it well, than to do all three and not really learn anything. Invite volunteers to perform their role-plays for the class.

8 Refusing Invitations. Page 239.

Review the instructions and sample language. Point out that when they refuse invitations this time, students will be opening with a positive comment at the beginning (*Thanks for asking...*) and adding a reason at the end (*I have other plans*). Encourage students to be creative in thinking of the reasons they add. At the end, invite volunteer pairs to role-play their conversations for the class.

Before You Read

1 Vocabulary Preview. Page 240.

Read the words aloud and have students circle the ones they don't know. Encourage students to explain the meanings of the words they do know. Students may want to come back to this vocabulary section after reading the selection to check again their understanding of the circled words.

Read

2 Making Inferences. Page 240. [on tape/CD]

Read together the instructions. Then play the tape or CD as students follow along in their books. Stop the tape or CD after every paragraph and have students complete the title for the paragraph. Then replay the tape as students read along in their books again. Stop again after each paragraph and ask students to identify the main idea. You may also want to check understanding and point out vocabulary words in each of the paragraphs.

Answers:

Titles:
B. A Mixture of Customs
C. Witches: A Symbol of Halloween
D. Halloween in North America
E. Halloween in Latin American Culture

Main Ideas:
A. The celebration began...
B. ...the Romans, Christians, and Celts.
C. There are many beliefs...
D. ... a children's holiday with costumes and candy.
E. ... is a holiday to welcome back the souls.

After You Read

3 Identifying Inferences. Page 242.

Review making inferences. Read and clarify the instructions as needed before asking students to complete the exercise. As you go over the answers with the group, have volunteers point out references in the readings for the stated and implied statements.

Answers: 1. X 2. O 3. X 4. O
5. O 6. X 7. O 8. O 9. X 10. O
11. O 12. X 13. O 14. X

4 Learning to Summarize. Page 242.

Review what a summary is. Read the instructions and call attention to the paraphrases of the important vocabulary. Arrange students in groups of five to summarize assigned paragraphs. Remind groups that the topic sentence gives the main idea of a paragraph and the other sentences give details. Allow 10-15 minutes for groups to prepare their summaries. Have a volunteer from each group read aloud its summary. If several groups have summarized the same paragraphs, compare and contrast the versions. Discuss any differences.

Sample Answers:

A The celebration of Halloween began in the Celtic culture centuries ago in areas of France and the British Isles. It was a festival at the beginning of winter. They believed that the Lord of the Dead called back the ghosts of the dead people on October 31. People wanted to chase away the bad ghosts, so they made big fires.

B Through the centuries, Halloween added customs from the Romans, Christians, and Celts. The Romans had a celebration at the end of harvest time. Christians had a religious holiday on November 1 to remember good people in their religion. The day before the holy day became "the holy evening" or All Hallow's Eve.

C There are many beliefs associated with witches, a common symbol of Halloween. In Britain, people believed that these old wise women could tell the future and use magic words. Others thought that witches had special meetings and could fly on brooms. Some Christians wanted to stop witches and the belief in witches.

D Today in North American, Halloween is a children's holiday with costumes and candy. Children dress up like ghosts, witches, and devils. They go to houses and say "Trick or treat!" They receive candy, apples, or other things from the people in the houses.

E In contrast to Halloween, the Days of the Dead is a holiday to welcome back the souls of dead relatives. It's not a scary or sad holiday in Latin American culture. It's held on November 1 and 2. People honor the dead by getting together at the graves, lighting candles, having picnics, making music, and telling stories.

Part 4 Writing

Before You Write

Exploring Ideas

Describing Holidays

1   Page 243.
   Sample Answers:
   Holiday: New Year's Eve;
   Time of Year: December 31;
   Activities: Parties, singing, dancing;
   Description of activities: People sing "Auld Lang Syne" and other traditional songs at parties and kiss at midnight.

2   Page 243.
   Invite students to share their methods for organizing the holidays into different groups. Write the various groupings on the board. Ask students if they can think of any other ways to group the material.

3   Building Vocabulary. Page 243.
   Sample Answers:
   Nouns: *custom, festival, masquerade;*
   Verbs: *dance, honor, gather;*
   Adjectives: *colorful, festive, noisy*

Organizing Ideas

Categorizing and Making an Outline

4   Page 244.
   To create their outlines, ask students to think about a holiday in which special foods are prepared and traditional songs, dances, or rituals are performed.

Ordering Information According to Importance

5   Page 245.
   Answers:
   1b. at home with family and friends
   2. Memorial Day
   3a. First Monday in September
   4. Labor Day
   4a. Third Monday in February

6   Page 247.
   Have students make an outline for the type of holiday that they are going to write about.

Write

Developing Cohesion and Style

Listing Information

7   Page 247.
   Answers:
   Transitional words from paragraph on page 246: *In addition; Another; A third important civic holiday; Besides these three civic holidays; also*

8 Page 247.

Answers:

Paragraph 1:

Salvadorans celebrate several civic holidays each year. The most important one is Independence Day on September 15. On this day, people parade in the streets, sing songs, and recite poems. <u>Another</u> important civic holiday is Labor Day. Labor Day is the first day in May. <u>Besides</u> Labor Day and Independence Day, Salvadorans also celebrate the birthday of José Matias Delgado, the "father of the country." <u>In addition to</u> these holidays, there are other minor holidays such as *Día de la Raza*.

Paragraph 2:

There are some traditional holidays in the United States that no one celebrates seriously. The <u>first</u> one is Ground Hog Day. Ground Hog Day is February 2. On this day, people look for ground hogs coming out of their nests in the ground. Traditional belief says that if the ground hog sees his shadow, there will be six more weeks of winter.

<u>Another</u> silly holiday is April Fool's Day. This holiday falls on April first. On this day, people play tricks on each other. <u>In addition to</u> Ground Hog Day and April Fool's Day, there is Sadie Hawkins Day. Sadie Hawkins Day is on November 13th. On this day, tradition says that women can ask men to marry them.

Unifying a Paragraph with Pronouns and Pronominal Expressions

9 Page 248.

Answers:

1. Independence Day
2. Memorial Day
3. Labor Day
4. Labor Day
5. students
6. The Fourth of July, Memorial Day, Labor Day

Using Nonrestrictive Relative Clauses

10 Page 249.

Answers:

1. Easter, which comes in the springtime, is a happy holiday.
2. The Fourth of July, which is known as Independence Day, is a time for big parades and fireworks.
3. Martin Luther King Day, which is our newest holiday, comes in January.
4. Halloween, which is an ancient British tradition, is a favorite children's holiday.
5. On New Year's Day, which is the first holiday of the year, there is a famous parade in Pasadena, California.
6. Ground Hog Day, which is in February, is not a serious holiday.

11 Page 250.

Answers will vary. Help students check their work for correct grammar.

Writing the First Draft

12 Page 250.

Have students choose a country and write their first drafts of a paragraph about holidays in that country. Remind them to use their outline from Activity 6 and the sentences they have written using nonrestrictive relative clauses from Activity 11. They should also include the transitional words they have learned to list information, such as *in addition to, besides, another,* and *the first, second, third,* or *last.*

Edit and Revise

Editing Practice

Punctuating Nonrestrictive Clauses

13 Page 251.
   Answers:
   1. Songkran, which is the Thai New Year, is on April 13.
   2. Eid-e-Ghorbon is a religious holiday in Iran, which is a Muslim country.
   3. Christmas, which is an important holiday in Christian countries, is usually a happy time.
   4. Bastille Day, which is on July 14, is a very important holiday in France.
   5. My birthday, which is February 24th, is a holiday in Mexico.
   6. Labor Day is the first weekend in September, which is also the beginning of school in the United States.
   7. Day of the Dead, which is an important holiday in many Christian countries, is not celebrated in the United States.
   8. Groundhog Day, which Americans celebrate on February 2nd, is not an official holiday.

Editing Your Writing

14 Editing Using a Checklist. Page 251.
   Have students make different editorial passes on their paragraph, using the checklist in the student book.

15 Peer Editing. Page 251.
   Use the suggestions in the student book to conduct peer conferences. Give pairs of students time to exchange papers and read each other's work. Students can write comments and suggestions in the margins of their partners' papers. Pairs can then reconvene and give each other verbal feedback, explaining the main points of their written comments. Afterwards, students can rewrite their paragraphs, incorporating the feedback as appropriate.

Writing the Second Draft

16 Page 251.
   Have students rewrite their paragraphs about holidays in their chosen country, based on the suggestions of their peers and teacher, as well as their own edits from Activity 14. Have students assess whether they feel their writing is improving.

Part 5 Grammar

A. Gerunds and Infinitives as Subjects
   Write this on the board.

   Infinitive = *to* + verb

   Gerund = verb + *ing*

   Write these sentences on the board and ask students to identify the subject of each one.

   Learning a new language isn't easy.

   It isn't easy to learn a new language.

   Call on students to read the examples and the notes in the Grammar Chart on page 252.

1 Page 252.
   Read the instructions and the example. Have students work individually.

   Answers:
   1. Blowing up balloons in hard.
   2. Making a birthday cake is fun.
   3. It takes time to decorate the house with balloons and colored streamers.
   4. It is traditional to sing, "Happy Birthday to You."
   5. Blowing out all the candles is not easy.
   6. It's very important to make a wish before you blow out the candles.
   7. It's exciting to open the presents.
   8. Being with all of your friends is great.
   9. Saying good-bye to your guests is sad.
   10. It isn't fun to wash the dishes after the party.

B. Verbs Often Followed by Gerunds or Infinitives

Write these sentences on the board. Tell the students to guess which sentence is incorrect and why. Then tell them to look at the Grammar Chart on page 253 to check their guesses. Put an X over the incorrect sentence.

We can't stand fishing.

We can't stand fish. (X)

We hate fishing.

We hate to fish.

2 Page 253.

Read the instructions and the example. Have students do the exercise individually. Then put them in pairs to compare answers.

Answers: 2. a 3. a 4. a 5. a 6. a 7. a

Video Activities: Puerto Rican Day Parade

Before You Watch

Discuss the questions with the whole class.

Sample Answers:

1. A parade is a procession of people often with music and costumes.

2. You can often see bands playing music, groups or clubs in uniforms, cars, floats, flags, horses, clowns, etc.

3. Puerto Rico is an island in the Caribbean. It's capital is San Juan. The people speak Spanish and study English in school. Puerto Rico is a commonwealth of the United States, so its people are American citizens. They use American money, etc. The climate is tropical. They produce sugar cane, citrus fruits, coffee. Many Puerto Ricans also live in the continental United States.

Culture Note

Puerto Rico is an island in the Caribbean. It is a territory of the United States. Puerto Ricans are U.S. citizens but they do not vote in presidential elections and Puerto Rico has no representation in Congress.

Watch [on video]

Have the students read the list. Then have them watch and check what they see. Replay the video for them to check their answers.

Answers:

1. the 500th anniversary of Columbus's discovery of Puerto Rico

2. spectators, a queen, a marching band, flag wavers, floats, police, the mayor of New York

Watch Again [on video]

Read the instructions. Play the video and have students complete the exercise. Put students in pairs to check their answers. Replay the video if needed.

Answers: 1. 500 years 2. proud 3. salsa 4. 20,000

After You Watch

Set a time limit of ten to fifteen minutes on the small-group discussions. Then invite the group captains to share their group's plans with the whole class.

Science and Technology

Part 1 Listening to Conversations

Before You Listen

1 Prelistening Questions. Page 256.

As students read and discuss the questions with their partners, you might ask them to take brief notes on their partner's answers. Then you can call on individuals to summarize how they and their partners make use of computers.

2 Vocabulary Preview. Page 256.

Read aloud the instructions and the list of words. You may wish to have students repeat the words after you. Then have them complete the exercise on their own.

Answers: 1. out of date   2. broke down
3. online   4. plug...in   5. research
6. typewriter   7. laptop   8. software
9. hardware   10. tricks

Listen

**3 Listening for Main Ideas. Page 257.
[on tape/CD]**

Read aloud the instructions for item 1. Remind students that the goal of the exercise is to listen only for main ideas. Ask them to look back at the picture on page 256 and explain that this picture illustrates one thing that happens in the recording they are going to hear. Have a student read the questions. Prompt students to ask about any questions they don't understand. Have a student read aloud the questions before you play the tape or CD. Play the tape or CD and have the students answer the questions. Then have them go over the answers in pairs.

Answers: 1. Her computer broke down.
2. research and writing   3. They're unnecessary.   4. No   5. She'll give her old computer to her parents and she'll teach them how to use e-mail.

Tapescript

Ming: Dad, my computer broke down again. I think I need a new one.

Dad: A new one? You've only had this one for three years.

Ming: Yeah, I know. But it's out of date already. I need a faster one with more memory.

Dad: You and your electronic toys…

Ming: It's not a toy, Dad. I need a computer for my schoolwork. I use it every day for research, for writing, for…

Dad: …for meeting guys online…

Ming: Nooo, I don't do that, don't worry. Anyway, I was thinking…how about a laptop? For Christmas, maybe?

Dad: Why a laptop?

Ming: Because I can take it to class to take notes, take it to the library…A lot of students have them. Believe me, it would make my life so much easier.

Dad: I don't get it. When I was in college, I did just fine with a notebook and a pen.

Ming: I know, I know. And you typed your papers on a typewriter.

Dad: That's right. No software, no hardware, nothing to plug in.

Ming: Okay, then here's another reason you should get me a computer. If you get me a new one, you can take my old one. Then I'll teach you and mom how to use e-mail. And then we can talk online every day.

Dad: Hmm. You think you can teach an old dog new tricks?

Ming: Sure I can. Even you!

Stress

**4 Listening for Stressed Words. Page 257.
[on tape/CD]**

Read the instructions and point out the blanks below where students will fill in the missing stressed words. Then point out the words they will use to fill in the blanks and go over the list together. Remind students to do two things: repeat after the speaker and write in the missing words. Then play the tape or CD again and ask students to fill in the missing words. After that, ask two students to read the dialogue aloud while the rest of the students correct their answers. Discuss any items that more than five people got wrong. Then have students practice reading the completed dialogue with partners.

After You Listen

5 Vocabulary Review. Page 258.

Ask different students to read aloud one question each. Have students raise their hands if they hear a question they don't understand. Invite another student to explain. Then give students about five minutes to complete the activity. Ask students to share with the class anything surprising they learn doing the exercise.

Pronunciation

The American /t/

Play the tape or CD that explains and gives examples of how to pronounce the American /t/. Then read the explanation again and demonstrate the /d/ sound in the sentences given. You may wish to have students repeat them after you.

6 Listening for the American /t/. Page 259. [on tape/CD]

Play the tape or CD and have students follow along in their books. Then ask students to close their books as they listen to the sentences again. After that, have them repeat the sentences after the recording.

7 Pronouncing the American /t/. Page 259.

Read the instructions and remind students not to look at their partner's answers as they work together. Then help students find partners and complete the activity on their own. Move around the room modeling pronunciation as needed.

Talk It Over

Discussing Technology in the Home

Ask students to form groups and discuss the four questions. To keep students moving, set time limits for each part of the assignment. You might allow five minutes for making the list in part 1, and a maximum of five minutes for each of the remaining three parts. Let students know when the time is up and prompt them to move along.

Part 2 Recalling Main Ideas

Before You Listen

1 Prelistening Questions. Page 261.

Read and discuss the instructions and questions with the whole class. Then help students form pairs and complete the activity. Set a time limit of five to ten minutes. Review the responses with the whole class.

2 Vocabulary Preview. Page 261.

Read the instructions and have students complete the activity individually. As you review the answers with the class, ask students to raise their hands if they are still having difficulty with any of the terms. Invite other students to explain these terms in their own words.

Answers: 1. g 2. a 3. f 4. b 5. c 6. d 7. e

Listen

3 Taking Notes on Main Ideas. Page 261. [on tape/CD]

Read the instructions and ask students to tell you the three things they should take notes on: good points, bad points, and the future of electric cars.

Possible Answers:

Good points: doesn't use gas, doesn't pollute the air, quiet, can use it in carpool lanes when driving alone

Bad points: not very fast, can't go very far, seats only two people, costs $20,000, not fancy, no air conditioning, not convenient, battery runs out after 60 miles, top speed is 65 miles per hour

Future: improved batteries, more recharge stations, special parking places for electric cars, more people will drive them, the price will go down

Tapescript

Hi. My name is Dave Escobar and my neighbors think I'm crazy. In fact, my friends think so too. I just bought a car for $20,000 that can't go very fast or very far or seat more than two people. It's not fancy; no air conditioning or anything like that. Maybe you guessed it: I've bought an electric car. And you know what? I really love it.

First of all, I feel good about not using any gas and not polluting the air. You know, here in California half the air pollution is caused by cars. *Gasoline* powered cars. We have to do something about that. Actually, Californians are already doing something. A new law says that by 2003, 10 percent of cars sold here must be electric. That may not sound like much, but it's a start.

Sure, my electric car isn't as convenient as my old one. For one thing, the battery runs out after about 60 miles—for me, that's about every three days. So that means I have to recharge it often. And I can't just go to any gas station like I used to. I have to find a special recharging station and leave the car there for several hours. And as I said, it's not the fastest car I've ever had. Its top speed is only about 65 miles per hour—which is okay because I only drive it around the city.

One good thing, though. My electric car is quieter than gas-powered cars. So it's cutting down on *noise* pollution too. Oh, and another advantage. When traffic is heavy, I can use the special "car pool lanes" on the freeway even if I'm driving alone.

All in all, I think electric cars are the wave of the future. I hope in a few years we'll have improved batteries, more recharge stations, and maybe even special parking spaces for people who drive electric cars. Then the number of people who'll buy them will increase and, for sure, the price will come down. And then we'll see if my friends and neighbors still think I'm "crazy."

4 Reviewing Notes. Page 262.

Read the instructions and discuss the Hints for Remembering. Then point out the three main points and the three details under each main point in the outline. Ask students to use their notes to complete the outline.

Answers:

I. Advantages

   A. doesn't use gas

   B. doesn't cause air or noise pollution

   C. can use carpool lanes when driving alone

II. Disadvantages

   A. doesn't go fast or far

   B. is inconvenient

   C. carries only two people

III. Future Developments

   A. improved batteries

   B. special parking places

   C. lower prices

5 Listening for Specific Information. Page 262.

Explain that students can use this listening opportunity to check the outline they have made and fill in anything they left out.

After You Listen

6 Summarizing Main Ideas. Page 262.

Read the instructions and help students find partners to complete the activity with. As they work, listen to different pairs, helping them with any aspects of the task that are proving difficult for them. If time permits, have one or more students present their summary to the class.

7 Vocabulary Review. Page 263.
This is an open-ended oral activity that reviews key vocabulary words and provides listening and speaking practice. Set a time limit of perhaps ten minutes. At the end, invite pairs to share any interesting points they discussed.

> ### Culture Note
> Psychologists have discovered a condition they call "Internet Addiction" in some teenagers and older people in the United States. Internet addicts find it necessary to use the Internet for several hours a day every single day. Some of them sleep as little as three or four hours a night so that they can spend more time accessing Websites and chatting with friends on the Web. One negative effect of this condition is that some people substitute electronic contact for face-to-face relationships and have no real friends at all.

Part 3 Reading

Before You Read

1 Discussing Pictures. Page 263.
Arrange students in small groups. Ask them to look at the pictures on page 263 and answer the questions. After the groups have finished their discussions, have a volunteer from each group report their responses. List vocabulary on the board as students describe the pictures. Help summarize the responses. Encourage students to identify places where they have seen these symbols or might see them.

Sample Answers:
1. Atomic energy; mechanics, chemistry, electricity, communications, biology, mathematics, radiation,

telecommunications, medicine, computer, engineering (physics)
2. Answers will vary.

2 Thinking about the Answers. Page 263.
Point out the title of the reading selection "Everyday Uses of Technology" and the illustrations on page 263. Then read the questions aloud and call on volunteers to suggest any ideas they have. Remind students that these questions will help guide them as they read the selection and work on the exercises. Point out key vocabulary: *controversial, issues, technology, computer, communicate, computer technology, medical technology, advances.* As students suggest answers, record students' responses and ideas on an overhead project or on a large piece of paper. Encourage students to develop their own pre-reading questions about the reading selection. You may want to review these questions and responses later after students have read the selection.

Sample Answers:
1. Some controversial issues are: genetic engineering, cloning, nuclear energy, mass media, high-tech medical treatments.
2. Computers can improve someone's social life and ability to communicate because they do not need to speak directly to a person. It can be done through a computer. You can contact more people throughout the world.
3. In the home, computer technology can be found in microwave oven programs, stoves, and other appliances, entertainment equipment, and even in cars.
4. Medical technology has advanced with computers to maintain and send patient information, sensors for diagnosing and monitoring patients in emergency situations, machines for CAT scans and DSA scans, machines for sonography, thermography, and lasers.

3 Vocabulary Preview. Page 264.

As you read the words aloud, ask students to circle the ones they don't know. You may want to have volunteers suggest the meanings of the new words. Encourage students to look for the words in the following reading. After completing the reading selection, have students come back to this list and check their understanding of the circled words.

Read

4 Everyday Uses of Technology. Page 264. [on tape/CD]

Play the tape or CD as students follow along in their books. You may want to stop the tape or CD after paragraphs to ask comprehension questions and to point out key vocabulary words. Listen a second time as students read along.

After You Read

5 Review of Outline Organization. Page 266.

Read the instructions aloud. Review the purpose, organization, and divisions of an outline. Then have students complete the outline using words and information from the reading selection. Students should then select the best statement of the main idea of the reading selection. Go over the answers together.

Answers:

I. A. 1. In homes
   B. 2. Use to look for potential dates or
       mates
       a. personal ads with photos on
          screen
       c. online video connections

II. A. 1. Person writes message and sends it
    2. computer dials server (central
       computer than collects and
       distributes electronic information
   B. Advantage: messages sent in a few
      seconds

III. A. 1. a. microwave oven
            c. dishwasher
            d. washing machine and dryer

III. A. 2. b. Televisions
            c. VCRs
       4. Family microcomputer

IV. Computers in medical sciences
    A. Computer use in ambulance by EMTs
       3. Technicians get advice on how to
          keep patient alive
    B. Doctors use to examine body
       2. b. Temperature (thermography)
          c. Radio waves
          d. Radio-active tracers
       3. Surgical procedures
          a. Cameras and lasers for heart
             surgery

Main idea of reading: 1

6 Understanding the Main Idea. Page 267.

Read the instructions. Review the difference between implied statements (inferences) and direct statements and talk about how writers may use them both. Then ask students to complete the exercise by identifying items that the writer stated or suggested and those items that the writer did not say or imply. Then discuss the answers with the whole class. Ask volunteers to point out parts of the reading that support their responses.

Answers: 1. O   2. X   3. X   4. O   5. X
6. O

7 Special Uses of Punctuation. Page 268.

After reading the instructions together, have students look for other examples of the punctuation and italics in the reading selection. Tell students to work individually to write the words or phrases to complete the sentences in Exercise 7. Go over the answers with the group.

Answers:

2. "Electronic bulletin board": a place for
   posting electronic messages

"Chat room": a place where people can meet and talk through the computer

Computer uses can put messages for others to read and read other people's messages. They can also talk to many different people about topics of interest to them.

3. "Personals": ads that people place on the computer.

"Digitized video segments": electronic forms of motion pictures.

"Live online video connections": movie connections that are broadcast through computers.

Computer uses might "meet" in nontraditional ways because they will not meet face-to-face or speak person-to-person. They can meet even though they are thousands of miles away from each other.

4. "E-mail": electronic mail—letters and messages.

"Servers": receive and give out information.

Computers "deliver" information from senders to receivers because the computer collects the information from the senders and stores and distributes the information to the receiver.

5. "Computer chips": small pieces of computer parts.

"Program": a person gives a plan to a computer—he or she teaches the computer to do something.

A household that is "programmed" with "computer chips" might begin making the coffee at a particular time, cooking a meal at a set time, washing dishes, washing and drying clothes. The machines would be programmed to begin their tasks at specific times.

6. "Sensors": things to read feelings.

"Slice through": CAT and DSA take pictures that are cross sections of the body and organs. They can take a view straight through as a knife would cut.

"Surgical procedure": a way of doing something in surgery.

Science is advancing in medical investigation and healthcare through the use of sensors to record how a patient is feeling and parts of the boy operating. Doctors can use machines to see the inside of organs and to identify exactly where a problem might be. They have many surgical procedures that don't require cutting into the body, so these procedures are safer and don't create other problems.

7. "Interactive media": This means that the media has an effect on the viewer or listener. The people will respond to the media.

"Genetic engineering": designing and building genes.

"High-tech" equipment: tools, machines, and appliances that use high technology (computers).

Some controversial issues and questions raised by "interactive media" are privacy, the controlling of minds, changing family life and personal relationships. In "genetic engineering", there questions about the effect the new genetically changed foods on people's health. There are questions about whether high-tech medical treatments will also be able to improve the health and happiness of people's lives along with letting them live for a longer time.

Discussing the Reading

8 Small Group Discussion. Page 270.
This activity allows students to use the vocabulary from the reading to talk about their own opinions and concerns about technology and science. Arrange students in groups of four. Set a time limit for the small group discussions. As groups talk about their answers together,

circulate among the groups, listening and giving assistance as needed. When all groups are finished, ask a volunteer from each group to summarize their ideas.

Answers will vary.

Part 4 Writing

Before You Write

Exploring Ideas

1 Discussing Computer Networks and Newsgroups. Page 271.

Have students read the article silently. Then ask volunteers to summarize the article in their own words. You can use the questions that follow the article to lead a discussion about computer networks and newsgroups.

2 Building Vocabulary. Page 272.
Sample Answers for Chart:
Nouns: cyberspace, Internet, privacy
Verbs: connect, boot, attach

1. upload
2. network
3. search engine
4. access
5. download
6. censor

Organizing Ideas

Internet Netiquette

3 Page 273.
Answers:
Information that should be deleted from the first article: The U.S. mail system has gotten so bad that I don't receive mail need, only stupid

advertisements. Now the same thing is happening to the Internet!

The last paragraph of the second message could be deleted in its entirety, as it strays too far from the topic.

4 Page 275.
Students should be able to see that the deleted information is not directly related to the discussion.

5 Page 275.
Answers:
The main idea of Cindy's message is: "It would be impossible to keep advertising out of the Internet." As a constructive suggestion, she proposes that advertisers and "consumers" of the Internet get together on-line to work out a solution that is agreeable to everybody.

6 Page 275.
Students' answers will vary.

Supporting Your Opinion

7 Page 275.
Answers:
Supporting example: Special discussion groups share information about different products.

Supporting reason: One of the freedoms we have is the freedom to make money.

8 Page 275.
Have students share their work with the class to elicit peer feedback. Evaluate the reasons and examples students give to support their opinion. Students should be careful not to support their opinions with unsubstantiated statements, but factual information or well-reasoned arguments.

9 Page 275.
Answers will vary.

Write

Developing Cohesion and Style

Unifying Your Writing with Synonyms and Pronouns

10 Page 276.
   Answers:
   1. electronic
   2. access
   3. censor
   4. criminal

Language for Giving Opinions and Suggestions

11 Page 277.
   Answer:
   In Cindy's message, she could rephrase a sentence near the end of the first paragraph in the following way to make it more polite: "We should make realistic rules to control advertising on the Net, not ban it completely."

   Answers will vary.

Writing the First Draft

12 Page 277.
   Have students write their first drafts of an e-mail message. Remind them to start with a topic line, give an opinion in the message, and support it with reasons. They should use synonyms and pronouns to unify their paragraphs. Students should include their topic line from Activity 9 and their opinion sentences from Activity 6.

Edit and Revise

Editing Practice

13 Spelling and Grammar in Computer Messages. Page 277.
   Sample Answer: Your point that the Internet is not like all other media is a good one. That is exactly why it should be given special treatment. If we follow Mr. Janovic's advice, the Internet will no longer be fun, interesting, or even useful. The Internet is not for children; it is for adults. If people want a Sesame-Street version of the Internet, they should make their own Net and not ruin ours.

Editing Your Writing

14 Editing Using a Checklist. Page 278.
   Have students make different editorial passes on their paragraph, using the checklist in the student book.

15 Peer Editing. Page 278.
   Use the suggestions in the student book to conduct peer conferences. Give pairs of students time to exchange papers and read each other's work. Students can write comments and suggestions in the margins of their partners' papers. Pairs can then reconvene and give each other verbal feedback, explaining the main points of their written comments. Afterwards, students can rewrite their messages, incorporating the feedback as appropriate.

Writing the Second Draft

16 Page 278.
   Have students rewrite their e-mails, based on the suggestions of their peers and teacher, as well as their own edits from Activity 14. Have students assess whether they feel their writing is improving.

Part 5 Grammar

A. Introduction to the Passive Voice

Write this sentence on the board. Ask students to tell you the subject and the object.

> *Lightning hit the tree.*

Then write this sentence on the board and ask students to tell you the subject.

> *The tree was hit by lightning.*

Write these sentences on the board and ask students to tell you which are passive voice and how they know.

> *The Internet is used by many people.*
>
> *The Internet is fast and convenient.*
>
> *Millions of e-mail messages are sent everyday.*
>
> *I often receive e-mail from my friends.*

Call on students to read the examples and the notes in the Grammar Chart on page 279.

1   Page 279.

Read the instructions and the examples. Have the class work together.

Answers: 2. A, P 3. P, A 4. P, A 5. A, P

B.   The Passive Voice: Uses

Write these sentences on the board.

> *The bank was robbed last weekend.*
>
> *I was arrested for speeding.*
>
> *The garbage is picked up every day.*
>
> *The dishes weren't washed yesterday.*

Tell the students to look at the uses of the passive voice in the Grammar Chart on page 280 and decide which use applies to each of the sentences.

C.   The Passive Voice with the Simple Present and the Simple Past Tenses

Write these sentences on the board.

> *We wash the floor every day.*
>
> *The floor is washed every day.*

Ask the students to tell you which sentence is in the passive voice. Change *floor* to *floors* and ask them what other changes need to be made.

> *The floors are washed every day.*

Then ask them to make the sentence negative.

> *The floors aren't washed every day.*

Begin the sequence above again with this past passive sentence:

> *The school was built in two months.*

Have the students change *school* to *schools* and then to the negative.

2   Page 280.

Read the instructions and the example. Have the class work together to do 2–5. Then have students work individually or in pairs to complete the exercise.

Answers: 2. linked 3. were sent
4. discovered 5. were taken 6. remained
7. was launched 8. became 9. orbit
10. were developed 11. was followed
12. links 13. is used 14. are made
15. are researched

Chapter 10

Video Activities: Sight for the Blind

Before You Watch
Read the instructions. Have students read the two questions. Discuss the first question as a class. Put students in small groups to discuss the second question.

Watch [on video]
Read the instructions. Have students read the items before having them watch the video. Play the video. Give students time to answer the questions. Play the video again, if necessary. Go over the answers as a class.

Answers:
1. Jerry is a blind man who got his sight back. Craig is a blind man who would like to see again.
2. It helps him see. He can see light.
3. 62, 25
4. 1

Watch Again [on video]
Read the instructions. Have students read the items before having them watch the video. Play the video and have students complete the exercise. Put students in pairs to check their answers. Replay the video if needed.

Answers: 1. c 2. c 3. a 4. b 5. b

After You Watch
Read the instructions. Put students in pairs to complete the story. Then have students read the story out loud.

Answers: were invented, could be used, were invented, was painted, invented, were divided, were made, have become, were developed, were made, could not be worn, became, were introduced, are worn

Placement Test

Listening/Speaking Section

Part 1 Listening

Listening 1

Circle the letter of the best response to each question.

Example

Who do you think are the two people talking?

a. A waiter and waitress working in a coffee shop.

b. An uncle and his nephew.

c. An aunt and her nephew.

d. An uncle and his niece.

1. Where does this take place?

a. In someone's house.

b. At work.

c. In a car.

d. In a coffee shop.

2. When does this take place?

a. After work.

b. Before work.

c. In the morning.

d. In the afternoon.

3. What does Mary want in her tea?

a. Milk.

b. Lemon juice.

c. Milk and lemon juice.

d. The information was not given in this listening passage.

4. What does Uncle Wayne want to drink?

    a. Milk.

    b. Milk and lemon.

    c. Lemon.

    d. This information was not included in the listening.

5. Uncle Wayne said that there was one bag left. What was in the bag?

    a. Lemons.

    b. A string attached to the label.

    c. Tea with little pieces of lemon.

    d. Tea.

Listening 2

Circle the letter of the best response to each question.

Example
How many radio announcers are there?

    a. 2 male and 1 female announcers.

    b. 2 male announcers.

    (c.) 1 male and 1 female announcer.

    d. 2 female announcers.

1. Based on the listening, what do you think XRKY is?

    a. A radio station.

    b. A TV station.

    c. A TV and radio station.

    d. A store that sells radios.

2. How many animals are missing?

    a. 1 dog and 2 cats.

    b. 2 dogs and 1 cat.

    c. 2 dogs and 2 cats.

    d. 1 dog and 1 cat.

3. Which of the animals were stolen?

    a. None of the animals were stolen.

    b. All of the animals were stolen.

    c. Oxen, the German Shepherd.

    d. Winston, the wire-haired terrier.

4. Who had a seeing-eye dog?

    a. Mr. Wilson.

    b. Mrs. Lincoln.

    c. The radio announcer.

    d. Mrs. Thompson.

5. What are listeners supposed to do if they find one of the dogs?

    a. Call the radio station.

    b. Call the police station.

    c. Call the local humane society.

    d. They don't say.

Listening 3

Circle the letter of the best word or words to complete each sentence.

Example

The speaker is _____.

    (a.) a man

    b. a woman

    c. a college student

    d. You can't tell if the speaker has a male or female voice.

1. This is an excerpt from a lecture in a _____.

    a. nutrition class

    b. business or marketing class

    c. supermarket staff room

    d. one-day seminar

2. Product placement is something students _____.

   a. should pay attention to in this class

   b. shouldn't pay attention to in this class

   c. don't need to know when they go to supermarkets

   d. need not pay attention to

3. The professor talked about _____.

   a. product placement outside of the United States

   b. product placement both in and out of the United States

   c. product placement in the United States

   d. products you shouldn't buy

4. The professor gave _____.

   a. candy as the only example

   b. candy as one of the examples

   c. examples taken directly from the textbook

   d. examples that would be on the test

5. The professor said that _____.

   a. all U.S. stores follow the same process for placing items in stores

   b. many U.S. stores place expensive items at eye level

   c. most U.S. stores place inexpensive items at eye level

   d. no U.S. stores place items at eye level

Part 2 Speaking

Look at the following questions. Circle the letter of the best response to each question.

Example

Do you know where I can get some stamps?

a. At the post office on Main Street.

b. At Marvin's Bakery.

c. I get three letters a week.

d. I need three stamps.

1. Why do you need to see the doctor today?

a. I am a nurse.

b. Dr. Bach will be in at 9:00.

c. I think I broke my elbow.

d. I have some medicine.

2. What do you eat on your diet?

a. Water is the least fattening food of all.

b. Apples, bananas, and oranges.

c. I need to lose weight.

d. Nutrition books and diet magazines.

3. How much is the subway fare?

a. Yes, I take the bus.

b. The ride is an hour long.

c. The ride costs one dollar.

d. The rides cost one dollar and ten cents.

4. What do you do?

a. Accounting does pay well.

b. I account.

c. I studied accounting.

d. I'm an accountant.

5. What is Mr. Hodge's problem?

  a. He is very happy.

  b. She is sad.

  c. He lost his job.

  d. He just won a million dollars.

6. What are you writing?

  a. An e-mail message.

  b. She's writing an e-mail message.

  c. Writing is hard work.

  d. I haven't gotten any of your writing.

7. Has she ever been there before?

  a. She's ever been there.

  b. He's been once.

  c. She's never been there.

  d. Where has she been?

8. What's your last name?

  a. My first name is Olga.

  b. Last names are often difficult to pronounce.

  c. Your last name is Jones.

  d. My family name is Smythe.

9. Where did Mildred buy her new dress?

  a. There are a couple of stores on 4th St.

  b. They have dresses on sale.

  c. At a cute little boutique.

  d. Sales are a good place to buy dresses.

10. Could you tell me where Hilda's Gym is?

  a. Hilda has owned the gym for a year.

  b. It's at 9th and Oak.

  c. I have trouble asking for directions.

  d. Gyms are often located in suburbs.

11. **Do you think that this jacket fits?**

    a. It's a beautiful color.

    b. She thinks the pants fit.

    c. They have three different sizes.

    d. It's a bit snug.

12. **Where were you on Saturday night?**

    a. I talked with my mother two days ago.

    b. In time for the jazz concert.

    c. The downtown area is beautiful.

    d. In a town near the mountains.

13. **What are your preferences?**

    a. They prefer going to the movies.

    b. I haven't really thought about it.

    c. I have no references.

    d. It's either black or white.

14. **How difficult is it to make an apple pie?**

    a. My dog eats apple pie.

    b. My mother says that it's pretty easy.

    c. She doesn't know.

    d. Apple pie tastes so much better than cherry pie.

15. **Did you understand what was on the test?**

    a. The first items were simple and the others were far too difficult.

    b. I hate exams.

    c. The professor gives wonderful lectures.

    d. I wonder how many people passed?

Reading Section

Part 1 Determining Meaning and Usage from Context

Circle the letter of the best word or words to complete each sentence.

Example

The patient was extremely _____ and had to be subdued.

    (a.) agitated

    b. sad

    c. lonely

    d. late

1. **Children who wish to _____ or achieve greatness must have drive and work hard.**

    a. drive a car

    b. fail

    c. excel

    d. go home

2. **Poodles, German Shepherds, Golden Retrievers are different types of _____.**

    a. canines

    b. felines

    c. dogs

    d. a and c

3. **If you are having trouble logging onto the Internet you might want to check out your _____.**

    a. modem

    b. video monitor

    c. word processing program

    d. none of the above

4. **Spending time reading newspapers and _____ is a good way to keep up with current events.**

    a. historical novels

    b. ancient texts

    c. classic books

    d. other periodicals

5. **She was a very _____ young child who could read university texts by the time that she was nine years old.**

    a. precocious

    b. illiterate

    c. developmentally delayed

    d. inadequate

Part 2 Reading Comprehension

Reading 1

The Visually Impaired

Individuals who are blind, or those who have low vision, as well as those with less severe visual impairments, have benefited from a variety of key developments that have occurred in Europe and the United States during the past couple of centuries. Low vision refers to individuals who have very limited sight and it does not have anything to do with whether items are high or low to the ground. The effort to assist the visually challenged began in the late 1700s, when a gentleman by the name of Victor Hauly committed himself to teaching the blind. This noble act occurred after he witnessed people being paraded around as court jesters or struggling on the streets as beggars. Mr. Hauly founded a residential school for blind children that featured teaching children how to read with raised print. Following the precedence set by Mr. Hauly, Mr. Samuel Gridley Howe founded the world renowned Perkins School for the Blind in 1821 in the U.S. A variety of curricula and methods were both piloted and refined at the Perkins School. Anne Sullivan and her well-known pupil, Helen Keller, spent several years at the Perkins School.

A little over a dozen years after the establishment of the Perkins School, a French man named Louis Braille created the Braille's system. The Braille system, as it is now referred to, is probably the most successful method for teaching touch-reading and has survived the test of time. It is simple, utilizing a six-dot cell system, but should never be perceived as simplistic.

In the second half of the nineteenth century, one of the major advances for the visually impaired was not targeted at blind or very low vision children but rather at children who appeared on the surface to have "normal" vision. In the 1860s, a Dutch ophthalmologist invented or developed the Snellen chart. This was an important creation since it was and currently still is the most widely used device for visual acuity screening of school age children.

The first major development for the severely visually impaired took place between 1900 and 1913. Classes in public schools were opened in Boston, Chicago, and Cleveland for children who were blind or had low vision. This was a significant development since several local school systems began to recognize that the government had an obligation to provide education for children with severe visual impairments. Following the establishment of the public school classes east of the Mississippi River, other school systems followed suit.

The next trend to provide blind individuals with government supported services occurred in 1932 when the U.S. Library of Congress made talking books available to all legally blind individuals. Also in the 1930s, a California school district employed itinerant teachers to help students with visual impairments function in regular education classrooms. During this time period, also in the U.S., there was the inauguration of orientation and mobility services including a white cane to help people function in the community.

In the second half of the 20th century, the Perkins braillewriter was invented at the Perkins School for the Blind. The braillewriter made it possible for individuals sitting at simple machines to transcribe books into a touch-reading format. This increased literacy among those with severe visual impairments. It is hoped that the advances for the visually impaired continue well into the 21st century.

Circle the letter of the best word or words to complete each sentence.

Example

The best title for this article could possibly be:

a. Key Developments Impacting those without Visual Impairments

b. Key Developments Benefiting those with Visual Impairments

c. The Visually Challenged in Your Community

d. People Who Help the Visually Impaired

1. **Individuals with low vision** _____.

   a. can only see things that are low to the ground

   b. have very minimal sight and can only see things that are low to the ground

   c. have very minimal sight

   d. none of the above

2. **There have been certain residential schools founded for the blind. These include** _____.

   a. the school founded by Mr. Hauly

   b. the school founded by Mr. Perkins

   c. the schools founded by Mr. Gridley Howe and Mr. Perkins

   d. the schools founded Mr. Hauly and Mr. Gridley Howe

3. All of the advances mentioned in this article took place in _____.

   a. Europe

   b. the United States

   c. the United States and Europe

   d. none of the above

4. The Snellen chart is an important development _____.

   a. because it helped children who were completely blind and had no vision

   b. because it only helped low vision children

   c. because it helped to identify children who both have visual impairments and attend regular public schools

   d. because an ophthalmologist was involved in the creation

5. Talking books are only available for those _____.

   a. who are legally blind

   b. who can not be legally blind

   c. who have hearing aids and are legally blind

   d. who have any visual impairments, even minor ones

Reading 2

The Critic's Corner

This week, I will be writing about a topic near and dear to my heart as well as the heart of my children. Don't underestimate the power or value of children's literature or "kiddie lit" as it is sometimes called. Many individuals find it surprising that children's literature, even books with little text, frequently encompass social themes that span from environmental studies to psychology or sociology. For example, "The Giving Tree" by Shel Silverstein is a very simple but elegant black and white picture book that tells the story of a boy and a tree that are mutually dependent upon one another. As the story unfolds, the man exploits the tree, while the tree remains gracious and benevolent towards the man. This book makes a powerful statement concerning man's disregard and downright callousness towards the environment.

Judith Viorst, a satirist, has written a charming picture book entitled "The Terrible, Awful, Horrible, No Good, Very Bad Day." Her work, illustrated with black and white drawings, deals with the frustrations confronting a very young boy. Through the voice of a child, she reveals the emotional issues impacting children including sibling rivalry, parental approval, and unrealistic teacher expectations. This book is invaluable for those wishing to study the psychological makeup of young children, mainly boys but also girls.

Another book with a minimal amount of print worth checking out is "A Chair for My Mother" by Vera Williams. The story of a family who has lost all of their belongings in a fire is told, in part, through brightly colored illustrations accompanied by text. The community pulls together to get the family back on their feet. In addition, the family helps itself reach a goal through hard work and stick-to-itiveness. This book addresses some key sociological support systems, including the extended family and the community.

So the next time you are in a bookstore or library, take a deep breath and a moment to stop and browse the children's book section.

Based on the article, select the best answer to each question.

Example

What is the main topic of this article?

    (a.) Children's Literature

    b. Remedies for Social Problems

    c. Environmental Studies

    d. none of the above

1. How does the writer of the article feel about children's literature?

    a. The writer believes that it is a frivolous genre that should be dismissed.

    b. The writer believes that it has a great deal of merit.

    c. It isn't clear.

    d. The writer feels that it should be rejected from people's hearts.

2. In the first paragraph the words *mutually dependent* are used. In this context, what does *mutually dependent* mean?

    a. Both sides do NOT need one another.

    b. One side needs the other.

    c. Both sides need one another.

    d. Everyone is dependent upon the environment.

3. Which book deals with issues impacting the environment?

    a. "The Giving Tree"

    b. "A Chair for My Mother"

    c. both a and b

    d. none of the above

4. Which books are illustrated with black and white drawings?

    a. "The Giving Tree"

    b. "The Terrible, Horrible, No Good, Very Bad Day"

    c. "A Chair for my Mother"

    d. a and b

5. According to the article, what can one assume?

    a. The writer has some familiarity with children's literature.

    b. The writer has no familiarity with children's literature.

    c. The writer doesn't want to read any more children's books.

    d. The writer checks out a lot of books from the library.

Writing Section

Part 1 Sentence Completion

Circle the letter of the best word, words, or phrase to complete each sentence. Be sure to look at the contents of each sentence.

Example

I want the pretty necklace _____.

(a.) that is on sale

b. who is on sale

c. what is on sale

d. where it is on sale

1. The restaurant has excellent food, _____.

a. so I never eat there

b. so I always eat there

c. I never eat there

d. I always eat there

2. I want to go to Mexico, _____.

a. but I have lots of money

b. but I don't speak Spanish fluently

c. so I speak Spanish fluently

d. I speak Spanish fluently

3. There's a movie theater _____ the left hand side of the street.

a. at

b. in

c. on

d. off

4. Louise screamed, _____

a. There's a fire upstairs!

b. "There's a fire upstairs!"

c. "That there is a fire upstairs!"

d. There's "a fire upstairs!"

5. She ate lunch _____.

   a. as soon she finished writing the report

   b. when the report ends

   c. while the report ends

   d. as soon as the meeting ended

6. The teacher_____ tells jokes in class is very popular.

   a. what

   b. whom

   c. that

   d. there

7. Another easy-to-prepare dish is quiche, _____.

   a. what is wonderful for lunch

   b. is brunch

   c. is wonderful for brunch

   d. which is wonderful for brunch

8. _____ I broke my leg, I have had a great deal of difficulty trying to get around.

   a. When

   b. Which

   c. Since

   d. What

9. She drinks a lot of plain water _____.

   a. because she desperately wants to gain weight

   b. because she desperately wants to lose weight

   c. but she desperately wants to lose weight

   d. when she desperately wants to gain weight

10. I can't go out for dinner tonight _____.

   a. because storms often come

   b. because of a storm that is due in at about eight o'clock

   c. because I love to go out for dinner

   d. because there will be a storm tomorrow at dinner time

Part 2 Organization

Read the following sentences. Circle the letter of the best sentence to follow the sentence given.

Example

This morning we ate the most wonderful waffles, brimming with blueberries, for breakfast.

    a. I like meat and potatoes.

    b. I eat blueberries every night.

    (c.) My husband made some wonderful French roast coffee to go with the waffles.

    d. I don't like coffee.

1. Children often have trouble getting up in the morning to go to school.

    a. For example, children love to get up in the morning.

    b. This probably wouldn't happen if they did not stay up as late at night.

    c. Once children get to school they can take naps.

    d. Children always like going to school and are anxious to be punctual.

2. The Mexican government wishes to curtail pollution in Mexico City.

    a. They will try a number of different approaches to increase this problem.

    b. I don't worry about pollution very much.

    c. The people who are north of the Mexican border think that their own pollution is severe.

    d. A wide variety of strategies impacting everyone from motorists to industrial polluters have been introduced.

3. It is very simple to make microwave popcorn.

    a. Popcorn always gets stuck between my teeth.

    b. I don't know how much popcorn costs.

    c. I buy popcorn when I go to the movies.

    d. All you have to do is know how to push the buttons on the outside of the microwave oven.

4. I firmly believe that children under the age of 21 should be prohibited from smoking.

    a. I think that smoking is something that young people enjoy doing.

    b. I really don't have any strong convictions one way or the other about teenage smoking.

    c. I was very poor and could not afford to do anything not even buy cigarettes for my mother.

    d. My heart aches when I see a teenager light up a cigarette.

5. Thank you so much for the gorgeous necklace.

    a. You should have bought something that was a little more expensive.

    b. Necklaces always look better on women who are much younger than I am.

    c. I have worn it several times and always receive compliments.

    d. Next time can we please go shopping for necklaces together?

Part 3 Writing

Your teacher will tell you if you should write a paragraph or an essay.

Write a Paragraph

Select one of the following topics and write a paragraph. Feel free to make some notes on a separate sheet of paper before you start writing.

1. Think of all of the different foods that you like to eat when you are at home. Please write about a food that you would serve to your guests.

2. Think about the different places that people go to on vacation. Please write about the location where you would like to go for your vacation.

3. Think about your favorite time of day. You might want to consider whether or not you are a morning or night person. Please write about your favorite time of day.

Write an Essay

Select one of the following topics. Write an essay about your selection.

1. Think about the different academic subjects that one can study in school. Think about one that you really liked and one that you did not like as well. Please write about a subject that you liked and compare it with one that you did not like as well. Be sure to comment on aspects such as the level of difficulty, the quality of instruction, etc.

2. Think about different people who have helped you over time and made a difference in your life. Please write about how they helped you and what your life might have been like if they had not been part of it.

3. Think about the different modes of transportation such as walking versus taking the subway. Please write about a mode of transportation that is quick and compare it to one that is very slow. Be sure to comment on the advantages and disadvantages of each.

Grammar Section

Part 1 Complete the Sentence

Circle the letter of the best word or words to complete each statement.

Example

I _____ from Boston.

   a. am

   b. were

   c. are

   d. is

1. Dick is the _____ determined person I have ever met.

   a. much

   b. most

   c. more

   d. many

2. She's a doctor and her life is never _____.

   a. bored

   b. boring

   c. bore

   d. board

3. Yes, they _____.

   a. haven't

   b. hasn't

   c. has

   d. have

4. What does Natasha _____?

   a. liked

   b. likes

   c. like to

   d. like

5. **Then, _____ June to September, it's very rainy.**

   a. in

   b. on

   c. at

   d. from

6. **Yes, she _____.**

   a. is

   b. not

   c. isn't

   d. doesn't

7. **The drugstore is to_____ the movie theater.**

   a. next

   b. the left of

   c. left of

   d. left and next

8. **Louisa loved the new book, and José _____.**

   a. also does

   b. does too

   c. did too

   d. didn't too

9. **You went to the movies last night, _____?**

   a. did not you

   b. didn't you

   c. don't you

   d. doesn't you

10. **Yes, he _____ at home last night.**

    a. were

    b. was

    c. weren't

    d. wasn't

11. **Excuse me, I need to buy _____ salt shakers.**

    a. some

    b. an

    c. a

    d. this

12. **Laura doesn't have _____ accounting experience.**

    a. any

    b. some

    c. the background in

    d. knowledge of

13. **Where are they _____?**

    a. gone to go

    b. go

    c. go to going

    d. going to go

14. **Yesterday, he said that his train will _____ at midnight.**

    a. arriving

    b. arrived

    c. arrive

    d. arrives

15. **They'll drop _____ their neighbor's house.**

    a. in

    b. on

    c. at

    d. by

16. **I have a doctor's appointment _____ November 10.**

    a. at

    b. on

    c. in

    d. from

17. I've _____ the Statue of Liberty.

    a. visited often

    b. visited recently

    c. recently visited

    d. ever visited

18. Mary doesn't like Indian food, _____.

    a. and either does Bob

    b. and Bob does too

    c. and Bob doesn't neither

    d. and Bob doesn't either

19. She didn't like the movie, _____?

    a. did she

    b. does she

    c. didn't she

    d. doesn't she

20. Her lemonade was _____ than his.

    a. more sweet

    b. sweeter

    c. many sweeter

    d. sweetest

21. We _____ them many times.

    a. spoke

    b. have spoken

    c. spoken to

    d. have spoken to

22. They haven't _____ anything being said.

    a. understand

    b. understood

    c. understanding

    d. understands

23. **Will you look _____ my pet parrots while I am on vacation?**
    a. on
    b. of
    c. in
    d. after

24. **My Aunt Elizabeth _____ the convent in 1985.**
    a. entered to
    b. has entered
    c. entered
    d. entered in

25. **She bathed _____ in a vat originally used to make wine.**
    a. himself
    b. herself
    c. hers
    d. she

Part 2 Find the Errors

Look at each item and select the letter below the word(s) containing the error.

Example

One of the reasons that I love him is that he <u>go</u> <u>to</u> visit <u>his</u> mother <u>every</u> Sunday.
         (a) b   c   d

1. The <u>latest</u> trends <u>in</u> fashion <u>designing</u> <u>was</u> revealed in the magazine *Sharp Dresser*.
       a   b   c   d

2. <u>This</u> afternoon, I received <u>an</u> extremely <u>thoughtfully</u> e-mail message from a <u>charming</u> young man.
    a   b   c   d

3. Mary <u>doesn't</u> <u>like</u> watching football <u>matches</u>, and <u>either</u> do I.
       a   b   c   d

4. Statistics <u>can be</u> very <u>misleading</u>, depending upon <u>who</u> presents them and how <u>their</u> presented.

                      a   b   c   d

5. She <u>adored</u> hamsters <u>and</u> guinea pigs <u>but</u> detested <u>mouses</u>.

        a   b   c   d

6. <u>No one</u> was more <u>surprising</u> than Henry <u>to discover</u> that his riding buddy had <u>become</u> engaged.

      a   b   c   d

7. <u>The</u> <u>fever</u> had not yet <u>broke</u> when the doctor <u>came</u> to visit.

   a   b   c   d

8. All <u>of the</u> students <u>believe</u> that they <u>should</u> get perfect <u>score</u> on their papers.

        a   b   c   d

9. <u>When</u> the telephone <u>ring</u>, I <u>always</u> race <u>to answer</u> it.

   a   b   c   d

10. Lisa is <u>happiest</u> <u>than</u> any of the <u>other</u> teen-age girls in <u>the</u> class.

        a   b   c   d

11. Tonight my mother will have a <u>big</u> dinner and she will tell everyone <u>to</u> eat <u>as many</u> as they want

                                   a   b   c

  or to have <u>as many</u> servings as they like.

           d

12. They <u>would</u> <u>have</u> gone to the concert, <u>so</u> it started <u>to rain</u> cats and dogs.

        a   b   c   d

13. If I <u>don't</u> have <u>none</u> money, I won't be able to do <u>any</u> shopping <u>this</u> weekend.

        a   b   c   d

14. <u>Last</u> semester Dr. Miller taught <u>a course</u> <u>who</u> was <u>nicknamed</u> Love and Glory.

   a   b   c   d

15. I love sweets <u>too</u> <u>much</u> <u>that</u> I'm ten <u>pounds</u> overweight.

        a   b   c   d

Name _____ Date _____

1. Listen and circle the reduced form. (10 points)

1. a. do b. to c. you

2. a. you b. do c. are

3. a. you b. do c. just

4. a. do b. can c. have

5. a. just b. have c. are

2. Make a conversation. Number the sentences in the correct order. (5 points)

___ C: You, too.

___ N: That's me!

_1_ A: Neil, this is my friend, Carlos.

___ C: Oh, yeah. You always sit in front.

___ N: Hi, Carlos. Nice to meet you.

___ N: We're in the same biology lecture, aren't we?

3. Write *T* for true statements and *F* for false statements. (5 points)

___ 1. Most colleges and universities don't want international students.

___ 2. International students only go to colleges and universities in the United States.

___ 3. International students bring different customs, ideas, and opinions to the schools.

___ 4. Most colleges and universities have resource centers, libraries, and other facilities for their students.

___ 5. All instructors dress casually and teach in a relaxed atmosphere.

4. Circle the letter of the correct word. (5 points)

1. Tuition _____ the fee or charge for instruction.

   a. are   b. is   c. pay

2. International students _____ hard.

   a. study   b. studies   c. is

3. Where _____ the Physical Education Office?

   a. are   b. is   c. find

4. Students with the highest scores on tests _____ the best universities.

   a. are   b. attend   c. attends

5. There _____ many international students in the United States.

   a. are   b. is   c. be

5. Complete the following sentences. (10 points)

1. A paragraph is a string of sentences organized around a single _____.

   a. word

   b. image

   c. topic

2. A topic sentence gives the _____ of a paragraph.

   a. conclusion

   b. main idea

   c. supporting detail

3. A fact is a _____.

   a. true statement

   b. popular idea

   c. idiomatic phrase

4. An opinion is a _____.

   a. personal belief

   b. topic sentence

   c. newspaper article

5. You can use the word *and* to connect _____.

   a. paragraphs

   b. phrases and sentences

   c. content and form

6. Match the questions with the appropriate answers. (5 points)

____ 1. What's your name?   a. He's over there.

____ 2. Who's that?   b. No, he's not.

____ 3. Where's your friend?   c. Andreas.

____ 4. Is he a history major?   d. No, he doesn't.

____ 5. Does he like school?   e. It's my sister.

7. Rewrite the following sentences in the negative. (10 points)

1. I like sugar in my coffee.

   _____

2. They are in the library.

   _____

3. This cookie is good!

   _____

4. She lives near me.

   _____

5. They have their books.

   _____

Name _____   **Date** _____

1. Listen and choose the correct answer. (10 points)

1. What does Don want to do?

    a. go swimming   b. go skiing   c. go snorkeling

2. What will the temperature be?

    a. in the 60s   b. 66 degrees   c. 60 degrees

3. Will it rain tomorrow?

    a. yes   b. no   c. maybe

4. What is true about Carrie?

    a. She never swims.   b. She can't swim.   c. She doesn't like to swim.

5. Does Don want to go swimming?

    a. yes   b. no   c. maybe

2. Choose the letter of the word that best completes each sentence. (5 points)

| a. hit the trail | b. muddy | c. humid | d. overnight | e. clear |

1. In spring the ground is often _____.

2. Let's _____ at sunrise!

3. _____ weather is best for sailing.

4. I like to stay home where there's air conditioning when it's _____.

5. It may get very cold _____.

3. Write *T* for true statements and *F* for false statements. (5 points)

___ 1. Weather conditions do not influence people's health, thinking, or feelings.

___ 2. Strong winds in Russia increase the number of strokes and heart attacks.

___ 3. Colds and flu are diseases that increase during warm weather.

___ 4. In northern regions, people feel less tired in the winter.

___ 5. Seasonal Affective Disorder may be caused by too little sun and light during the daytime.

4. Circle the letter of the correct word. (5 points)

1. The earth's climate _____ slowly.

   a. are changing   b. is changing   c. change

2. Global warming and El Niño _____ an effect on the earth and weather.

   a. has   b. is having   c. are having

3. The temperature of the earth _____ up.

   a. going   b. is going   c. are going

4. Cars and factories _____ more carbon dioxide into the air.

   a. are putting   b. is putting   c. putting

5. We _____ some of the problems.

   a. are causing   b. is causing   c. causing

5. Complete the following sentences. (10 points)

1. An adjective is a word that describes a _____.

   a. noun

   b. pronoun

   c. verb

2. The words *on*, *in*, and *under* are _____.

   a. verbs

   b. articles

   c. prepositions

3. *Near the door* is _____.

   a. a prepositional phrase

   b. a sentence

   c. a preposition

4. The words *a* and *an* are _____.

   a. indefinite articles

   b. definite articles

   c. limited articles

5. The word *the* is a _____.

   a. indefinite article

   b. definite article

   c. limited article

6. Read the paragraph and fill in the blanks with one of the following choices. Note that only one choice is possible in each blank. (5 points)

there is	there is a	there isn't a	there isn't any	there are	there aren't any

I love camping in the country. I have a favorite place that I go to every year. No one else knows about my

place so _____ other people there. It is very peaceful. _____ just a lot of quiet there. _____
          1   2   3

beautiful waterfall. At the bottom of the waterfall _____ small pond for swimming. In the pond
                                                4

_____ sharp rocks so you have to be careful. _____ fish, though, so you can't go fishing.
    5   6

_____ great view of the ocean from the campsite. _____ a few problems with this place. You
      7   8

have to bring in all your own drinking water because _____ drinking water there. Also, you have to
                                                 9

hike to it because _____ road to it.
            10

7. Circle the correct modal. (10 points)

A: I'm going to the beach this afternoon. (Can / May) you come with me?
                                                  1

B: I'm not sure. I (might / will) have too much homework. I'm waiting to see how much my teacher
                      2

gives us.

A: You (will / can) do your homework on the beach. I (won't / may not) bother you. I (can't / may)
          3   4   5

even take homework, too.

B: Let me think about it. I (may / 'll) tell you after school. OK?
                        6

A: Well, that (can / may) be too late because I only have room for one other person in my car. I
                    7

(might / can) run into someone else who wants to go. You never know.
        8

B: OK, then. I ('ll / won't) go. (Might / Can) you pick me up at 3:00?
          9   10

A: Sure. See you then.

Name _____   **Date** _____

1. Listen and circle the correct answer. (10 points)

1. 14   40

2. 16   60

3. 17   70

4. 15   50

5. 13   30

2. Match each word or phrase in Column 1 with the correct completion in Column 2. (5 points)

____ 1. express   a. checks

____ 2. a pound of   b. sauce

____ 3. take   c. discount

____ 4. aisle   d. 5:00

____ 5. mushroom   e. line

____ 6. 10%   f. a day

____ 7. 50 cents   g. diet

____ 8. until   h. steak

____ 9. two cups   i. 12

____ 10. on a   j. off

3. Write *T* for true statements and *F* for false statements. (5 points)

____ 1. A person's diet is his or her usual food choices.

____ 2. All people like fast food because it is inexpensive and convenient.

____ 3. Fast food is always healthful.

____ 4. Foods with high nutritional value have a lot of fiber, vitamins, and minerals.

____ 5. The global diet is becoming less healthful.

4. Circle the letter of the correct word. (5 points)

1. Food should _____ fresh and natural.

    a. is   b. be   c. being

2. Families are _____ more meals at home.

    a. prepare   b. prepares   c. preparing

3. Many people like to _____ on candy and cookies.

    a. snack   b. snacking   c. snacks

4. Food companies are _____ more nutritious food.

    a. produce   b. produces   c. producing

5. Too much fat and sugar can _____ health problems.

    a. increase   b. increases   c. increasing

5. Number the sentences in a logical order.   (10 points)

_____ Typical dishes include turkey, yams, and cranberry sauce.

_____ On this day, American families usually sit down to a big meal.

_____ Thanksgiving is a traditional holiday.

_____ It falls on the third Thursday of November.

_____ Thanksgiving is my favorite holiday because I love to eat and be with my family.

6. Circle the correct words. (15 points)

Hiroshi: There's (no / any) fruit in the refrigerator and we need (some / any) meat. We also need
                  1   2

          (a little / many) tea. And there isn't (much / many) milk.
              3   4

Asako: All right. Get (many / a lot of) soda, too. And how about (some / any) cookies? And get
                         5   6

          (a / some) spaghetti, too.
             7

Asako: Okay but (may / would) you please buy (some / a lot) ice cream and (a / some) newspaper?
                       8   9   10

Hiroshi: One more thing. I don't have (some / any) money. (Will / Can) I borrow some from you??
                                    11   12

Asako: Sure. There's (some / any) money on the kitchen table. Take as (many / much) as you need. I
                    13   14

          don't need (many / much) cash today.
             15

Name _____   **Date** _____

1. Listen and write the full form of each reduced form you hear. (10 points)

1. I've _____ _____ go now.

2. _____ _____ planning to go out?

3. _____ _____ give me a lift?

4. _____ _____ use Mario's car?

5. I _____ _____ visit my sister in the hospital.

2. Make a conversation. Number the sentences in the correct order. (5 points)

___ A: Then do I turn right?

___ A: Yes. Are they on Walnut Street?

_1_ A: I'm looking for the tennis courts.

___ B: Do you know how to get to Walnut and First?

___ B: No. You have to walk west two blocks.

___ B: No. They're at the corner of Newbury and First.

3. Match each word with its meaning. (5 points)

___ 1. advantages

___ 2. tourists

___ 3. the countryside

___ 4. to motion

___ 5. gestures

___ 6. impolite

___ 7. confused

___ 8. seldom

___ 9. straight

___ 10. sense of direction

a. not often; rarely

b. to give a direction or signal

c. rude; discourteous

d. people who travel for pleasure

e. without turns or curves

f. things that are helpful or useful

g. a feeling or understanding of how to find places

h. a rural regions without large cities

i. movements of the arms, hands, or head

j. mixed-up; disordered

4. Write *T* for true statements and *F* for false statements. (5 points)

___ 1. People around the world give directions the same way.

___ 2. Tourists in Japan get confused because there are no street names.

___ 3. In the American Midwest, people give directions in distances.

___ 4. In Los Angeles, California, people measure distances in miles, kilometers, and blocks.

___ 5. Everywhere people use body language to give directions.

5. Complete the following sentences. (10 points)

1. The salutation of a letter usually begins with _____.
   a. sincerely
   b. dear
   c. the date

2. To close an informal letter to someone you don't know very well, use_____.
   a. Best wishes,
   b. Love,
   c. Fondly

3. Prepositions often show _____.
   a. place, direction, and distance
   b. color, shape, and size
   c. subject, verb, and object

4. The order of a date is _____.
   a. day, year, month
   b. year, day, month
   c. month, day, year

5. Most letters begin with _____.
   a. Dear
   b. Regards
   c. Yours

6. Circle the correct verb form. (10 points)

Alice: Let's have dinner at that new Italian restaurant tonight.

Maria: I can't. I (am going to / will) go to the movies with Bill. Call Tina. Maybe she (is going to / will)
                             1   2

         go with you.

Alice: Tina's busy too. Her parents (are arriving / will arrive) tomorrow. She (is going to / will) clean
                                          3   4

         her house tonight.

Maria: Well, what (are you doing / will you do) tonight?
                            5

Alice: Maybe I (am going to / will) stay home and watch television.
                      6

Maria: (Aren't you / Won't you be) lonely?
                7

Alice: Of course not and you (aren't being / won't be) very late.
                       8

Maria: We (will be / are being) home by 10:30.
              9

Alice: Okay. Don't forget your umbrella. It (is going to rain / is raining) later tonight.
                           10

Maria: Don't worry. I'll take it.

7. Fill in the blanks with one of the prepositions in the box. (5 points)

after	at	during	on	until

1. What do you like to do _____ weekends?

2. My class starts _____ 8:00 in the morning, so I have to get up early.

3. We're all going to the movies _____ dinner. Would you like to join us?

4. Jorge starts working at 5:00 in the afternoon and he doesn't finish _____ midnight.

5. The library is open from 7:00 AM to 11:30 PM _____ the week, but on weekends the
    hours are 8:00 AM to 10:00 PM.

Chapter 5 Quiz

Name _____   **Date** _____

1. Listen to the pairs of words. Circle the sound of *-ed* you hear. (10 points)

____ 1. /d/ /t/ /id/   ____ 6. /d/ /t/ /id/

____ 2. /d/ /t/ /id/   ____ 7. /d/ /t/ /id/

____ 3. /d/ /t/ /id/   ____ 8. /d/ /t/ /id/

____ 4. /d/ /t/ /id/   ____ 9. /d/ /t/ /id/

____ 5. /d/ /t/ /id/   ____10. /d/ /t/ /id/

2. Match each statement with its use. (5 points)

Statement   **Use**

____ 1. I need you to...   a. make a polite request

____ 2. No way.   b. make a strong refusal

____ 3. Can you please...   c. make a strong request

____ 4. I don't mind....   d. show something isn't a problem for you

____ 5. I'm sorry. I can't...   e. make a polite refusal

3. Match each word with its meaning. (5 points)

____ 1. relatives   a. to decrease in value

____ 2. couples   b. customary way of doing things

____ 3. divorces   c. to provide money and other necessary things for care of others

____ 4. widow   d. to take into a family through a legal process

____ 5. decline   e. people related through marriage or family

____ 6. adopt   f. the legal ending of a marriage

____ 7. traditional   g. a family group that includes cousins, aunts, uncles, grandparents, and so on

____ 8. nuclear family   h. two people who are married or very close

____ 9. extended family   i. a family group of just parents and children

____10. support   j   a woman whose husband has died

4. Write *T* for true statements and *F* for false statements. (5 points)

____ 1. There are only two types of families: extended families and nuclear families.

____ 2. Many women had to go to work outside of the home during World War II.

____ 3. After World War II, families become more traditional with the father working and the mother staying at home.

____ 4. The divorce rate declined and the birthrate increased since the 1960s.

____ 5. The family structure will probably change more in the future.

5. Number the sentences in a logical order. (10 points)

____ The separation was difficult, but I think it was good for us.

____ We went to the school together until the end of high school.

____ I have a twin brother.

____ I was born in 1979.

____ When we graduated, we went to different colleges.

6. Circle the correct words. (15 points)

How (did we live / we lived) fifty years ago? Well, life was a little different. We (don't / didn't)
    1   2

(have / had) so many machines. We (listen / listened) to the radio and we (watching / watched) TV
   3   4   5

but it wasn't in color. Who (maked / made) dinner? My mother (makes / made) it and my sister
                               6   7

(helps / helped) her. The boys in the family never (did / done) housework.
  8   9

Before I (get / got) married, I never (have / had) to clean or cook. But when I (become / became) a
        10   11   12

husband, I (begin / began) to help around the house. What (did I do / I did)? Everything! And I
        13   14

(learning / learned) that housework is not easy!
    15

Midterm Quiz

Name _____   **Date** _____

1. Listen and write *T* for true and *F* for false. (10 points)

____ 1. Harold is Andy's advisor.

____ 2. The steak was expensive.

____ 3. Andy bought a little ice cream.

____ 4. Andy bought some produce.

____ 5. Harold enjoys shopping for groceries.

2. Write the letter of the stressed word in each sentence. (5 points)

____ 1. <u>How</u> <u>are</u> you <u>doing</u>?
     A   B   C

____ 2. I have <u>to</u> <u>go</u> <u>home</u> now.
     A B C

____ 3. <u>Can</u> I <u>help</u> <u>you</u>?
     A   B   C

____ 4. <u>How</u> <u>about</u> <u>you</u>, Richard?
     A   B   C

____ 5. Those apples <u>are</u> three <u>for</u> a <u>dollar</u>.
           A   B   C

3. Circle the letter of the correct word. (5 points)

1. Food should _____ fresh and natural.

   a. is   b. be   c. being

2. Families are _____ more meals at home.

   a. prepare   b. prepares   c. preparing

3. Many people like to _____ on candy and cookies.

   a. snack   b. snacking   c. snacks

4. Food companies are _____ more nutritious food.

   a. produce   b. produces   c. producing

5. Too much fat and sugar can _____ health problems.

   a. increase   b. increases   c. increasing

4. Circle the letter of the correct word. (5 points)

1. I prefer to ask _____ directions.

    a. to   b. for   c. in

2. You should turn left _____ the big hotel.

    a. at   b. on   c. in

3. The post office is _____ the bus stop.

    a. across from   b. for   c. from

4. Go another mile _____ a northeast direction.

    a. at   b. for   c. in

5. Some people will lead you _____ the post office.

    a. of   b. to   c. at

5. Number the sentences in a logical order. (10 points)

____ There is an old section of San Juan and a new section.

____ San Juan is the capital of Puerto Rico.

____ I live in the old part of town.

____ It is made entirely of stone and is very beautiful.

____ There is a military fort in my neighborhood.

6. Choose the correct completion for each sentence. (15 points)

1. My brother and I _____ students at this university.

    a. am

    b. are

    c. being

2. He _____ five languages!

    a. speaks

    b. speak

    c. is speaking

3. Where _____?

    a. you study

    b. do you study

    c. study you

4. There are _____ many students from Korea here.
   a. is
   b. be
   c. are

5. I'm looking for _____ glasses. Have you seen them?
   a. Tom's
   b. Toms
   c. Toms'

6. I can't talk to you now. I _____.
   a. studying
   b. study
   c. am studying

7. There aren't _____ soft drinks in the refrigerator. I'll buy some.
   a. much
   b. some
   c. many

8. Can I have _____ salt for my French fries?
   a. some
   b. any
   c. much

9. How _____ sisters and brothers do you have?
   a. often
   b. much
   c. many

10. We _____ take a long vacation when school is over.
    a. going to
    b. be going to
    c. are going to

11. Don't forget your umbrella. I think _____ tonight.
    a. it's raining
    b. it's going to rain
    c. rains

12. I was really tired last night. I fell asleep _____ my favorite television program!
    a. until
    b. in
    c. during

13. I telephoned my parents _____.
    a. tomorrow
    b. last night
    c. right now

14. What _____ on your trip to San Francisco?
    a. did you see
    b. you saw
    c. did you saw

15. I went to a party last night and _____ too much!
    a. eated
    b. eat
    c. ate

Name _____   **Date** _____

1. **Read the list below. Then listen to the tape and write B for mistakes Bill makes and F for mistakes Frannie makes. (10 points)**

    _____ putting on makeup at the table

    _____ not leaving a tip

    _____ reading at the table

    _____ saying something tastes awful

    _____ taking food from someone else's plate

2. **Make a conversation. Number the sentences in the correct order. (5 points)**

    ___ A: Like what?

    _1_ A: Is this your first trip to the United States?

    ___ B: And people take food home from restaurants for their dogs.

    ___ B: Yes, and I'm amazed by some of the things I've seen.

    ___ B: For one thing, people put ketchup on eggs.

    ___ A: Even I think that's a little bizarre.

3. **Match each word with its meaning. (5 points)**

    _____ 1. achievement

    _____ 2. weapon

    _____ 3. invent

    _____ 4. agree

    _____ 5. polite

    _____ 6. rude

    _____ 7. significant

    _____ 8. pleasantly

    _____ 9. proud

    _____10. magnificent

    a. something used to fight

    b. to have the same opinion

    c. without good manners

    d. nicely; agreeably

    e. excellent; grand

    f. feeling happy about something you own or have done or are part of

    g. meaningful; important

    h. with good manners

    i. to create something new

    j. something that is difficult to do

4. Write _T_ for true statements and _F_ for false statements. (5 points)

___ 1. The fine arts include architecture, music, literature, paintings, and sculpture.

___ 2. Some early important inventions were in media—TV, CDs, and the Internet.

___ 3. All important scientific and technological discoveries were in the Americas.

___ 4. Some points of culture are universal, such as food and media.

___ 5. Because of cultural diversity, people around the world celebrate the same things.

5. Complete the following sentences. Circle the letter of the answer. (10 points)

1. The words _before_ and _after_ are _____.

   a. time words

   b. articles

   c. clauses

2. The word _while_ can be used to describe _____.

   a. one action that happened after another

   b. two actions separated by time

   c. two actions in progress at the same time

3. The phrase _as soon as_ is used to show _____.

   a. that one action happened immediately after another

   b. two actions that are dependent on each other

   c. the reason for an action

4. A quotation shows _____.

   a. descriptive words

   b. a character's exact words

   c. the author's opinion

5. The first word of a quote always starts with a ____.

   a. capital letter

   b. preposition

   c. vowel

6. Circle the correct word. (10 points)

Gary: How many countries (have you visited / did you visit) so far?

1

Mike: I (have been / was) in about 20 countries. I (have traveled / traveled) through most of Europe

2   3

and several countries in Asia.

Gary: (Have you been /Did you go) to Africa?

4

Mike: Not yet. I (have gone / am going to go) next year.

5

Gary: What's your favorite place?

Mike: That's hard to say. I (love / have loved) Paris. It's really beautiful. And of course, I

6

(have always enjoyed / am always enjoying)India because of its delicious food.

7

Gary: Where (are you going / have you gone) next?

8

Mike: To China. I (wasn't / haven't been) there. I (went/ haven't been) to Japan last year, but not to

9   10

China.

7. Unscramble the sentences. (5 points)

1. to   ever   you   New   York   been   have

_____ ?

2. returned   he   just   Washington   from   has

_____ .

3. sushi   never   we   eaten   have

_____ .

4. yet   she   has   Rome   seen

_____ ?

5. Spanish   classes   we   started   recently   have

_____ .

Name _____   **Date** _____

1. Listen and answer the questions. (10 points)

1. What kind of show is it?

   a.   a drama series   b.   a quiz show   c.   a reality-based show

2. What is the main idea?

   a.   Alan's been in a car accident.

   b.   Roger has been in a car accident.

   c.   Melanie has been in a car accident.

3. Who agrees with Alan's opinion?

   a.   Julia   b.   Sarah   c.   Roger

4. Whose opinion don't we know?

   a.   Roger   b.   Julia   c.   Alan

5. Who disagrees with Alan?

   a.   Julia   b.   Sarah   c.   Roger

2. Match each statement with its use. (5 points)

Statement	Use
___ 1. There are no good movies being made today.	a. disagreeing (informal)
___ 2. I think you're absolutely right.	b. disagreeing (formal)
___ 3. Oh, come on!	c. expressing an opinion
___ 4. Oh, I think it depends on who's in the movie.	d. not sure
___ 5. I don't feel the same way.	e. agreeing

3. Match each word with its meaning. (5 points)

____ 1. behavior   a. a center of attention or interest

____ 2. concentration   b. feeling hopeful and happy about something

____ 3. reactions   c. not feeling content or happy about something

____ 4. tension   d. giving close attention to something

____ 5. focus   e. feeling excited or worried because of a strange situation

____ 6. beneficial   f. a response to something

____ 7. dissatisfied   g. mental or nervous pressure

____ 8. envious   h. feeling unhappy because another person has something you want

____ 9. suspenseful   i. the actions or conduct of a person

____ 10. optimistic   j. helpful

4. Write *T* for true statements and *F* for false statements. (5 points)

____ 1. Television and the other visual media are never helpful to people.

____ 2. In families that watch a lot of television, there may be little communication between the family members.

____ 3. Watching a lot of television can help a person think better and be more logical.

____ 4. The violence on television may give people bad dreams.

____ 5. Some people believe that television is more real, so normal life seems boring to them.

5. Number the sentences in a logical order. (10 points)

____ It tells about two people who meet on a ship.

____ Titanic is a love story and a tragedy.

____ Then, the ship hits an iceberg and begins to sink.

____ Unfortunately, Jack dies but Rose survives.

____ They fall in love at first sight.

6. Circle the correct words. (15 points)

Two roommates got home from work a while ago. One roommate is watching TV and the other is listening to music.

Maria: What a day! People (used / were using) the machines every minute, and the noise (was / is)
1   2

terrible. Did you have a hard day too?

Lisa: I sure did. Remember last night that I told you I had a lot of work to do today? Well, I just

(get / got) to work when the telephone (rang / was ringing). It was Mr. Stevens. He
3   4

(was wanting / wanted) to know something about the Kelly contract. I (found / was finding)
5   6

the contract and read it to him. Then while I (was hanging up / hung up) my coat, Nancy
7

(was coming / came) into the office. She (was / was being) very upset. Her computer
8   9

(wasn't working / didn't work) and she (was needing / needed) to use it immediately. So, I
10   11

(told / was telling) her that she could use mine. I couldn't do any work, so I (was sitting / sat)
12   13

and reading the newspaper when my boss (was walking / walked) in! He (was / was being)
14   15

very unhappy.

Name _____   **Date** _____

1. Listen and choose the correct answer. (10 points)

1. Event: a. dinner   b. concert   c. movie

2. Location: a. club   b. theater   c. restaurant

3. Date and time: a. June 3rd at 8:00   b. June 1st at 6:00   c. June 1st at 8:00

4. Total cost: a. two dollars   b. sixteen dollars   c. twenty dollars

5. Remember to bring: a. ID   b. a jacket   c. an umbrella

2. Make a conversation. Number the sentences in the correct order. (5 points)

___ A: Well I've been looking around for a few weeks.

___ B: You're kidding! So soon?

_1_ A: Guess what? I lost my job.

___ B: Oh no! That's awful!

___ B: Congratulations! I know you'll enjoy the change.

___ A: No, it isn't. I'm starting a new job on Monday.

3. Match each word with its meaning. (5 points)

____ 1. mate   a. having an unfriendly behavior

____ 2. interview   b. features or qualities of a person

____ 3. examine   c. not hopeful or confident

____ 4. reply   d. to look at or study carefully

____ 5. potential   e. to complete or write in information

____ 6. aggressive   f. to talk to face-to-face; to have a conversation with

____ 7. characteristics   g. partner; companion

____ 8. optimistic   h. hopeful; expecting the best

____ 9. fill out   i. possible

____ 10. discouraged   j. to say an answer

4. Write *T* for true statements and *F* for false statements. (5 points)

___ 1. In arranged marriages, parents choose who their children will marry.

___ 2. People can search for partners on the Web.

___ 3. You can meet people with similar interests in special interest clubs.

___ 4. In computer dating, a person matches you with someone of similar interests.

___ 5. People place personal ads in newspapers in video-dating clubs.

5. Number the sentences from most general to most specific. (10 points)

_____ She also works so that she can pay her tuition.

_____ Adrianne has had a very busy year.

_____ She has been going to school full time.

_____ In addition, she is getting married in June.

_____ Her fiancé is very understanding, because he's a student, too.

6. Circle the correct words. (15 points)

How long (do / have) I (live / lived) here? I've been (lived / living) in the
         1   2   3

United States (since / for) 1987. (I / I've) (been / have) learning a lot. In general, I've
                4   5   6

(been / being) happy here. But I've been (feel / feeling) lonely (since / for) a while.
     7   8   9

(Since / While) I (rent / rented) this apartment, I've (meet / met) some of the
   10   11   12

neighbors in the building but I (didn't / haven't) made any new friends there yet.
                              13

On the other hand, I've been (dated / dating) an American (for / since) the last
               14   15

six months. We (have become / became) very close.
       16

Name _____   **Date** _____

1. **Listen and circle the correct answers. (10 points)**

   1. The groundhog is a (cat / wild animal / shadow).

   2. Groundhog's day is celebrated during the (fall / winter / spring).

   3. Where was Groundhog's day first celebrated? (Pennsylvania / Germany / America)

   4. If the groundhog sees his shadow, there will be (two / four / six) more weeks of winter.

   5. Groundhog's Day was first celebrated (over 200 years ago / over 100 years ago / six years ago).

2. **Write *I* in front of each sentence that *makes* an invitation.**
   Write *A* in front of each sentence that *accepts* an invitation.
   Write *R* in front of each sentence that *refuses* an invitation. (5 points)

   ____ 1. I'd love to.

   ____ 2. I wish I could, but I have a class.

   ____ 3. Why don't we go to the movies?

   ____ 4. I'm sorry but I can't.

   ____ 5. That sounds great!

3. **Match each word with its meaning. (5 points)**

   ____ 1. invitation   a. thankfulness

   ____ 2. hospitality   b. to observe an occasion with special festivities

   ____ 3. appreciation   c. a spoken or written way of asking a person to do
                                      something

   ____ 4. etiquette   d. to recommend or suggest

   ____ 5. advise   e. complex; having many details

   ____ 6. grateful   f. kind treatment of guests

   ____ 7. appropriate   g. rules of behavior

   ____ 8. considerate   h. thankful

   ____ 9. celebrate   i. proper; suitable

   ____10. elaborate   j. thoughtful; thinking of others' feelings

4. Write *T* for true statements and *F* for false statements. (5 points)

___ 1. Customs for dinner parties are the same around the world.

___ 2. In nearly all cultures, it's a nice idea to bring a gift to the host of a party.

___ 3. Before eating at a dinner party, guests often talk and have some snacks.

___ 4. If you are the host of a party, you should spend all your time in the kitchen preparing the food.

___ 5. A host doesn't want his or her guests to be comfortable.

5. Complete the following sentences. (10 points)

1. *In addition to, besides, first, second,* and *third* are examples of _____.
   a. transitional words
   b. quantifiers
   c. adjectives

2. A restrictive clause gives information that is _____ to identify the subject.
   a. necessary
   b. unncecessary
   c. useless

3. A nonrestrictive clause gives _____.
   a. necessary information
   b. additional information
   c. false information

4. Use _____ to separate a nonrestrictive clause from the rest of the sentence.
   a. commas
   b. periods
   c. parentheses

5. You can use _____ to avoid repeating the same words again and again.
   a. prepositions
   b. nouns
   c. pronominal expressions

6. Circle the correct words. (10 points)

(Celebrate / Celebrating) on January 1st is the custom all over Europe, but instead of (they stay / staying)
　　　　1　　　　　　　　　　　　　　　　　　　　　　　　　　　　　　　　　　　2

home and (to get / getting) excited (watch / watching) football on TV, the Italians (going / go) to
　　　　　3　　　　　　　　　　　4　　　　　　　　　　　　　　　　　5

church that day. When I was in Italy, I saw people (brought / bringing) gifts to friends and I remember
　　　　　　　　　　　　　　　　　　　　　　　　　　　6

them (toast / toasting) the New Year with wine. After (visit / visiting) with friends and family, everyone
　　　　7　　　　　　　　　　　　　　　　　　　　　8

goes home tired but happy. (Experiencing / Experience) Italian culture first-hand was a real pleasure.
　　　　　　　　　　　　　　　　　9

(Return / Returning) there some day is a dream of mine.
　　　10

7. Choose the part of each sentence that has an error in it. (5 points)

1. We started to doing the assignment before we understood it.

2. The music continued play until midnight.

3. Everyone here prefers on go to the movies, not to the soccer game.

4. My girlfriend loves to preparing delicious meals for me.

5. Please continue to working. I won't disturb you.

Name _____   **Date** _____

1. Listen and circle the letter of the correct answer. (10 points)

1. What is Gloria showing Michael how to do?
   a. Repair the answering machine
   b. Set up the answering machine

2. What problem does he have?
   a. He can't find the "Select" key.
   b. He can't find the "Enter" key.

3. How many rings does Michael choose?
   a. four
   b. six

4. What kind of announcement does Michael make?
   a. a short one
   b. a long one

5. What is the last step they do?
   a. Set the day and time.
   b. Check Michael's greeting.

2. Number the sentences in the correct order. (5 points)

___ A: That's it?

_1_ A: My printer won't work. What should I do?

___ B: That should solve the problem

___ B: First you turn off the printer and the computer.

___ A: Wait. I don't just turn off the printer?

___ A: Thanks!

___ B: No. Turn them both off. Then turn them on again.

3. Match each word with its meaning. (5 points)

____ 1. radiation

____ 2. treatments

____ 3. distribute

____ 4. controversial

____ 5. interactive

____ 6. high-tech

____ 7. automatically

____ 8. monitoring

____ 9. interference

____ 10. invade

a. causing argument or debate

b. to enter by force or to spread harm through

c. involving advanced scientific devices and machines

d. the act of getting in the way of something

e. ways of giving medical care

f. watching over and keeping track of

g. to give out; to supply

h. nuclear energy; waves of light and energy

i. relating to a computer program in which a person and computer act on or affect each other

j. in a manner that is self-operating

4. Write *T* for true statements and *F* for false statements. (5 points)

____ 1. Everyone agrees that technology is always good.

____ 2. E-mail is an electronic way to write letters.

____ 3. Most families in the U.S. have many appliances and machines that use computer technology.

____ 4. Some examples of computer technology in the medical sciences are sensors, CAT scans, and laser surgery.

____ 5. Computers and television are going to improve relationships between people.

5. Complete the following sentences. (10 points)

1. A word that has the same or similar meaning is _____.
   a. an antonym
   b. a synonym
   c. a homonym

2. *It, they, this,* and *these* are _____.
   a. nouns
   b. names
   c. pronouns

3. An e-mail topic is just like the _____ of a composition.

    a. title

    b. conclusion

    c. signature

4. You should always support an opinion with _____.

    a. other people's opinions

    b. connecting sentences

    c. reasons and examples

5. The phrases *should, need to,* and *it would be better if* are _____ as *must.*

    a. less polite

    b. more polite

    c. just as polite

6. Complete the text with the passive or active form of the verbs in parentheses. Remember to think about the correct tense (present, past, and so on). (15 points)

From our point of view in the 21st century, we can see that many important scientific milestones

_____ (make) in the 20th century. Scientists _____ (send) men to the moon. They
1

                                                     2

_____ (find) cures for many diseases and _____ (develop) powerful personal
3   4

computers. In short, people's lives _____ (make) a lot easier through the advances of modern
5

science. However, some people now _____ (believe) that our environment
6

_____ (hurt) by technology. They say that human lives _____
7   8

(not enrich) by some of these inventions and discoveries. For example, they _____ (point)
9

out that the water _____ (pollute) by industry and that the ozone layer _____
10   11

(damage) by the exhaust from millions of car engines and smokestacks. Furthermore, they _____
12

(claim) television _____ (have) a very negative effect on young children in the 20th century.
13

They _____ (blame) television for many social evils. However, science cannot be blamed alone.
14

After all, the scientists only _____ (give) people what they asked for.
15

Final Quiz

Name _____   **Date** _____

1. Listen and choose the correct answer. (10 points)

___ 1. This is:

    a. a statement   b. a question   c. an exclamation

___ 2. This is:

    a. a statement   b. a question   c. an exclamation

___ 3. This is:

    a. a statement   b. a question   c. an exclamation

___ 4. This is:

    a. a statement   b. a question   c. an exclamation

___ 5. This is:

    a. a statement   b. a question   c. an exclamation

2. Make a conversation. Number the sentences in the correct order. (5 points)

___ B: Then I advise you to talk with your counselor.

___ A: You're right. She'll be able to help. You're really smart!

_1_ A: I can't decide which college to go to. What should I do?

___ B: Try talking with your friends.

___ B: So are you.

___ A: But I already did that. I just got more confused.

3. Write the entertainment category you would use to find things to do. Use the choices from the box. (5 points)

Live theater	TV programming	Radio
Recitals/concerts	Neighborhood movies	Clubs

1. I want to watch my favorite soap opera and the local news show. _____

2. I want to see a play acted out by people on stage. _____

3. I want to watch a new film with some friends. _____

4. I want to listen to an orchestra perform music by Mozart and Handel. _____

5. I want to go out with some friends to listen to a small band, dance, and have something to eat.

_____

4. VCR Instructions: Number the following statements in the proper order. (5 points)

_____ Turn off the TV and VCR when you are finished.

_____ Insert a video cassette.

_____ Press the PLAY button.

_____ Turn on the TV and set the VCR channel.

_____ Use the Tracking Control to adjust the picture or sound.

5. Number the sentences in the most logical order. (10 points)

_____ Most people celebrate by having barbecues and watching fireworks.

_____ Civic holidays are also known as public holidays.

_____ On this day, we celebrate our independence from Great Britain.

_____ It falls on the fourth of July.

_____ The most important civic holiday is Independence Day.

6. Choose the correct completion for each sentence. (15 points)

1. I _____ to California, but not to Oregon.
   a. have travel
   b. have traveled
   c. have traveling

2. My car _____ down twice last week.
   a. broke
   b. was breaking
   c. has broken

3. What unusual foods _____?
   a. you have eaten
   b. have you eaten
   c. have eaten

4. At nine o'clock last night, Marcella _____ care of her little sister.
   a. was taking
   b. is taking
   c. took

5. I didn't hear the phone ring. My roommate _____ loud music and I _____ a shower.
   a. was playing . . . was taking
   b. played . . . was taking
   c. played . . . took

6. Matt and Jason _____ hard on their project last night.
   a. was been working
   b. was working
   c. were working

7. This building has been here _____ 1850.
   a. for
   b. since
   c. during

8. Our neighbors _____ loud music for hours! I can't stand it any more!
   a. have played
   b. have been played
   c. have been playing

9. Carlos _____ animals since he was a little boy.

    a. has been liking

    b. likes

    c. has liked

10. _____ outdoors in nice weather is great!

    a. Be

    b. Being

    c. To being

11. The thief _____ last night.

    a. was arrested

    b. arrested

    c. is arrested

12. The business was founded _____ a simple farmer.

    a. by

    b. on

    c. to

13. We _____ to the radio and then went to bed.

    a. were listened

    b. have listened

    c. listened

14. Rob loves his car. Every day it _____ and _____.

    a. was washed . . . polish

    b. was washed . . . polished

    c. is washed . . . polished

15. Who _____ the transistor _____ by?

    a. was...invented

    b. is...invented

    c. is...inventing

Placement Test Answer Keys

Listening/Speaking Section

Part 1 Listening

Listening Number 1

Tapescript

Wayne: Morning, Mary.

Mary: Good Morning, Uncle Wayne.

Wayne: What kind of tea would you like?

Mary: I'm not really sure.

Wayne: Let me see what we have in the house.

Mary: I really liked the Ceylon tea that I had yesterday afternoon after work.

Wayne: I think we have one bag left. What do you want in your tea?

Mary: There's half a lemon in the refrigerator.

Wayne: Oh, I'll get it for you.

Example: d

1. a
2. c
3. b
4. d
5. d

Listening Number 2

Tapescript

This is the XRKY radio lost pet announcements.

Female Announcer: Tonight our announcements include a missing cat and two dogs. Mrs. Lincoln's black and white nine-month-old kitten, Blacky, was lost yesterday morning next to the high school.

Male Announcer: Mr. Wilson's German shepherd is a seeing-eye dog. The shepherd is named Oxen and is wearing a black color and has a scar over his left eye. It is extremely rare for a seeing-eye dog to disappear. Mr. Wilson is blind in both eyes and cannot get around without his dog. Oxen was lost in the Green Acres neighborhood. Winston, a wire-haired terrier, was stolen from Mrs. Thompson's back yard. Winston is a prize winning purebred worth about three thousand dollars.

Female Announcer (first announcer): If you have any information, please call the radio station. The police station no longer handles missing animal reports. The humane society's phone is broken and won't be repaired for a week.

Example: c

1. a
2. b
3. d
4. a
5. a

Listening Number 3

Tapescript

Male Announcer: This evening I am going to talk about product placement. Product placement is probably one of the most important concepts I will cover this semester. In the United States special care is taken when placing items in different parts of the supermarket. For example, candy is generally placed next to the cashier or check out counter. This is because customers are often likely to grab a candy bar while waiting in line. Children, who are waiting in line with their parents, often pester their parents for to buy candy for them. Another example has to do with the placement of expensive products. Many stores, not all, will place expensive product at eye level. Your imported shampoos are placed at a level where they are clearly visible and people can easily reach for them. Please note that I am not supporting or endorsing cheap items over expensive ones. As your homework assignment you must go to a large supermarket and see where the over-the-counter medicine is placed. I look forward to seeing you next Tuesday night.

Example: a

1. b
2. a
3. c
4. b
5. b

Part 2 Speaking

Example: a

1.	c	9.	c
2.	b	10.	b
3.	c	11.	d
4.	d	12.	d
5.	c	13.	b
6.	a	14.	b
7.	c	15.	a
8.	d		

Reading Section

Part 1 Determining Meaning and Usage from Context

Example: a

1. c
2. d
3. a
4. d
5. a

Part 2 Reading Comprehension

Reading 1
Example: b

1. c
2. d
3. c
4. c
5. a

Reading 2
Example: a

1. b
2. c
3. a
4. d
5. a

Writing Section

Part 1 Sentence Completion

Example: a

1.	b	6.	c
2.	b	7.	d
3.	c	8.	c
4.	b	9.	b
5.	d	10.	b

Part 2 Organization

Example: c

1. b
2. d
3. d
4. d
5. c

Part 3 Writing Test Rubric

The following rubric on page 164 is to be used if you request a writing sample from your students. See page 120 for prompts.

Please rank on a scale from 0 to 5. Use 0 to describe a student's writing that does NOT match the descriptor given. Use 5 to describe a student's writing that perfectly matches the descriptor given. It is very helpful if you note examples of the student writing.

Name _____   **Date** _____

Writing Areas	Rating and Examples
Content	
Sufficient detail and a variety of adjectives have been included.	
The writing is interesting.	
Sufficient information has been provided.	
The writing is well developed.	
The writing is thought provoking.	
The vocabulary used would be appropriate for an academic paper or class.	
Organization	
The writing contains a clear beginning, middle and end.	
The sentences are organized in a logical order.	
The paragraphs are organized in a logical order.	
Cohesion and Style	
Tenses are used consistently and/or appropriately.	
Transitions are used appropriately.	
The style used is appropriate for an academic paper.	
Grammar	
All sentences are correct. There are no run on sentences or fragments.	
All word forms, such as irregular verb forms and plurals, are correct.	
Relative clauses are used correctly and positively contribute to the writing.	
Complex sentences are used correctly and positively contribute to the overall presentation.	
Form	
Capital letters are used correctly.	
Periods and commas are used correctly.	
Sentences are properly indented.	
The forms are used correctly and add to the overall presentation.	

Grammar Section

Part 1 Complete the Sentence

Example: a

1.	b	14.	c
2.	b	15.	d
3.	d	16.	b
4.	d	17.	c
5.	d	18.	d
6.	a	19.	a
7.	b	20.	b
8.	c	21.	d
9.	b	22.	b
10.	b	23.	d
11.	a	24.	c
12.	a	25.	b
13.	d		

Part 2 Find the Errors

Example: a

1.	d	9.	b
2.	c	10.	a
3.	d	11.	c
4.	d	12.	c
5.	d	13.	b
6.	b	14.	c
7.	c	15.	a
8.	d		

Answer Keys and Tapescripts for Chapter Quizzes

Chapter 1

Tapescript for Exercise 1

1. We hafta get something to eat.
2. How're you feeling?
3. Jim will meetcha at the library.
4. I k'n do it this afternoon.
5. Jus' wait a minute please.

Answers

1) 1b, 2c, 3a, 4b, 5a
2) 3, 6, 1, 5, 2, 4
3) 1F, 2F, 3T, 4T, 5F
4) 1b, 2a, 3b, 4b, 5a
5) 1c, 2b, 3a, 4a, 5b
6) 1c, 2e, 3a, 4b, 5d
7) 1. I don't like sugar in my coffee.
   2. They aren't in the library.
   3. This cookie isn't good!
   4. She doesn't live near me.
   5. They don't have their books.

Chapter 2

Tapescript for Exercise 1

Don: You know Carrie, maybe we could go to the beach tomorrow.

Carrie: But the radio said the temperature is going to be in the 60s. That's too cold to swim. And they also said it was going to rain.

Don: No, I heard the weather forecast. They said there was a chance of rain.

Carrie: You're right. The truth is I'm a pretty good swimmer, but really don't care for swimming.

Don: That's hard for me to understand. I can't wait to get in the water.

Answers

1) 1a, 2a, 3c, 4c, 5a
2) 1b, 2a, 3e, 4c, 5d
3) 1F, 2T, 3F, 4F, 5T
4) 1b, 2c, 3b, 4a, 5a
5) 1a, 2c, 3a, 4a, 5b
6)
   1. there aren't any
   2. There is
   3. There is a
   4. there is a
   5. there are
   6. There aren't any
   7. There is a
   8. There are
   9. there isn't any
   10. there isn't a
7)
   1. Can
   2. might
   3. can
   4. won't
   5. may
   6. 'll
   7. may
   8. might
   9. 'll
   10. Can

Chapter 3

Tapescript for Exercise 1

1. I need 14 peaches to make pies for the party.
2. The market sold 60 pounds of apples this afternoon.
3. They're selling tomatoes for 70 cents apiece!
4. Cook the steak for about 15 minutes.
5. We have 13 bottles of water left.

Answers

1) 1. 14, 2. 60, 3. 70, 4. 15, 5. 13
2) 1e, 2h, 3a, 4i, 5b, 6c, 7j, 8d, 9f, 10g
3) 1T, 2F, 3F, 4T, 5F
4) 1b, 2c, 3a, 4c, 5a
5) 4, 3, 1, 2, 5
6)
   1. no
   2. some
   3. a little
   4. much
   5. a lot of
   6. some
   7. some
   8. would
   9. some
   10. a
   11. any
   12. Can
   13. some
   14. much
   15. much

Chapter 4

Tapescript for Exercise 1

1. I've gotta go now.
2. Arya planning to go out?
3. Couldja give me a lift?
4. Kinya use Mario's car?
5. I hafta visit my sister in the hospital.

Answers

1)
   1. got to
   2. Are you
   3. Could you
   4. Can you
   5. have to
2) 5, 3, 1, 2, 4, 6
3) 1f, 2d, 3h, 4b, 5i, 6c, 7j, 8a, 9e, 10g
4) 1F, 2T, 3T, 4F, 5T
5) 1b, 2a, 3a, 4c, 5a
6)
   1. am going to
   2. will
   3. are arriving
   4. is going to
   5. are you doing
   6. will
   7. Won't you be
   8. won't be
   9. will be
   10. is going to rain
7)
   1. on
   2. at
   3. after
   4. until
   5. during

Chapter 5

Tapescript for Exercise 1

1. called   called
2. pushed   pushed
3. missed   missed
4. started   started
5. learned   learned
6. waited   waited
7. shopped   shopped

8. needed   needed

9. sounded   sounded

10. stayed   stayed

Answers

1) 1. /d/   6. /id/
      2. /t/   7. /t/
      3. /t/   8. /id/
      4. /id/   9. /id/
      5. /d/   10. /d/

2) 1c, 2b, 3a, 4d, 5e

3) 1e, 2h, 3f, 4j, 5a, 6d, 7b, 8i, 9g, 10c

4) 1F, 2T, 3T, 4F, 5T

5) 5, 3, 2, 1, 4

6) 1. did we live   9. did
      2. didn't   10. got
      3. have   11. had
      4. listened   12. became
      5. watched 13. began
      6. made   14. did I do?
      7. made   15. learned
      8. helped

Midterm Quiz

Tapescript for Exercise 1

Harold: Hey Andy, let's go out for dinner.

Andy: No Harold, let's stay home. I just did the food shopping and I spent a lot of money.

Harold: What did you get?

Andy: Well, the steak was on sale—only $9.99 a pound—so I got two pounds.

Harold: $9.99 a pound! We could get two whole dinners plus dessert for $9.99 at Gino's.

Andy: And the ice cream was on sale so I bought four gallons.

Harold: Well, I do like ice cream...

Andy: And I got some bread, too.

Harold: Since you bought all that stuff, I guess we should eat at home. Did you get any vegetables or fruit?

Andy: On, no. I forgot. But I think we have some salad from last week.

Harold: Oh, boy. Just what I want. Week-old salad.

Andy: You know, maybe you should do the food shopping next week.

Harold: No, that's OK. You can do it. I'd rather complain about shopping than do it.

Answers

1) 1F, 2T, 3F, 4F, 5F

2) 1C, 2C, 3B, 4C, 5C

3) 1b, 2c, 3a, 4c, 5a

4) 1b, 2a, 3a, 4c, 5b

5) 2, 1, 3, 5, 4

6) 1b, 2a, 3b, 4c, 5a, 6c, 7c, 8a, 9c, 10c, 11b, 12c, 13b, 14a, 15c

Chapter 6

Tapescript for Exercise 1

Bill: I really like this restaurant. Don't you?

Franny: I guess so. Hey! Is it OK if I take some of your french fries?

Bill: Well . . . OK. Didn't you have enough to eat?

Franny: Yeah, I guess so. But my meal was terrible.

Bill: Well, I didn't notice the food much. I got really interested in this story in the newspaper.

Franny: Yeah, I do that sometimes. Are you ready to go?

Bill: Yeah. I'll pay the bill on the way out. I'm not going to bother leaving any money for the waiter.

Franny: Can you wait just a minute? I want to put on my lipstick before we leave the table.

Bill: Sure. No problem.

Franny: OK. Let's go.

Bill: Where to?

Franny: Let's get some ice cream from that stand on the corner.

Answer Keys

Answers

1) F, B, B, F, F
2) 3, 1, 6, 2, 4, 5
3) 1j, 2a, 3i, 4b, 5h, 6c, 7g, 8d, 9f, 10e
4) 1T, 2F, 3F, 4T, 5F
5) 1a, 2c, 3a, 4b, 5a
6)
  1. have you visited
  2. have been
  3. have traveled
  4. Have you been
  5. am going to go
  6. love
  7. have always enjoyed
  8. are you going
  9. haven't been
 10. went
7)
  1. Have you ever been to New York?
  2. He has just returned from Washington.
  3. We have never eaten sushi.
  4. Has she seen Rome yet?
  5. We have recently started Spanish classes.

Chapter 7

Tapescript for Exercise 1

Alan: Oh, Julia! I can't believe it. I let Roger borrow my new car for an hour and he crashes it into a tree!

Julia: Oh, no Alan! Roger had your car? My Roger? How is he?

Alan: Oh, he's OK, Julia. Nobody got hurt. But my car . . . Thirty-two thousand dollars. That's a lot of money, you know! Roger is totally crazy!

Julia: Roger's not crazy! Where is he, poor boy?

Alan: Who knows. He's probably hiding from me if he's smart.

Julia: Now Alan. I'm sure he feels bad about it. I'm sure he'll pay you back. I just hope he's OK.

(pause)

Sarah: Hi, Roger. Hi, Julia.

Alan & Julia: Hi / Hi, Sarah.

Sarah: You look unhappy. What's up?

Alan: Well Sarah...Roger borrowed my car and crashed it into a tree. He's OK but the car isn't.

Sarah: Your new car? Well, don't worry. Your insurance will pay for it.

Julia: That's all you can say? Roger was almost killed!

Sarah: I'm sure he'll be OK.

Alan: That's more than you can say for my car.

Answers

1) 1a, 2b, 3b, 4a, 5a
2) 1c, 2e, 3a, 4d, 5b
3) 1i, 2d, 3f, 4g, 5a, 6j, 7c, 8h, 9e, 10b
4) 1F, 2T, 3F, 4T, 5T
5) 2, 1, 4, 5, 3
6)
1. were using	9. was
2. was	10. wasn't working
3. got	11. needed
4. rang	12. told
5. wanted	13. was sitting
6. found	14. walked
7. was hanging up	15. was
8. came	

Chapter 8

Tapescript for Exercise 1

Male voice: (over phone) Open Air Theater. Can I help you?

Female voice: Yes, uh, do you have any tickets left for the Big Band show next week?

Male voice: Yes, we do. Which night are you interested in?

Female voice: Tuesday, I think.

Male voice: I'll check. (pause)

Male voice: I don't have anything left for Tuesday, but there are some for Wednesday.

Female voice: That's Wednesday, June 1st?

Male voice: That's right. June 1st at 8:00 p.m.

Female voice: That sounds fine. I'd like two tickets please.

Male voice: OK. That'll be $16 for the tickets plus a service charge of two dollars per ticket, so your total comes to 20 dollars. And how would you like to pay for your tickets?

Female voice: Can I pay for them the night of the concert?

Male voice: Certainly. Be sure to get her half an hour early—7:30—to pick them up.

Female voice: Ok. Thanks.

Male voice: And don't forget to bring a jacket. It sometimes gets cool outside before the show's over.

Female voice: Thanks, I will. Good-bye.

Male voice: Bye.

Answers

1) 1b, 2b, 3c, 4c, 5b
2) 5, 4, 1, 2, 6, 3
3) 1g, 2f, 3d, 4j, 5i, 6a, 7b, 8h, 9e, 10c
4) 1T, 2T, 3T, 4F, 5F
5) 3, 1, 2, 4, 5
6)
1. have
2. lived
3. living
4. since
5. I've
6. been
7. been
8. feeling
9. for
10. Since
11. rented
12. met
13. haven't
14. dating
15. for
16. have become

Chapter 9

Tapescript for Exercise 1

Every year on February 2nd Americans celebrate Groundhog Day. On this day, so the story goes, you should go out and look for a groundhog—a wild animal about the size of a housecat. If the groundhog can see its shadow, it means there will be six more weeks of winter. If it can't see his shadow, spring will come early. This holiday, which comes halfway between the beginning of winter and the beginning of spring, was brought to American by German immigrants who arrived in America in the 1700s. The first official celebration of Groundhog's Day was on February 2, 1886 in Pennsylvania.
[SOURCE: http://www.stormfax.com/ghogday.htm]

Answers

1)
1. wild animal
2. winter
3. Germany
4. six
5. over 200 years ago
2) 1A, 2R, 3I, 4R, 5A
3) 1c, 2f, 3a, 4g, 5d, 6h, 7i, 8j, 9b, 10e
4) 1F, 2T, 3T, 4F, 5F
5) 1a, 2a, 3b, 4a, 5c
6)
1. Celebrating
2. staying
3. getting
4. watching
5. go
6. bringing
7. toasting
8. visiting
9. Experiencing
10. Returning
7)
1. to do or doing
2. playing or to play
3. prefers to go or prefers going
4. to prepare or preparing
5. to work or working

Chapter 10

Tapescript for Exercise 1

Gloria: This answering machine is really easy to set up.

Michael: Oh, good. What do I do?

Gloria: Well, first you have to set the number of rings.

Michael: How do I do that?

Gloria: You press the "Select" button. Then you press a number key.

Michael: I'm confused. I see the "Enter" button, but where's the "Select" button?

Gloria: Here it is. Now you press the number of rings you want.

Michael: OK. "Select." . . . "Six" . . .

Gloria: So far, so good. Now press "Exit" to go on to the next step.

Michael: "Exit" OK. Now do we set the day and date?

Gloria: Not yet. First we put in your outgoing message. Press "Record" and just make your announcement.

Michael: "Record".... This is Mike. Please leave a message.

Gloria: Good work. Now we'll check your greeting. Press "Star one one."

Michael: OK. "Star one one"...

Michael: (recorded voice) This is Mike. Please leave a message.

Gloria: Congratulations. Now we can set the day and time.

Michael: Let's do that tomorrow. I've had enough for today.

Answers

1) 1b, 2a, 3b, 4a, 5b
2) 5, 1, 6, 2, 3, 7, 4
3) 1h, 2e, 3g, 4a, 5i, 6c, 7j, 8f, 9d, 10b
4) 1F, 2T, 3T, 4T, 5F
5) 1b, 2c, 3a, 4c, 5b
6)
   1. were made
   2. sent
   3. found
   4. developed
   5. were made
   6. believe
   7. was hurt
   8. were not enriched
   9. point
   10. was polluted
   11. was damaged
   12. claim
   13. had
   14. blame
   15. gave

Final Quiz

Tapescript for Exercise 1

1 That's your roommate, isn't it? (rising intonation)

2. You like pizza, don't you? (falling intonation)

3. Don't touch that dog! (exclamatory intonation)

4. The teacher was late, wasn't she. (falling intonation)

5. You're not leaving early, are you? (rising intonation)

Answers

1) 1b, 2a, 3c, 4a, 5b
2) 4, 5, 1, 2, 6, 3
3)
   1. TV programming
   2. Live theater
   3. Neighborhood movies
   4. Recitals/concerts
   5. Clubs
4) 5, 2, 3, 1, 4
5) 5, 1, 4, 3, 2
6) 1b, 2a, 3b, 4a, 5a, 6c, 7b, 8c, 9c, 10b, 11a, 12a, 13c, 14c, 15a

_____	5.	chronic	e.	the ways in which sound and visual images can be sent out to many people
_____	6.	diagnosis	f.	a statement that has not yet been proved
_____	7.	media	g.	a system that keeps people of different races separated
_____	8.	category	h.	a small piece of equipment
_____	9.	refugee	i.	a group or a class
_____	10.	apartheid	j.	existing over a long period of time

3. Read these selections from a lecture. Choose the best phrase to complete the sentences. (5 points)

a. According to historians

b. As I was saying

c. Before I forget

d. In other words

e. It has always seemed to me

Today I want to talk about the fight for civil rights in the United States. Even before the Civil War...

_____, let me say that there's a film being shown tonight on Dr. Martin Luther King.
　　　1

It's at 8:00 in the Student Union, and it's free. _____, the issue of slavery very important
　　　　　　　　　　　　　　　　　　　　　　　　　　　　　　　　　2

in the early days of the Republic . . .

_____, the issues of the Civil War were complex. The war was not just a battle between the
　　　3

Northern states and the Southern states. _____, people disagreed with each other within
　　　　　　　　　　　　　　　　　　　　　　　　4

the various states as well. One example of this is Virginia, which eventually divided into two states,

Virginia and West Virginia, over these issues . . .

_____, even though historians can't prove it, that the Civil War could have been avoided if...
　　　5

4. Match each word with its meaning. (5 points)

_____ 1. depict   a. following standards of moral behavior

_____ 2. breakthrough   b. completely grown or developed

_____ 3. deterrent   c. an article that gives the opinion of the editor

_____ 4. rights   d. describe or represent

_____ 5. holy   e. shocking news about improper behavior

_____ 6. ethical   f. sudden and exciting discovery

_____ 7. editorial   g. something that prevents an action

_____ 8. mature   h. understanding without reasoning or proof

_____ 9. scandal   i. sacred; important for religious reasons

_____ 10. intuition   j. something that a person has a moral or legal claim to

5. Write *T* for true statements or *F* for false statements. (5 points)

_____ 1. Art never has practical or functional uses.

_____ 2. Memories aren't always true.

_____ 3. Ethical questions about medical technology are difficult to answer.

_____ 4. Editorials express opinions.

_____ 5. Juries are used in every legal system.

6. Circle the letter of the correct answer. (10 points)

1. Which sentence is incorrect?

   a. Neither situations are ideal.

   b. Neither situation is ideal.

   c. Neither situation is an ideal one.

2. Which sentence correctly uses the passive voice?

   a. The sun orbits by nine planets.

   b. The sun is orbited by nine planets.

   c. The sun is orbiting by nine planets.

3. Which sentence is the correct indirect speech form for this sentence: The faith healer said, "Trust me and I will cure you."

   a. The faith healer told me he will cure me.

   b. The faith healer tells me he is going to cure me.

   c. The faith healer told me he would cure me.

4. Which sentence is not correct?

    a. The bank, which is protected by security guards, was robbed yesterday.

    b. The bank, that is protected by security guards, was robbed yesterday.

    c. The bank, protected by security guards, was robbed yesterday.

5. Which of these sentences is correct?

    a. If I was rich, I should travel all over the world.

    b. If I am rich, I will travel all over the world.

    c. If I were rich, I would travel all over the world.

7. Indicate whether the sentence is correct or incorrect. Then rewrite the incorrect sentences to make them correct. (15 points)

_____   1.   For me, the goodest movies are comedies.

_____   2.   She didn't sing as beautiful as she usually does.

_____   3.   Texas is a lot hotter Colorado.

_____   4.   It's been many years since astronauts were first send to the moon.

_____   5.   A new gym is being built where the stadium used to be.

_____   6.   Your term paper should be write on a computer.

_____   7.   Measles which is usually a childhood disease is rarely harmful to children.

_____   8.   Summer is the season when I love to travel.

_____   9.   The professor that I like so much is going to move to a different university

_____   10.   They decided going to the movies instead of to the basketball game.

_____   11.   I need to get my brother lend me some money.

_____   12.   I went to the computer lab, but no one could help me there.

_____   13.   If you ate more this morning, you wouldn't have gotten hungry before lunch!

_____   14.   I didn't know you were going to the store! You could have picked up some bread for me.

_____   15.   I wouldn't have taken this course if I knew that it would be so difficult.

Placement Test Answer Keys

Listening/Speaking Section

Part 1 Listening

Listening Number 1

Tapescript

Wayne: Morning, Mary.

Mary: Good Morning, Uncle Wayne.

Wayne: What kind of tea would you like?

Mary: I'm not really sure.

Wayne: Let me see what we have in the house.

Mary: I really liked the Ceylon tea that I had yesterday afternoon after work.

Wayne: I think we have one bag left. What do you want in your tea?

Mary: There's half a lemon in the refrigerator.

Wayne: Oh, I'll get it for you.

Example: d

1. a
2. c
3. b
4. d
5. d

Listening Number 2

Tapescript

This is the XRKY radio lost pet announcements.

Female Announcer: Tonight our announcements include a missing cat and two dogs. Mrs. Lincoln's black and white nine-month-old kitten, Blacky, was lost yesterday morning next to the high school.

Male Announcer: Mr. Wilson's German shepherd is a seeing-eye dog. The shepherd is named Oxen and is wearing a black color and has a scar over his left eye. It is extremely rare for a seeing-eye dog to disappear. Mr. Wilson is blind in both eyes and cannot get around without his dog. Oxen was lost in the Green Acres neighborhood. Winston, a wire-haired terrier, was stolen from Mrs. Thompson's back yard. Winston is a prize winning purebred worth about three thousand dollars.

Female Announcer (first announcer): If you have any information, please call the radio station. The police station no longer handles missing animal reports. The humane society's phone is broken and won't be repaired for a week.

Example: c

1. a
2. b
3. d
4. a
5. a

Listening Number 3

Tapescript

Male Announcer: This evening I am going to talk about product placement. Product placement is probably one of the most important concepts I will cover this semester. In the United States special care is taken when placing items in different parts of the supermarket. For example, candy is generally placed next to the cashier or check out counter. This is because customers are often likely to grab a candy bar while waiting in line. Children, who are waiting in line with their parents, often pester their parents for to buy candy for them. Another example has to do with the placement of expensive products. Many stores, not all, will place expensive product at eye level. Your imported shampoos are placed at a level where they are clearly visible and people can easily reach for them. Please note that I am not supporting or endorsing cheap items over expensive ones. As your homework assignment you must go to a large supermarket and see where the over-the-counter medicine is placed. I look forward to seeing you next Tuesday night.

Example: a

1. b
2. a
3. c
4. b
5. b

Part 2 Speaking

Example: a

1.	c	9.	c
2.	b	10.	b
3.	c	11.	d
4.	d	12.	d
5.	c	13.	b
6.	a	14.	b
7.	c	15.	a
8.	d		

Reading Section

Part 1 Determining Meaning and Usage from Context

Example: a

1. c
2. d
3. a
4. d
5. a

Part 2 Reading Comprehension

Reading 1

Example: b

1. c
2. d
3. c
4. c
5. a

Reading 2

Example: a

1. b
2. c
3. a
4. d
5. a

Writing Section

Part 1 Sentence Completion

Example: a

1.	b	6.	c
2.	b	7.	d
3.	c	8.	c
4.	b	9.	b
5.	d	10.	b

Part 2 Organization

Example: c

1. b
2. d
3. d
4. d
5. c

Part 3 Writing Test Rubric

The following rubric on page 176 is to be used if you request a writing sample from your students. See page 118 for prompts.

Please rank on a scale from 0 to 5. Use 0 to describe a student's writing that does NOT match the descriptor given. Use 5 to describe a student's writing that perfectly matches the descriptor given. It is very helpful if you note examples of the student writing.

Name _____   **Date** _____

Writing Areas	Rating and Examples
Content	
Sufficient detail and a variety of adjectives have been included.	
The writing is interesting.	
Sufficient information has been provided.	
The writing is well developed.	
The writing is thought provoking.	
The vocabulary used would be appropriate for an academic paper or class.	
Organization	
The writing contains a clear beginning, middle and end.	
The sentences are organized in a logical order.	
The paragraphs are organized in a logical order.	
Cohesion and Style	
Tenses are used consistently and/or appropriately.	
Transitions are used appropriately.	
The style used is appropriate for an academic paper.	
Grammar	
All sentences are correct. There are no run on sentences or fragments.	
All word forms, such as irregular verb forms and plurals, are correct.	
Relative clauses are used correctly and positively contribute to the writing.	
Complex sentences are used correctly and positively contribute to the overall presentation.	
Form	
Capital letters are used correctly.	
Periods and commas are used correctly.	
Sentences are properly indented.	
The forms are used correctly and add to the overall presentation.	

Grammar Section

Part 1 Complete the Sentence

Example: a

1.	b	14.	c
2.	b	15.	d
3.	d	16.	b
4.	d	17.	c
5.	d	18.	d
6.	a	19.	a
7.	b	20.	b
8.	c	21.	d
9.	b	22.	b
10.	b	23.	d
11.	a	24.	c
12.	a	25.	b
13.	d		

Part 2 Find the Errors

Example: a

1.	d	9.	b
2.	c	10.	a
3.	d	11.	c
4.	d	12.	c
5.	d	13.	b
6.	b	14.	c
7.	c	15.	a
8.	d		

Answer Keys and Tapescripts for Chapter Quizzes

Chapter 1

Tapescript for Exercise 1

Lecturer: Now this is a good place for me to introduce you to something called plagiarism. Plagiarism is a serious problem at American universities. First, let me spell it for you; it's p-l-a-g-i-a-r-i-s-m. OK, what is plagiarism? Well, I just said that when you write a term paper, it has to be in your own words. That means you can't copy your paper or even small parts of your paper from another student or a book or the Internet. If you do, if you copy, that's plagiarism. Plagiarism is cheating, and it's absolutely forbidden. If you plagiarize and get caught, the punishment can be very serious. You can fail the course or even get kicked out of the university. As I said, this is a very serious thing and you need to be very careful about it.

OK; does anyone have questions at this point about types of university courses, about course requirements, or about plagiarism? No? Then let's stop here and take a break.

Answers

1) 2, 5, 6, 7, 8
2) 1a, 2b, 3d, 4e, 5c
3) 1d, 2c, 3c, 4a, 5a
4) 1F, 2F, 3T, 4T, 5T
5) 1. secondary
   2. graduate
   3. primary
   4. vocational
   5. college preparatory
6) 1c, 2a, 3c, 4c, 5b
7) 1a, 2c, 3a, 4b, 5c
8) 1b, 2a, 3b, 4a, 5b

Chapter 2

Tapescript for Exercise 1

Lecturer: How many of you are familiar with the name Jeff Bezos? OK, how about Amazon.com? Have you heard of that? Well, Amazon.com is the world's first and largest Internet bookstore, and Jeff Bezos is the man who started Amazon.com back in 1995. Five years later, Amazon.com was serving millions of customers in 120 different countries. Amazing, right? And this is the reason why in 1999, Jeff Bezos was selected as Time Magazine's Person of the Year, a very great honor.

Now, Jeff Bezos is actually not the topic of my lecture today, but he is a perfect example of my topic, which is entrepreneurs. That's entrepreneurs, spelled e-n-t-r-e-p-r-e-n-e-u-r-s. It's a French word meaning a person who starts a completely new business or industry, um, someone who does something no one else has done before, or who does it in a completely new way, like Jeff Bezos, who started the very first Internet bookstore. Entrepreneurs like Jeff Bezos are very highly respected in American society and, I think, in many other countries too. So in today's lecture I want to talk about three things. First, the characteristics of entrepreneurs, I mean what kind of people they are. Second, the kind of background they come from. And third, the entrepreneurial process, that is, the steps entrepreneurs follow when they create a new business.

OK, let's begin by looking at the characteristics, or, um the qualities, of entrepreneurs. There are two qualities that I think all entrepreneurs have in common. First, entrepreneurs have vision. I mean that they have the ability to see opportunities that other people simply do not see. Let's look again at the example of Jeff Bezos. One day in 1994, he was surfing the Internet when suddenly he had a brilliant idea: Why not use the Internet to sell products? Remember, at that time, no one was using the Internet in that way. After doing some research, Bezos decided that the product he wanted to sell was books. That's how Amazon.com got its start.

The other quality that I think all entrepreneurs possess is that they are not afraid to take risks. I mean they're not afraid to fail. As an example, let me tell you about Frederick Smith, who founded Federal Express, the company that delivers packages anywhere in the United States overnight. Smith first suggested the idea for his company in a college term paper. Do you know what grade he got on it? A "C"! But this didn't stop him, and today his company is worth more than two billion dollars and employs more than 25,000 people.

Answers

1) Wording may vary.
   I. Intro
      A. Example: Jeff Bezos. Amazon.com.
      B. Definition of an entrepreneur: *A person who starts a new business or industry*
   II. *Characteristics of entrepreneurs*
      A. Vision
         1. Definition: *The ability to see opportunities that others do not see*
         2. Example: Jeff Bezos's idea of selling products on the Internet
      B. *Not afraid to take risks.*
         1. Definition: Not afraid to fail
         2. Example: *Frederick Smith, Federal Express, got a bad grade on his business idea in a term paper*

   2) 1c, 2d, 3e, 4b, 5a
   3) 1c, 2b, 3a, 4c, 5c
   4) 1a, 2c, 3d, 4e, 5b
   5) 1F, 2F, 3T, 4F 5F
6)1b, 2c, 3a, 4a, 5c

7)
1. had better
2. shouldn't
3. must
4. might/may/could; may/might/could
5. must
6. could; should/ought to; could/may/might
7. may/might/could; should/had better/ought to
8. couldn't
9. had to
10. must not
11. don't have to be

Chapter 3

Tapescript for Exercise 1

Lecturer: OK, this brings me to my second main point: Why? I mean what has caused this change in the U.S. economy? First of all, why has the number of manufacturing jobs decreased? Can anyone guess? Yes?

Student 1: Uh, robots? Robots replacing factory workers?

Lecturer: OK, good. Robots or in other words, automation. A lot of the work that our parents and grandparents used to do by hand is now done by machines like computers or computerized robots. Anything else besides automation? Another reason?

Student 2: I would say foreign competition. I mean, most manufacturing is now done outside of the U.S., in China, or Malaysia, you know, countries where the labor costs are cheaper.

Lecturer: That is exactly correct. Most manufacturing these days _is_ being done outside the United States. To give you just one statistic, between March 1998 and November 1999, a period of just 20 months, more than half a million U.S. manufacturing jobs were moved to Asia. But on the other hand, what about service jobs? Why have those increased so much? Well here again

there are two basic causes. First, the number of service jobs has increased because of technology. Think about it. With all the new machines, well, someone has to sell them and install them and fix them when they break, right? None of those jobs existed 25 or 30 years ago.

And the other reason why there are so many new service jobs is that the American population is changing. The population is changing. For example, because people are living longer and longer, they need more medical services, right? So the fastest-growing jobs include things like nursing and home medical workers. Also, another example, since most married women now work outside the home, there's a much greater need for services such as restaurants and day-care centers.

Answers
1) 1b, 2a, 3c, 4a, 5b
2) 1c, 2a, 3d, 4e, 5b
3)
1. effect
2. cause
3. effect
4. effect
5. cause
4) 1c, 2e, 3d, 4a, 5b
5) 1F, 2T, 3F, 4F, 5T
6) 1c, 2b, 3a, 4a, 5b
7) 1b, 2a, 3a, 4a, 5c
8) 1a, 2b, 3a, 4b, 5b

Chapter 4

Tapescript for Exercise 1

Lecturer: The rich are really different from the rest of us. For one thing, they have so much money they can buy almost anything. British rock star Elton John once spent $5,500,000 in less than two years. During that period he spent $240,000 just on flowers for his house. On the other hand, the rich have a lot of problems that the rest of us don't. One example is the amount of tax they have to pay. American billionaire Howard Hughes saved a lot of money while he was alive. When he died, 70% of his money went to the U.S. government in taxes—a total of 336 million dollars!

Answers

1) 1b, 2b, 3a, 4b, 5b
2) 1d, 2e, 3b, 4a, 5c
3) 1c, 2c, 3a, 4d, 5b
4) 1a, 2e, 3c, 4b, 5d
5) 1T, 2F, 3F, 4F, 5T
6) 1a, 2c, 3c, 4b, 5a
7) 1. The teacher calls on him every day but he rarely knows the answer.
   2. We thought about the problem but we couldn't find a good solution.
   3. Please pick up your clothes and put them away.
   4. We'll get through with this work by 5 o'clock.
   5. She was satisfied with her grades.
8) 1. with
   2. to
   3. of
   4. on
   5. about

Chapter 5

Tapescript for Exercise 1

Lecturer: Finally, the last area of behavior that I want to mention today is gift-giving. Everybody likes to receive gifts, right? So you may think that gift-giving is a universal custom and there's not much variation from culture to culture. But actually, the rules of gift-giving can be very complicated, and not knowing them can result in great embarrassment. In the United States, if you're invited to someone's home for dinner, bring wine or flowers or a small item as a present. Americans generally don't give gifts in business situations. On the other hand, the Japanese, like many other Asian people, give gifts quite frequently, often to thank someone such as a teacher or doctor for their kindness. In the Japanese culture, the tradition of gift-giving is very ancient. There are many detailed rules for everything from the

color of the wrapping paper to the time of the gift presentation. Another interesting fact about gift-giving is that many cultures have strict rules about gifts you should not give. For example, never give yellow flowers to people from Iran, or they will think you hate them!

Answers

1) 1b, 2a, 3b, 4a, 5c
2) 1c, 2e, 3a, 4b, 5d
3) 1b, 2b, 3a, 4a, 5b
4) 1e, 2a, 3c, 4d, 5b
5) 1T, 2F, 3T, 4F, 5T
6) 1c, 2a, 3a, 4b, 5a
7) 1. Correct
   2. New maps quickly become out-of-date after / as soon as they are produced.
   3. The U.N. will have many more members if the number of countries grows.
   4. When nations have their own special interests, it is difficult for them to cooperate. (Completions of the independent clause will vary.)
   5. After we finish this project, we will help you with yours.

Midterm Quiz

Tapescript for Exercise 1

Lecturer: OK, now first of all, to begin, let's talk about the American job market and how it has changed. Without any question, the most important change in the 20th century was the shift, the um, change, from a manufacturing economy to a service economy. What do these two terms mean? Um, it's very simple. A manufacturing economy is one that produces a large number of things, or products. People who produce things like cars, furniture or clothing are working in a manufacturing economy. Have you got that? But on the other hand, a service economy is one in which most workers provide services, I mean that they do something instead of making something. Some examples of service workers include your doctor, your hair stylist, um...airline pilots, salesclerks, and of course everybody working in the computer industry. All the people who design and program and service computers, all of them are part of the service economy.

So again, my point is that the United States has changed from a manufacturing economy to a service economy. You can see this clearly if you take a look at the graph on job restructuring. Let's look at those statistics... You can see that the percentage of manufacturing jobs has gone down dramatically since the beginning of the 20th century, and it will continue to decrease in the 21st century. And what about service jobs? At the same time that the percentage of manufacturing jobs has gone down, there has been a great increase in the percentage of service jobs. Basically, one hundred years ago, 80% of workers worked in agriculture or manufacturing; but today, as we start the 21st century, only about 20% do, while 80% provide services. And you can see that by the year 2020, the percentage of service workers will increase to 90%; in other words, within 20 years, nine out of ten workers in the United States will supply services and not products.

OK, this brings me to my second main point: Why? I mean what has caused this change in the U.S. economy? First of all, why has the number of manufacturing jobs decreased? Can anyone guess? Yes?

Answers

1) 1c, 2a, 3d, 4b, 5c
2) 1f, 2e, 3a, 4j, 5h, 6d, 7b, 8i, 9c, 10g
3) 1b, 2d, 3c, 4a, 5d
4) 1h, 2i, 3d, 4g, 5e, 6a, 7j, 8b, 9f, 10c
5) 1T, 2F, 3F, 4T, 5F
6) 1c, 2b, 3a, 4a, 5a
7) 1. Be quiet when you come in tonight. The baby will be sleeping.
   2. I won't use my car unless you help me pay for the gas.
   3. Correct

4. Correct
5. You should/ought to/had better/must/have to do all of the assignments if you want to get a good grade.
6. I looked everywhere, but I couldn't find my chemistry book.
7. Correct
8. Have you taken your final exam yet?
9. How is your brother? I haven't seen him for a long time.
10. Correct
11. I disagree with you. American food can be very good.
12. Who does this computer belong to?
13. If you need help, just ask me. (Completion of the independent clause will vary.)
14. You will need warmer clothes when winter comes.
15. Correct

Chapter 6

Tapescript for Exercise 1

Host: How are baby boomers different from their parents? I mean, do they spend their money differently from the way their parents did?

Harris: Very differently. You have to remember that the parents of the boomers grew up in the 1920s and 1930s. The years between World War I and World War II were very difficult, especially after the stock market crashed in 1929. Then came the Great Depression. Most people were poor, and there weren't enough jobs. But in contrast to that, the baby boomers were born <u>after</u> World War II, when the U.S. economy was very strong. And it's still strong today, the strongest it's ever been. As a result, first of all, baby boomers like to spend their money instead of putting it in the bank. I mean they save very little, compared to their parents. Second, boomers use a lot of credit; that is to say, they use credit cards instead of paying cash for things. And third, baby boomers have much more free time than their parents did.

Host: OK, so the baby boomers have a very different lifestyle from their parents. They have a lot more money to spend than their parents did. What do they spend it on?

Harris: I'll give you several examples. First, what do you think is the biggest expense for people between the ages of 40 and 55?

Host: Uh... housing?

Harris: Right. People in this age group spend between 25 and 40 percent of their income on housing, depending on where they live. In addition, they spend a lot of money on furniture and appliances, you know, refrigerators, dishwashers, washing machines, and so on.

Answers

1) 1b, 2b, 3c, 4a, 5a
2) 1S, 2D, 3D, 4S, 5S
3) 1d, 2a, 3e, 4b, 5c
4) 1e, 2c, 3a, 4d, 5b
5) 1T, 2F, 3T, 4F, 5F
6) 1b, 2c, 3c, 4b, 5a
7) 1. tall
   2. friendlier
   3. faster
   4. better
   5. the most interesting
   6. more optimistic
   7. excitable
   8. more rapidly
   9. more often
   10. recently
   11. more depressed
   12. sociable
   13. more sociable
   14. most irritable
   15. healthiest/most healthy

Chapter 7

Tapescript for Exercise 1

Joshua: Now many people are sure that the full moon can cause unpredictable or even violent behavior. Back in 1977, a psychiatrist named

Arnold Lieber wrote a book called *The Lunar Effect*, which stated that crime rates seem to increase at the time of the full moon. For example, a woman named Sarah Jane Moore tried to kill then U.S. president, Gerald Ford, during a full moon. At least two research studies examined thousands of murders and other violent crimes and showed that they occur more frequently at the time of the full moon. One study involved 11,613 cases of aggravated assault, which is when one person attacks another person with a weapon like a gun or a knife. These attacks took place over a period of five years, and the research showed that they occurred more often around the full moon. Many police officers agree that there is a connection between violent behavior and the occurrence of the full moon.

Dr. Lieber also proposed that the full moon is related to depression. As an example, he states that in 1977, nine people committed suicide during a full moon by jumping off the Golden Gate Bridge in San Francisco. One study published in 1980 showed an increase in the number of people who try to poison themselves on the day of the full moon. And many people who work in mental hospitals complain that patients are more irritable and difficult to handle at the time of the full moon.

Answers

1) 1a, 2c, 3c, 4a, 5b
2) 1d, 2c, 3b, 4a, 5e
3) 1E, 2E, 3O, 4E, 5E
4) 1d, 2e, 3b, 4a, 5c
5) 1T, 2F, 3F, 4T, 5F
6) 1a, 2c, 3b, 4b, 5c
7) 1. have been developed
   2. have been sent
   3. has been explored
   4. have been photographed
   5. have not been started
8) 1. are being trained
   2. is being designed
   3. are being programmed
   4. are building
   5. is improving

9) 1. Should; spend
   2. must be/should be started
   3. must/should use
   4. might be wasted
   5. should/could be spent;
      should/could be saved

Chapter 8

Tapescript for Exercise 1

Woman: Last night I got the scare of my life. I was walking home from work at about 10:00 when I heard a really loud crash. I looked up and saw there had been an accident and a man had been thrown from the car and was lying on the sidewalk. At first, I didn't know what to do. Then I remembered that you're supposed to check to see if the person is conscious. So I ran over to him and asked, "Are you OK? Can you talk?" He didn't say anything, so I checked to see if he was breathing and he was. I told a woman who had stopped beside me to call 911 right away. Then the man asked softly, "What happened?" I told him to lie still and that help would be there soon.

Answers

1) 3, 5, 1, 2, 4
2) 1a, 2b, 3b, 4b, 5a
3) 1R, 2G, 3R, 4R, 5G
4) 1c, 2e, 3d, 4a, 5b
5) 1F, 2F, 3T, 4T, 5F
6) 1c, 2a, 3b, 4a, 5b
7) 1. whose
   2. when
   3. which
   4. that
   5. that
   6. who
   7. that
   8. where
   9. that
   10. whose
8) 1. Dr. Moore, who still makes house calls, is highly respected in our community.
   2. My sister is attending medical school in Boston, where there are many teaching hospitals.
   3. Dr. Alexander, who(m) I just saw last week, has been my family's doctor for twenty years.
   4. People with diabetes, whose pancreas does not function properly, must take a hormone called insulin every day.
   5. When my daughter got sick I took her to a pediatrician that/who/whom my neighbor recommended.

Chapter 9

Tapescript for Exercise 1

Argument 1

There are several advantages to going to school 12 months of the year.

Argument 2

I don't think our school library is good at all.

Argument 3

Classes should be no more than 45 minutes long.

Argument 4

English is a really hard language.

Argument 5

Students should never be late to class.

Answers

1) 1c, 2e, 3a, 4d, 5b
2) 1b, 2a, 3a, 4b, 5b, 6a, 7b, 8a, 9b, 10a
3) 1b, 2c, 3a, 4e, 5d
4) 1F, 2F, 3F, 4F, 5T
5) 1b, 2b, 3c, 4a, 5a
6) 1. to see
   2. to leave
   3. to going
   4. watching
   5. to stop
7) 1. to help
   2. do
   3. use
   4. mow
   5. to see

Chapter 10

Tapescript for Exercise 1

Speaker: OK, as I was saying, the Universal Declaration of Human Rights contains a detailed list of people's civil rights. Article 1, for example, says that all human beings are born free and equal. In addition, the Declaration states that every person should have freedom of movement, freedom of speech, and freedom of religion. Furthermore, the Declaration prohibits slavery and torture, and it also prohibits discrimination against minority groups.

The second group of articles deals with economic rights. Article 23, for instance, states that everyone has a right to work and to be paid for work, and furthermore, that everyone has the right to equal pay for equal work; in other words, if men and women are doing the same work, they should be paid at the same level.

The next category, social rights, mainly deals with education. The Declaration states that everyone has a right to education and that parents have a right to choose the kind of education they want for their children.

Finally, in the area of cultural rights, the Declaration states that people have the right to participate in the cultural, artistic, and scientific life of their communities. This means that countries like Cuba that control literature and art aren't respecting their people's human rights, according to the Declaration.

Answers

1) Wording of answers will vary, and there are often several correct answers.
   1. (Only one item is required. Possible answers follow.)
      All human beings are born free and equal.
      Every person has freedom of movement, freedom of speech, freedom of religion, and freedom from slavery and torture.
      No discrimination against minority groups.
   2. (Two items are required.)
      Everyone has the right to work.
      Everyone has the right to equal pay for equal work.
   3. (Only one item is required. Possible answers follow.)
      Everyone has the right to an education.
      Parents have a right to choose the kind of education they want for their children.
   4. (Only one item is required. Possible answers follow.)
      Everyone has the right to participate in the cultural, artistic, and scientific life of their communities.
      Governments can't control literature.
      Governments can't control art.
2) 1b, 2e, 3d, 4a, 5c
3) 1c, 2b, 3e, 4d, 5a
4) 1e, 2c, 3d, 4a, 5b
5) 1F, 2T, 3F, 4F, 5T
6) 1c, 2b, 3b, 4a, 5a
7) 1. should / could have studied
   2. should / could have taken
   3. wouldn't / might not have been
   4. should / could have read
   5. should / could have talked
8) 1. had listened
   2. would / might have been
   3. had agreed
   4. would / might/could have saved
   5. would / might/could have done

Final Quiz

Tapescript for Exercise 1

Lecturer: Now, that brings us to treatments for insomnia. Obviously, if you have trouble sleeping the first thing you should do is avoid coffee, tea, and cigarettes in the evening. You should also avoid alcohol. Many people say that a glass of beer or wine helps them sleep, and that may be true once in a while. But drinking alcohol every night is dangerous because after a while it stops working and, as everyone knows, alcohol is addictive. You should also avoid sleeping pills for the same reason, because they are addictive. These are the things you <u>shouldn't</u> do if you have insomnia. Now, what <u>should</u> you do?

Some methods that doctors recommend are, first, listening to relaxation tapes or soft music. Second, you can try self-hypnosis, which is easy to learn. Then there's always TV; many people like to watch TV when they can't sleep. And reading a boring book can also be very effective. That reminds me, your textbooks finally arrived in the bookstore. No, really, please buy them as soon as possible because we'll start using the book next Monday. Anyway, where was I? Oh yes. Treatments for insomnia. What really works for chronic insomnia is taking care of the <u>cause</u>. What I mean is, if stress is the cause of a person's insomnia, it's important to find out where that stress is coming from and to work on lowering the stress. In many cultures people do this with the help of a professional therapist. If therapy doesn't work, medication may be the answer, and luckily there are some wonderful new drugs on the market that aren't addictive.

Answers

1) 1b, 2c, 3a, 4b, 5a
2) 1c, 2h, 3a, 4f, 5j, 6b, 7e, 8i, 9d, 10g
3) 1c, 2b, 3a, 4d, 5e
4) 1d, 2f, 3g, 4j, 5i, 6a, 7c, 8b, 9e, 10h
5) 1F, 2T, 3T, 4T, 5F
6) 1a, 2b, 3c, 4b, 5c
7)
1. For me, the best movies are comedies.
2. She didn't sing as beautifully as she usually does.
3. Texas is a lot hotter than Colorado.
4. It's been many years since astronauts were first sent to the moon.
5. Correct
6. Your term paper should be written on a computer.
7. Measles, which is usually a childhood disease, is rarely harmful to children.
8. Correct
9. Correct
10. They decided to go to the movies instead of the baseketball game.
11. I need to get my brother to lend me some money.
12. Correct
13. If you had eaten more this morning, you woulnd't have gotten hungry before lunch !
14. Correct
15. I wouldn't have taken this course if I had known that it would be so difficult.